STUDY GUIDE

James Swofford
University of South Alabama

STUDY GUIDE

to accompany

Modern Principles:
MICROECONOMICS

Cowen ■ Tabarrok

WORTH PUBLISHERS

Study Guide
by James Swofford
to accompany
Cowen ■ Tabarrok: *Modern Principles: Microeconomics*

ISBN 13: 978-1-4292-3170-1
ISBN 10: 1-4292-3170-X

First Printing 2009

Printed in the United States of America

Worth Publishers
41 Madison Avenue
New York, NY 10010
www.worthpublishers.com

Contents

Key to Corresponding Chapter Numbers

	Microeconomics	Economics	Macroeconomics
The Big Ideas	Chapter 1	Chapter 1	Chapter 1
Supply and Demand	Chapter 2	Chapter 2	Chapter 2
Equilibrium: How Supply and Demand Determine Prices	Chapter 3	Chapter 3	Chapter 3
Elasticity and Its Applications	Chapter 4	Chapter 4	
The Price System: Signs, Speculation and Prediction	Chapter 5	Chapter 5	
Price Ceilings	Chapter 6	Chapter 6	
Price Floors, Taxes and Subsidies	Chapter 7	Chapter 7	
International Trade and Globalization	Chapter 8	Chapter 8	Chapter 18
Externalities: When Prices Send the Wrong Signals	Chapter 9	Chapter 9	
Profits, Prices and Costs under competition	Chapter 10	Chapter 10	
Monopoly	Chapter 11	Chapter 11	
Price Discrimination	Chapter 12	Chapter 12	
Cartels, Games, and Network Goods	Chapter 13	Chapter 13	
Labor Markets	Chapter 14	Chapter 14	
Getting Incentives Right: Lessons for Business, Sports, Politics, and Life	Chapter 15	Chapter 15	
Stock Markets and Personal Finance	Chapter 16	Chapter 16	Chapter 9
Public Goods and the Tragedy of the Commons	Chapter 17	Chapter 17	
Economics, Ethics, and Public Policy	Chapter 18	Chapter 18	
Political Economy	Chapter 19	Chapter 19	

Preface

This **Study Guide** is designed for use with *Modern Principles: Microeconomics* by Tyler Cowen and Alex Tabarrok. Economics is not just an interesting subject for study, it is an integral part of life—from shopping at the local grocery store to buying a house to understanding national and local legislation. To help you reach your goal of understanding economics, this study guide includes a number of exercises that involve active learning and repetition. Together, these activities will enhance your learning of text material and will help you to evaluate your understanding of important concepts.

Have you ever taken a test thinking you were well prepared only to discover that you really didn't understand a particular concept? Ideally, working through a study guide chapter will enable you to actively learn the text chapter's contents while also discovering and focusing on material you thought you had mastered but had not.

Why Learn About. . .?

Each chapter begins with a brief motivational introduction. Some chapters have a hypothetical dialog between an instructor and his or her students. Other chapters explain why the material is important and lists categories of people who are most likely to be interested in the chapter topics—for example, consumers, businesspeople—making it clear that most of economics will be useful to you even in the years following graduation. These motivational introductions are intended to pique your interest in the chapter contents and so to motivate you to read on.

Summary and Key Terms

Each summary contains only the essential points of the chapter, including useful tables and graphs from the text. To make the material easier for you to digest, the summary is deliberately brief and straightforward. Reading the summary does not replace reading the text. However, it will help solidify your understanding of the text material.

For your convenience, the key terms in the text chapter are listed separately and defined.

Traps, Hints, and Reminders

This short section first identifies concepts that from experience we have found can be difficult for undergraduate students new to economics. Helpful hints for understanding that material are then provided. The section also includes information about concepts that we think are among the most important.

Practice Exercises: Learn by Doing

When you feel comfortable that you understand the chapter contents, try to complete these practice exercises, using your own words. These exercises include some questions (marked with an asterisk [*]) that duplicate the text end-of-chapter questions. Answers to these exercises are provided at the end of the chapter. In addition, the topic or topics covered by the question are given, so that you can check the text when you don't understand a topic. Remember: learning is best when it is active.

Multiple-Choice and Short-Answer Questions

Each chapter contains a self-test review, which includes about 20 multiple-choice questions and about 10 short-answer questions. Answers are provided at the end of the chapter. The short-answer questions are very similar to the practice exercises. We feel that repetition can help you continue to learn right though this section. The self-test review is yet another opportunity for active learning.

Acknowledgements

A number of people and institutions have greatly contributed to the writing of this study guide. I want to thank the University of South Alabama, Mobile, Alabama, for granting me a sabbatical leave during the fall term of 2009. Thanks also go to the department of economics of Lund University in Lund, Sweden, that invited me to be a visiting scholar during my sabbatical. In addition to getting scholarly work done while in Sweden, my visit to Lund gave me time away from the usual distractions of life to get a very good jump on writing this study guide.

I would also like to thank my wife Cindy who put the eyes of a noneconomist on each chapter and found many places to help make this study guide more readable.

Finally, I would like to thank my colleague Mitch Mitchell who shared ideas and encouragement with me during the writing of both study guides for **Modern Principles**. I would also like to thank Paul Shensa for all his encouragement in this project and helping us decide on the structure of the study guide. I thank Tom Acox and Matt Driskill who worked the closest with us on writing and formatting the chapters. We also wish to thank Laura McGinn and Stacey Alexander for their assistance in producing this study guide.

Jim Swofford
2009

STUDY GUIDE

1

The Big Ideas

Why Learn about Economics?

Economics is a difficult subject, not just because it involves learning lots of material, but because it is way of thinking. So, why would anyone want to learn about economics? Economics is a requirement for many business majors because it helps them think about trade-offs, prices, costs, and labor markets.

Who else would want to learn about economics? Political science majors will want to learn about economics because so much policy is based on it. Nursing majors will be interested in economics because they will want to understand the incentives of policy makers, doctors, patients, health maintenance organizations (HMOs), and other nurses. A sociology or anthropology major might want to understand why some countries are so rich and others are so poor. Environmental science majors need to know economics because there is often a trade-off between industry and the environment.

Summary

This chapter discusses the reasons for studying economics and the ten key (big) ideas in economics.

Institutions are overall rules for making rules. These include the rule of law, democracy, the Constitution, and property rights. Good institutions provide good **incentives**. Incentives are things that encourage people to act a certain way. Good institutions encourage people to save, work, and innovate.

Trade-offs are the idea that in order to get one thing, you must give up something else. The benefits that you give up are called the **opportunity cost**. Economists think about trade-offs at the *margin*. "Margin" means small change.

Sometimes governments implement *price controls*. Price controls are government intervention with prices. Price controls can limit how high a price can go, or they can limit how low a price can go.

Booms and busts are periods of economic expansion and contraction. During a boom, the economy is thriving. During a bust the economy is not doing well. During a boom, output is high and unemployment is low. Though the economy may go up and down in the short term, hopefully it is experiencing economic growth in the long term. *Economic growth* is a long-run increase in a country's ability to produce more goods and services.

The *central bank* is a nation's banking authority. It is usually responsible for controlling the money supply, as well as for conducting monetary policy. That might include taking actions to promote economic stability, low **inflation**, and full employment. When the central bank prints too much money, inflation occurs. Inflation is a general increase in prices.

Key Terms

incentives are rewards and penalties that motivate behavior

opportunity cost of a choice is the value of the opportunities lost

inflation is a general increase in prices

Traps, Hints, and Reminders

Opportunity cost is a trap for students because it has the word "cost" in it, but it is really the "benefit" foregone. This is a common test question.

Marginal analysis is changing by small units. Many of the later chapters also discuss marginal analysis. The opposite of marginal analysis is all or nothing. Think of it this way—rarely do people drive at the exact speed limit or go as fast as their car will go. Many people choose how fast they want to drive (within limits).

For example, you might decide to drive 9 miles per hour (mph) over the speed limit, but you choose not to drive as fast as your car can go. So, why not drive 10 mph over the speed limit instead of 9 mph? Because at 10 mph over the speed limit you are more likely to get pulled over by a traffic patrol officer. The cost of going 9 mph over the speed limit (instead of 10 mph over) is low. In addition, speeding tickets are considerably more expensive for driving 10 mph over the speed limit than 9 mph for driving over.[1] The benefit of going 9 mph over the speed limit is high (since it will get you to your destination faster). Make sure that you read all of the above closely, as understanding the fine details of benefits and costs can be confusing.

Marginal thinking is thinking about making a small change. You will sometimes hear the expression "thinking at the margin." Being "at the margin" is a similar term that means that you are only a small change away from being in a new category. If your professor says that you are at the margin between a "C" and a "D," this means that you are right between the two grades. A bit more work would mean a "C," while a bit less work would mean a "D."

---

[1] The authors of this study guide and Worth Publishers do not endorse speeding of any kind. Driving over the speed limit is dangerous, and besides, getting a speeding ticket is not good for your driving record or your insurance payment!

Practice Exercises: Learning by Doing

1. Why are test questions about opportunity cost difficult for students?

2. What evidence is there that "direct incentives" matter more than "appeals to sensitivity"? Use an example from the text.

3. How could a drug be "too safe"?

4. Why are lost wages counted in the opportunity cost of college, but your college food bill is not?

Multiple-Choice Questions

1. Opportunity cost is

   a. the cost of your next-best alternative.

   b. the cost of your second-next-best alternative.

   c. the benefit of taking your best alternative.

   d. the benefit from all your other alternatives.

2. A baseball star has been drafted to play major league baseball and is offered a $100,000 signing bonus; a young mathematician in need of advanced training could make $30,000 working now; and an aspiring accountant could make $15,000 working now. They all attend Big State U for their freshman year. Which one has the highest opportunity cost?

   a. the baseball player

   b. the future mathematician

   c. the future accountant

   d. They all have equal opportunity costs.

3. Which of the following is a marginal choice?

   a. the decision to build a new factory or not

   b. the decision to hire one more worker

   c. the decision to explore the oceans

   d. the decision to learn how to speak Spanish

4. Which of the following is not listed in your text as a benefit of economic growth?

   a. longer life expectancy

   b. more rights for women

   c. better vacations

   d. more fairness

5. If governments decide to ban high prices during catastrophes, then economists would predict that during catastrophes

   a. people would be happy because they are getting all their goods for low prices.

   b. fewer goods will be available and people will have to wait.

   c. suppliers will bring in even more goods at low prices.

   d. suppliers will not be affected in any way by the rule.

6. Economic growth is measured by

  a. how happy the populace is getting.

  b. the increase in how much a country can produce.

  c. the increase in the number of people employed in a country.

  d. the increase in the amount of taxes in a country.

7. Why is North Korea poorer than South Korea?

  a. Countries farther from the equator are poorer.

  b. All of the capitalist countries are conspiring against North Korea.

  c. South Korea has institutions that provide incentives for innovations and investment.

  d. North Korea is too mountainous for companies to build factories.

8. According to your text, the Great Depression was

  a. prolonged by bad policy.

  b. a natural occurrence in a capitalist society.

  c. caused by a famine in India.

  d. caused by the beginning of World War II.

9. The central bank of the United States is called

  a. Bank of America.

  b. the National Bank of the United States.

  c. the Federal Reserve.

  d. Washington Mutual.

10. When the central bank prints too much money,

  a. people cannot get paper anymore.

  b. inflation occurs.

  c. prices fall too fast.

  d. All of the answers are correct.

11. Which of the following is not a reason that central banking is hard?

  a. There is often a time lag between when the central bank changes policy and when the effects of the changes are known.

  b. It is difficult to foresee the future.

  c. A central bank often has conflicting goals.

  d. There are not enough hard challenges to make central banking interesting.

12. A student attends the local college instead of working as a customer service representative making $20,000. Tuition is $15,000. Books and fees are $2,000. He lives at home. What is the out-of-pocket cost of going to college for this student?

    a. $15,000

    b. $17,000

    c. $20,000

    d. $37,000

13. A student attends the local college instead of working as a customer service representative making $20,000. Tuition is $15,000. Books and fees are $2,000. He lives at home. What is the opportunity cost of going to college for this student?

    a. $15,000

    b. $17,000

    c. $20,000

    d. $37,000

14. Good institutions

    a. eliminate trade-offs.

    b. align self-interest with the social interest.

    c. eliminate incentives.

    d. eliminate self-interest.

15. The Boudreaux family and the Williams family are both making decisions about pets. The Boudreaux family is deciding whether or not to keep all 20 pets that currently live on their farm or to move to the city and get rid of all their pets. The Williams family has one cat and one dog. The Williams are thinking of getting one more dog. Which family is thinking "at the margin"?

    a. Neither family is thinking at the margin.

    b. the Williams family

    c. the Boudreaux family

    d. Both families are thinking at the margin.

16. Your professor has a strict grading rule. An average grade from 90 to 100% is an "A." An average grade from 80 to 89.99% is a "B." An average grade from 70 to 79.99% is a "C." There are no pluses or minuses. Patty has an average grade of 89.95 before the final exam. Selma has an average grade of 85 before the final exam. Which student is "on the margin"?

    a. Patty

    b. Selma

    c. both Patty and Selma

    d. neither Patty nor Selma

17. Jerome's favorite flavor of ice cream is chocolate. His second-favorite flavor is black cherry, and his third-favorite is coffee. If he cannot get one of those flavors, he would rather not eat ice cream. If Jerome goes to a well-stocked ice cream store and gets chocolate, what is his opportunity cost?

a. There is never an opportunity cost when you eat ice cream.

b. chocolate

c. black cherry

d. coffee

18. Bubba's average tax rate is 20%, but his marginal tax rate is 30%. If Bubba works an extra hour, what is his tax rate on that extra hour?

a. 20%

b. 25%

c. 25.87%

d. 30%

19. Tyra's favorite TV shows, in order of preference, are *America's Next Top Model*, *America's Funniest Home Videos*, and *CSI*. If each show is an hour and she wants to study for one hour this week, what is the opportunity cost of studying?

a. Giving up *America's Next Top Model*, *America's Funniest Home Videos*, and *CSI*.

b. Giving up *America's Next Top Model*.

c. Nothing: it is free to watch TV.

d. Giving up *CSI*.

20. If prices are rising in general, that is known as

a. deflation.

b. inflation.

c. rationing.

d. appreciation.

Short-Answer Questions

21. Sarah moves to a new city. She gets an apartment that costs $6,000 a year. Her food costs are $6,000 a year. Her job pays $28,000 a year. She is thinking of giving up her job and going to the local college full-time, including summers. Tuition, fees, and books will cost $20,000 a year. What is the opportunity cost of going to college?

22. Elizabeth is dating Jeremy, but she is also thinking of going back to her high school boyfriend, David. Since Jeremy does not charge her to date him, is there any cost to Elizabeth?

23. Could a car be too safe? Explain.

24. If you do not have lunch with your friends at the school cafeteria and instead eat a "free lunch" given by an on-campus recruiter, what was the cost of the lunch?

25. What is a trade-off? How are trade-offs related to opportunity cost?

26. What are institutions, and how are they related to incentives?

27. From 1949 to 1990 Germany was separated into two countries. The German Democratic Republic (East Germany) was a communist country. The Federal Republic of Germany (West Germany) was a capitalist country. Despite similar history and culture, West Germany had more innovations and inventions than East Germany did. Why might this be?

28. What are price controls?

29. How is the production of innovative ideas different from the production of other goods?

30. What are booms and busts?

31. What is a central bank and how does it cause inflation?

Answer Key

Answers to Practice Exercises: Learning by Doing

1. During the stress of an exam, students sometimes forget that opportunity cost is the benefit foregone. It is easy for students to get definition questions and application-type questions wrong.

   Topic: Big Idea Three: Trade-offs Are Everywhere

2. Paying ship captains for prisoners delivered to Australia alive instead of for prisoners loaded on to ships provided an incentive to bring prisoners to Australia alive. This incentive worked much better than simply asking ship captains to bring prisoners alive.

   Topic: Big Idea One: Incentives Matter

3. When we make drug companies prove that their products are super safe, we miss out on the opportunity to have some risky drugs available on the market that can save some lives.

   Topic: Big Idea Three: Trade-offs Are Everywhere

4. When you go to college full-time, you miss out on the benefit of earning money by working full-time. Regardless of whether you go to college or work, you would still eat.

   Topic: Big Idea Three: Trade-offs Are Everywhere

Answers to Multiple-Choice Questions

1. c, Topic: Opportunity Cost

2. a, Topic: Opportunity Cost

3. b, Topic: Big Idea Four: Thinking on the Margin

4. d, Topic: Big Idea Six: The Importance of Wealth and Economic Growth

5. b, Topic: Big Idea Five: Tampering with the Laws of Supply and Demand Has Consequences

6. b, Topic: Big Idea Six: The Importance of Wealth and Economic Growth

7. c, Topic: Big Idea Seven: Institutions Matter

8. a, Topic: Big Idea Eight: Economic Booms and Busts Cannot Be Avoided but Can Be Moderated

9. c, Topic: Big Idea Ten: Central Banking Is a Hard Job

10. b, Topic: Big Idea Nine: Prices Rise When the Government Prints Too Much Money

11. d, Topic: Big Idea Ten: Central Banking Is a Hard Job

12. b, Topic: Opportunity Cost

13. d, Topic: Opportunity Cost

14. b, Topic: Big Idea Two: Good Institutions Align Self-Interest with the Social Interest

15. b, Topic: Big Idea Four: Thinking on the Margin

16. a, Topic: Big Idea Four: Thinking on the Margin

17. c, Topic: Opportunity Cost

18. d, Topic: Big Idea Four: Thinking on the Margin

19. d, Topic: Opportunity Cost

20. b, Topic: Big Idea Nine: Prices Rise When the Government Prints Too Much Money

Answers to Short-Answer Questions

21. If Sarah goes to college, she gives up $28,000 a year in salary and the use of $20,000 (for tuition, fees, and books). She has to pay for her apartment and food whether or not she is in college. Sometimes students are confused about opportunity cost, including only the tuition, but could not Sarah have spent the $20,000 on something else? Thus, her opportunity cost is $48,000.

    Topic: Big Idea Three: Trade-offs Are Everywhere

22. Yes, Elizabeth has opportunity cost. When she dates Jeremy, she gives up dating David.

    Topic: Big Idea Three: Trade-offs Are Everywhere

23. Yes, if a car is made so safe that no one can afford to drive it. This could lead to people missing the financial benefits that owning a car brings or being in unsafe situations. For example, having a car enables people to drive to work. If people could not afford to buy cars to commute to work, this could put a restriction on job opportunities. Also, if people living in areas prone to natural catastrophes (such as forest fires or floods) cannot afford to buy cars, they may not be able to escape during an emergency situation.

    Topic: Big Idea Three: Trade-offs Are Everywhere

24. You endure the presentation from the on-campus recruiter and give up lunch with your friends. The benefit of enjoying lunch with your friends is the opportunity cost.

    Topic: Big Idea Three: Trade-offs Are Everywhere

25. A trade-off is the idea that when you do one thing, you cannot do something else. You cannot study economics and watch TV. You do one or the other. The benefit you forego is the opportunity cost.

    Topic: Big Idea Three: Trade-offs Are Everywhere

26. Institutions are overarching rules that govern the way that rules are made. They can be thought of as rules for making rules. Some institutions, such as communism, are set up so that everyone benefits from your hard work. That type of institution would provide you with less of an incentive to work hard. Other institutions, such as those found in capitalist countries, have laws that give you the right to the benefits of your hard work. Those types of institutions provide an incentive to work hard.

Topic: Big Idea Seven: Institutions Matter

27. West Germany's capitalism provided the right incentives for people to invent and innovate. In West Germany, if people worked hard, then they were able to save more money and benefit. In East Germany's communist system, whether or not people worked hard, invented, or innovated, their financial status did not change. As a result, this type of system did not provide incentives.

Topic: Big Idea Seven: Institutions Matter

28. Price controls are government rules that limit how high or low a price can go.

Topic: Big Idea Five: Tampering with the Laws of Supply and Demand Has Consequences

29. Innovative ideas are easily replicable. Regular goods are not. If you invent a new way to harness solar energy, everyone who sees that invention can use it (and pay you for patent usage). If you bake a pizza and more people eat that pizza, then less pizza will be available for you to eat. More people seeing pizza does not mean that there is more pizza.

Topic: Big Idea Seven: Institutions Matter

30. Booms and busts are the economic cycles. The most famous bust was the Great Depression.

Topic: Big Idea Eight: Economic Booms and Busts Cannot Be Avoided but Can Be Moderated

31. The central bank is a nation's banking authority. It is usually responsible for controlling the money supply, as well as for conducting monetary policy. Responsibilities might involve taking actions, such as keeping inflation low, to maintain economic stability. Inflation is a general increase in prices. When the central bank prints too much money, inflation occurs. The Federal Reserve is the central bank of the United States.

Topic: Big Idea Ten: Central Banking Is a Hard Job

2

Supply and Demand

Why Learn about Supply and Demand?

As the authors say in the text, if you understand little else, you may rightly claim to be literate in economics if you understand supply and demand. If you fail to understand supply and demand, you will understand little else in economics. Thus, supply and demand are the fundamental building blocks of economics.

Supply and demand can be used to understand many human interactions, ranging from the supply and demand of oil (gasoline) for automobiles to the supply and demand of human organs for transplanting.

Who will be interested in supply and demand?

> Elected public officials and candidates for political office that implement programs (affecting taxes and taxpayers), set prices for city services (such as buses), or need to understand the economic effects of government policies

> Businesspeople who want to decide how much to produce and at what price to sell their product

> Students of economics, who, as the authors say in the text, will be lost if they fail to understand this chapter

Summary

This chapter covers supply and demand. A **demand curve** is a function that shows the quantity demanded at different prices. As shown in Figure 2.1, **quantity demanded** is the quantity buyers are willing and able to buy at a particular price.

Figure 2.1

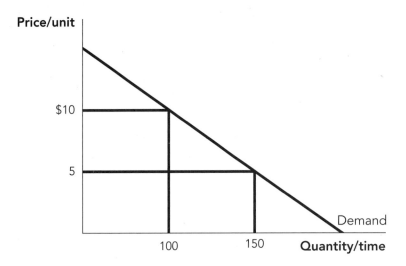

Demand curves are typically downward sloping, implying that if the price falls, the quantity demanded increases. In Figure 2.1, if the price falls from $10 to $5, the quantity demanded increases from 100 units to 150 units. Similarly, if the price rises from $5 to $10, then the quantity demanded decreases from 150 units to 100 units.

Consumer surplus is the consumer's gain from exchange, or the difference between the maximum price a consumer is willing to pay for a certain good and the market price. For example, if you are willing to pay $1,000 for a Super Bowl ticket, and the market price is $480, then your consumer surplus is $520 = $1,000 − $480.

In Figure 2.2, the **total consumer surplus** is measured by the area beneath the demand curve and above the price.

Figure 2.2

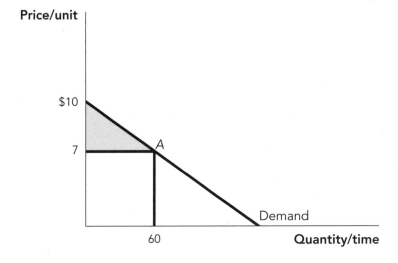

With a market price of $7, the total consumer surplus is the triangle determined by points $7, A, and $10, and it is shaded. The amount of this area can be calculated using the formula for the area of a triangle, which is (height × base)/2. In this example, the height is $3 = $10 − $7 and the base is 60. The height × base is $180 = $3 × 60. The total consumer surplus is $90 = $180/2.

It is important to understand what things cause demand to shift when they change. If, in Figure 2.3, the demand curve shifts from D_1 to D_3, then it is said that demand has increased. This means at every price the quantity of the good that people want to buy is larger. If, in Figure 2.3, the demand curve shifts from D_1 to D_2, it is said that demand has decreased. This means at every price the quantity of the good that people want to buy is smaller.

Figure 2.3

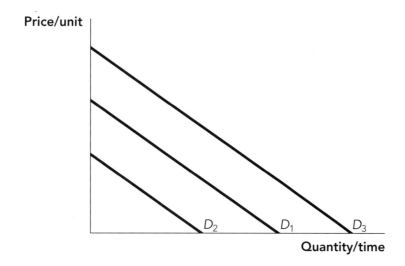

Among the important things that shift demand are changes in consumer income, population, the price of substitutes and complements, expectations, and tastes (how desirable a good is at a specific point in time).

For some goods, when consumer incomes rise, demand increases. These goods are called **normal goods**. For other goods, when consumer incomes rise, demand decreases. Such goods are called **inferior goods**.

If, when the price of another good goes up and the demand for the original good rises, then the two goods are called **substitutes**. Consumers use one good instead of the other and buy more of the now relatively cheaper of the two goods. If, when the price of another good goes up and the demand for the original good falls, then the two goods are called **complements**. Consumers use the two goods together and buy less of both goods when the price of one of them rises.

If population, tastes (desire) for a good, and the expected future price of the good all increase at the same time, then the demand for the goods will also increase. Again that would be a shift like D_1 to D_3, as shown in Figure 2.3.

A **supply curve** is a function that shows the quantity supplied at different prices. In Figure 2.4, **quantity supplied** is the quantity that sellers are willing to sell at a particular price.

Supply curves are typically upward sloping, implying that if the price rises, then the quantity supplied also increases. In Figure 2.4, if the price rises from $5 to $15, then the quantity supplied increases from 50 units to 200 units. Similarly in Figure 2.4, if the price were to fall from $15 to $5, then the quantity supplied would decrease from 200 units to 50 units.

Figure 2.4

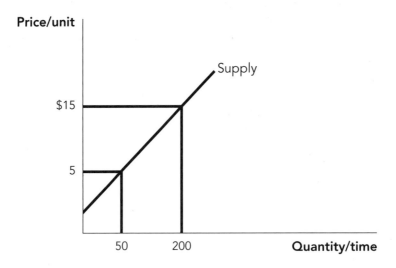

Producer surplus is the producer's gain from exchange, or the difference between the market price and the minimum price at which a producer would be willing to sell a certain quantity. For example, if you are willing to sell your car for $10,000 and the market price is $15,000, then your producer surplus would be $5,000 = $15,000 − $10,000 on that transaction.

Total producer surplus is measured by the area above the supply curve and below the price, as shown in Figure 2.5.

Figure 2.5

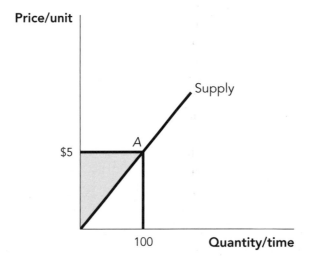

With a market price of $5, the total producer surplus is the triangle determined by points $5, A, and the origin 0,0. Again, the amount of this area can be calculated using the formula for the area of a triangle, which is (height × base)/2. In this example, the height is $5 and the base is 100. The height × base is $500 = $5 × 100. The total consumer surplus is $250 = $500/2.

As with demand, it is important to understand what things will cause supply to shift when they change. If, in Figure 2.6, the supply curve shifts from S_1 to S_3, it is said that supply has increased. This means at every price the quantity of the good that sellers want to sell is larger. If, in Figure 2.6, the supply curve shifts from S_1 to S_2, it is said that supply has decreased. This means at every price the amount of the good that sellers want to sell is smaller.

Figure 2.6

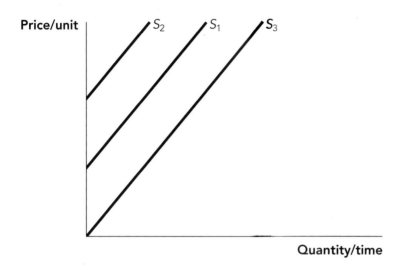

Among the important things that shift supply are technological change, changes in the price of inputs in production, taxes and subsidies, changes in expectations, entry and exit of producers, and changes in opportunity costs.

If a technology involved in producing calculators improves, then the supply of calculators increases. Similarly, if the price of any input involved in producing calculators falls, then the supply of calculators increases.

If the government taxes the production of calculators, then the supply of calculators decreases. With the tax added, it costs the producer more money to supply calculators. A subsidy is the negative of a tax. If the government subsidizes the production of calculators, then the supply of calculators increases. With the subsidy factored in, it costs the producer less money to produce calculators.

When producers expect a higher price for the product tomorrow (future markets), they have less incentive to sell today (current markets). To the extent that producers can store their product, they will reduce supply today so that they can sell more in the future (when prices are expected to be higher).

An increase in the number of producers also increases supply. For any given amount of supply, if a new producer comes into the market, the supply is increased. Similarly, when any producer leaves the market, this causes a decrease in the amount supplied. In a similar manner, opportunity costs can affect supply. For example, if a self-employed glazier accepts a job installing air-conditioning units that pays more than a job installing glass and mirrors, then the opportunity cost of installing glass and mirrors has increased. The glazier left the business of glass and mirror installation, thereby reducing supply in that market.

Key Terms

demand curve a function that shows the quantity demanded at different prices

quantity demanded the quantity that buyers are willing and able to buy at a particular price

consumer surplus the consumer's gain from exchange, or the difference between the maximum price a consumer is willing to pay for a certain good and the market price

total consumer surplus the area beneath the demand curve and above the price

normal good a good for which demand increases when income increases

inferior good a good for which demand decreases when income increases

substitutes two goods are substitutes if a decrease in the price of one good leads to a decrease in the demand for the other good

complements two goods are complements if a decrease in the price of one good leads to an increase in the demand for the other good

supply curve a function that shows the quantity supplied at different prices

quantity supplied the quantity that sellers are willing and able to sell at a particular price

producer surplus the producer's gain from exchange, or the difference between the market price and the minimum price at which a producer would be willing to sell a particular quantity

total producer surplus the area above the supply curve and below the price

Traps, Hints, and Reminders

Consumer surplus and producer surplus should not be confused with a surplus on a market. Though these terms have the word "surplus" in them, they are not related to surplus on a market or quantity supplied greater than quantity demanded (these concepts will be discussed in Chapter 3).

Inferior goods are not necessarily substandard goods. They are simply goods that are negatively related to consumer income. If a person became rich enough, he or she might buy fewer small jets and more custom-fitted commercial jets. This implies that the small jet might be an inferior good to some people at a certain income level, but says nothing about the quality.

Whether goods are complements or substitutes is up to the consumer. To you, butter and margarine may be substitutes, but for the heart patient only margarine is acceptable, and for the pastry chef only butter will be used. You may think of peanut butter and grape jelly as complements, that is, you may only use them together on bread. However, someone else may think of them as substitutes, that is, he may put only peanut butter on his toast and not jelly.

On a supply curve, any increase in supply is a shift to the right and down. This can be confusing. With supply or demand, "increase" or "decrease" describes the change along the quantity axis. Thus, an increase in supply is a shift to the right and down, because that moves supply to the right (that is, increasing quantities) along the quantity axis. Similarly, a decrease in supply is a shift up and to the left, because that moves supply to the left (that is, decreasing quantities) along the quantity axis.

A *subsidy* is a negative tax, that is, the government is giving someone money rather than taking it away. You could also think of a tax as a negative subsidy. So quite naturally, taxes and subsidies have opposite effects on supply. That is, a tax on a product decreases supply, while a subsidy for a product increases supply.

The *area of a triangle* is one-half the height times the base. The area of a triangle can be calculated as (1/2) × height × base (or .5 × height × base).

Practice Exercises: Learning by Doing

1. What is a demand curve? What is quantity demanded? Draw a demand curve on the graph below and use it to explain what a demand curve shows.

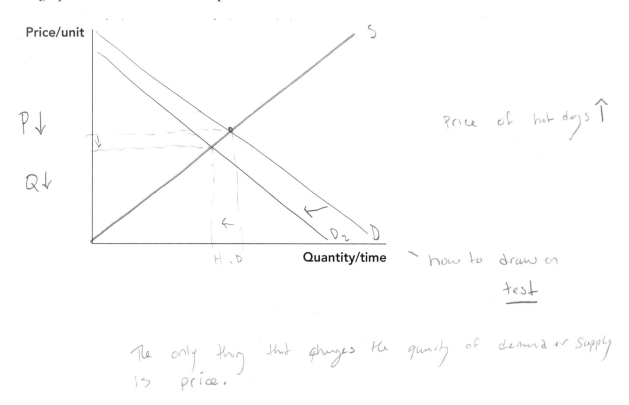

The only thing that changes the quantity of demand or supply is price.

2. What is a supply curve? What is quantity supplied? Draw a supply curve on the graph below and use it to explain what a supply curve shows.

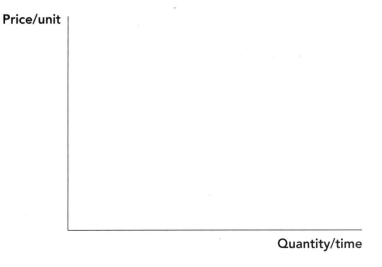

Price/unit

Quantity/time

3. What is consumer surplus? If the market price for a calculator was $10, the most that Bob was willing to pay was $20, the most that Kaitlin was willing to pay was $15, and the most that Cindy was willing to pay was $8, how much consumer surplus did each get?

4. How is total consumer surplus measured? On the graph below, mark the total consumer surplus at a market price of $10. Then calculate the amount of total consumer surplus.

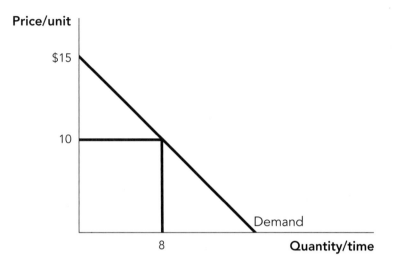

5. What is producer surplus? If the market price of a used textbook is $80, the least that Bob was willing to sell for was $90, the least that Kaitlin was willing to sell for was $40, and the least that Cindy was willing to sell for was $25, how much producer surplus did each get?

6. How is total producer surplus measured? On the graph below, mark the total producer surplus at a market price of $10. Then calculate the amount of total producer surplus.

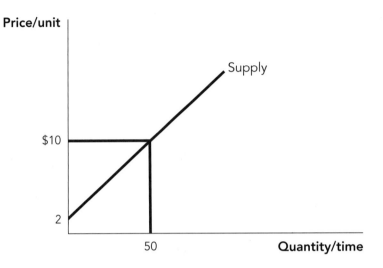

7. On the first graph below, draw an increase in demand.

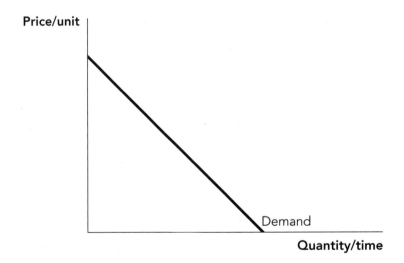

On the next graph below, draw a **dec**rease in demand.

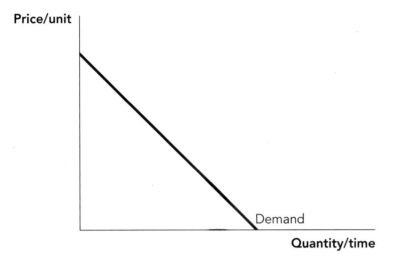

8. What are some of the important **thin**gs that cause demand to change when they change? Why do they cause **dem**and to change? And what is the direction of the change in demand **c**aused by each?

9. On the first graph below, draw an **in**crease in supply.

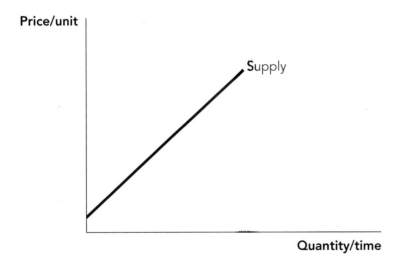

On the next graph below, draw a decrease in supply.

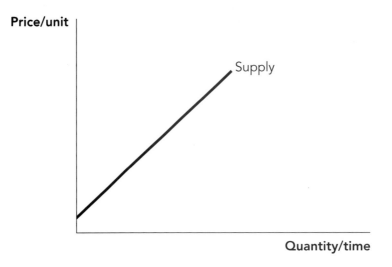

10. What are some of the important things that cause supply to change when they change? Why do they cause supply to change? And what is the direction of the change in supply caused by each?

★11. When the price of Apple computers goes down, what probably happens to the demand for Windows-based computers?[1]

Multiple-Choice Questions

1. If the price of oil rises, then
   a. the quantity of oil demanded falls.
   b. the demand for oil rises.
   c. the supply of oil rises.
   d. All of the answers are correct.

---

[1] Questions marked with a ★ are also end-of-chapter questions.

2. A demand curve shows

   a. the maximum willingness to pay for particular quantities.

   b. quantity demanded at different prices.

   c. different combinations of prices and quantities that consumers are able and willing to buy.

   d. All of the answers are correct.

3. If the most Tom is willing to pay for an ice cream cone is $5 and the market price is $2, then by purchasing an ice cream cone, Tom will get a consumer surplus of

   a. $2.

   b. $3.

   c. $5.

   d. $10.

Figure 2.7

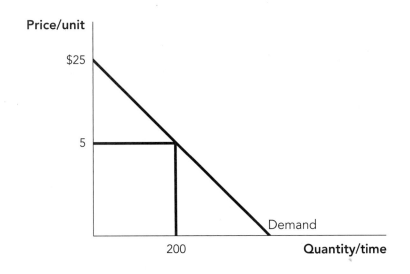

4. In Figure 2.7, if the market price is $5, then the consumer surplus is

   a. $25.

   b. $500.

   c. $1,000.

   d. $2,000.

5. If consumer incomes rise, then the demand for

   a. inferior goods increases.

   b. normal goods decreases.

   c. inferior goods decreases.

   d. complements decreases.

6. If peanut butter and jelly are complements, then an increase in the price of peanut butter will cause
   a. an increase in the price of jelly.
   b. a decrease in the demand for jelly.
   c. an increase in the demand for peanut butter.
   d. a decrease in the demand for peanut butter.

7. If the price of a substitute for butter rises, then
   a. the demand for butter increases.
   b. the demand for butter decreases.
   c. the price of butter falls.
   d. the supply of the substitute decreases.

8. Inferior goods are
   a. substandard.
   b. those with expected future price decreases.
   c. those that are negatively related to consumer income.
   d. those that few people buy.

9. If the price of oil is expected to fall in the future, then
   a. the demand for oil today decreases.
   b. the demand for oil in the future decreases.
   c. the supply of oil today decreases.
   d. the supply of oil in the future increases.

10. If tastes for a good goes up due to a fad, then
    a. the current price falls.
    b. the good is a normal good.
    c. the supply of the good decreases.
    d. the demand for the good increases.

11. If the price of oil falls, then
    a. the supply of oil decreases.
    b. the quantity of oil demanded decreases.
    c. the demand for oil increases.
    d. the quantity of oil supplied decreases.

12. Quantity supplied is
    a. negatively related to price.
    b. the amount of a good that sellers are willing and able to sell at a particular price.
    c. price without the willingness to sell.
    d. All of the answers are correct.

13. Producer surplus is

    a. the difference between the market price and the minimum price at which a producer would be willing to sell a particular quantity.

    b. the difference between the maximum price that a consumer would be willing to pay for a particular quantity and the market price.

    c. when the quantity supplied is greater than the quantity demanded.

    d. when the quantity demanded is greater than the quantity supplied.

Figure 2.8

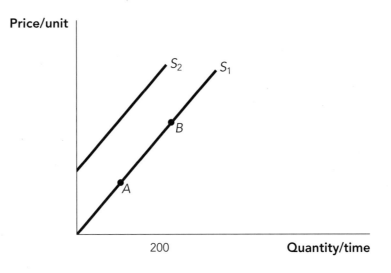

14. In Figure 2.8, an increase in supply is

    a. a move from point A to point B on S_1.

    b. a move from point B to point A on S_1.

    c. a shift from S_2 to S_1.

    d. a shift from S_1 to S_2.

15. If technology increases, then the

    a. supply curve decreases.

    b. demand curve decreases.

    c. supply curve increases.

    d. demand curve increases.

16. If the price of an input, such as the number of autoworkers, increases, then

    a. the supply of cars will decrease.

    b. the supply of cars will increase.

    c. the price of cars will decrease.

    d. the supply of autoworkers will decrease.

17. If firms expect the price of their product to increase in the future, then

    a. the demand today will decrease.

    b. the price today will decrease.

    c. the price in the future will decrease.

    d. the supply today will decrease.

18. If a firm's opportunity cost of producing a product increases, then the supply of that product will

    a. increase as the number of firms in the industry grows.

    b. decrease as the number of firms in the industry grows.

    c. increase as the number of firms in the industry falls.

    d. decrease as the number of firms in the industry falls.

19. If Al's Used Cars sells a car for a market price of $10,000 and the minimum that they would have sold it for was $4,000, then the producer surplus of Al's Used Cars is

    a. $4,000.

    b. $6,000.

    c. $10,000.

    d. $40,000,000.

Figure 2.9

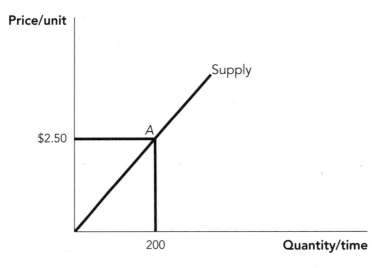

20. In Figure 2.9, total producer surplus is

    a. $2.50.

    b. $197.50.

    c. $250.

    d. $500.

Short-Answer Questions

21. What is a demand curve? What is **qu**antity demanded?

22. What is a supply curve? What is **qu**antity supplied?

23. What is consumer surplus? How **is t**otal consumer surplus measured?

24. What is producer surplus? How **is to**tal producer surplus measured?

25. If the market price for a good is **$6** and the maximum that Tom is willing to pay is $8, what is his consumer **surplus**? Assume that the market price is $6 and 50 units are sold. The demand **c**urve hits the vertical axis at $9. What is the total consumer surplus?

26. If the market price for burgers is **$7** and the minimum that Big Bun Burgers would have sold a burger for is $4, **t**hen what is the producer surplus of Big Bun Burgers on a burger? If the **mar**ket price is $7, all local burger restaurants sell 400 burgers, and the supply **cur**ve passes through the origin, then what is the total producer surplus?

27. Describe and graph an increase in demand. What might cause an increase in demand for a good?

28. Describe and graph a decrease in supply. What might cause a decrease in supply of a good?

29. When does the demand for an inferior good rise? What does it mean for a good to be normal or inferior? What does it *not* mean when it is said that a good is normal or inferior?

30. What determines if two goods are complements or substitutes? Are two goods always substitutes or complements?

Answer Key

Answers to Practice Exercises: Learning by Doing

1. A demand curve is a function that shows the quantity demanded at different prices. Quantity demanded is the quantity that demanders are willing and able to buy at a particular price. The demand curve should be drawn with a negative slope. The demand curve should demonstrate that price decreases lead to increases in quantity demanded.

   Topic: The Demand Curve for Oil

2. A supply curve is a function that shows the quantity supplied at different prices. Quantity supplied is the amount of a good that sellers are willing and able to sell at a particular price. The supply curve should be drawn with a positive slope. The supply curve should demonstrate that price increases lead to increases in quantity supplied.

   Topic: The Supply Curve for Oil

3. Consumer surplus is the consumer's gain from exchange, or the difference between the maximum price the consumer is willing to pay for a certain quantity and the market price. Bob received a consumer surplus of $10 = $20 − $10 from buying a calculator. Kaitlin received a consumer surplus of $5 = $15 − 10 from buying a calculator. Cindy received zero consumer surplus from buying a calculator, because the exchange would not take place. Cindy's potential consumer surplus was negative, that is, −$2 = $8 − $10.

   Topic: Consumer Surplus

4. Total consumer surplus is measured by the area beneath the demand curve and above market price. The area between demand and market price should be marked on the graph. The calculation for total consumer surplus is $20 = ($15 − $10) × 8 × (½).

   Topic: Consumer Surplus

5. Producer surplus is the producer's gain from exchange, or the difference between the market price and the minimum price at which a producer would be willing to sell a particular quantity. Bob received zero producer surplus from selling the textbook, because the exchange would not take place: his potential consumer surplus was negative, that is, -$10 = $80 − $90. Kaitlin received a producer surplus of $40 = $80 − $40 from selling the textbook. Cindy received a producer surplus of $55 = $80 − $25 from selling the textbook.

   Topic: Producer Surplus

6. Total producer surplus is measured by the area above the supply curve and below market price. The area between supply and market price should be marked on the graph. The calculation for total producer surplus is $200 = ($10 − $2) × 50 × (½).

   Topic: Producer Surplus

7. In the first graph, the new demand curve should be above and to the right of the old demand curve. In the second graph, the new demand curve should be below and to the left of the old demand curve.

Topic: What Shifts the Demand Curve?

8. For normal goods, demand increases as income rises because the consumer buys more of the good. For inferior goods, demand decreases as income rises because the consumer shifts to other goods. For substitutes, demand rises when the price of the other good increases, because the consumer substitutes one good for the other. For complements, demand falls when the price of the other good increases, because the consumer uses the two goods together. If population, taste (desire) for a good, and expected future prices each increase, then the demand for the good will also increase. More buyers mean more demand. Increased taste means that each person wants more of the good. Consumers will try to buy today because the good is expected to be more costly in the future.

Topic: What Shifts the Demand Curve?

9. In the first graph, the new supply curve should be to the right of and below the old supply curve. In the second graph, the new supply curve should be above and to the left of the old supply curve.

Topic: What Shifts the Supply Curve?

10. If technology improves, or if the prices of inputs decline, supply increases because production is cheaper. A tax increase makes production more costly and decreases supply, while a subsidy makes production cheaper and increases supply. If a firm expects a higher price in the future, then to the extent its product is not perishable, the firm will reduce supply today to sell later when the price is expected to be higher. The more firms in the market, the greater the supply, since each supplier adds to the supply. Finally, if the opportunity cost for suppliers rises, some suppliers will leave the business for the higher-valued opportunity, thereby reducing supply in the first industry.

Topic: What Shifts the Supply Curve?

11. Apple computers and Windows-based computers are likely substitutes. Thus, when the price of Apple computers falls, the demand for Windows-based computers likely falls. In this scenario, some consumers will purchase Apple computers rather than Windows-based computers. These consumers would most likely have purchased Windows-based computers when the Apple computers were more expensive.

Topic: What Shifts the Demand Curve?

Answers to Multiple-Choice Questions

1. **a, Topic: The Demand Curve for Oil**

2. **d, Topic: The Demand Curve for Oil**

3. **b, Topic: Consumer Surplus**

4. **d, Topic: Consumer Surplus**

5. c, Topic: What Shifts the Demand Curve?

6. b, Topic: What Shifts the Demand Curve?

7. a, Topic: What Shifts the Demand Curve?

8. c, Topic: What Shifts the Demand Curve?

9. a, Topic: What Shifts the Demand Curve?

10. d, Topic: The Demand Curve for Oil

11. d, Topic: The Supply Curve for Oil

12. b, Topic: Producer Surplus

13. a, Topic: Producer Surplus

14. c, Topic: What Shifts the Supply Curve?

15. c, Topic: What Shifts the Supply Curve?

16. a, Topic: What Shifts the Supply Curve?

17. d, Topic: What Shifts the Supply Curve?

18. d, Topic: What Shifts the Supply Curve?

19. b, Topic: Producer Surplus

20. c, Topic: Producer Surplus

Answers to Short-Answer Questions

21. A demand curve is a function that shows the quantity demanded at different prices. Quantity demanded is the quantity that buyers are willing and able to buy at a particular price.

    Topic: The Demand Curve for Oil

22. A supply curve is a function that shows the quantity supplied at different prices. Quantity supplied is the quantity that sellers are willing and able to sell at a particular price.

    Topic: The Supply Curve for Oil

23. Consumer surplus is the consumer's gain from exchange, or the difference between the maximum price a consumer is willing to pay for a certain quantity of goods and the market price. Total consumer surplus is measured by the area beneath the demand curve and above the price.

    Topic: Consumer Surplus

24. Producer surplus is the producer's gain from exchange, or the difference between the market price and the minimum price at which a producer would be willing to sell a certain quantity. Total producer surplus is measured by the area above the supply curve and below the price.

    Topic: Producer Surplus

25. Tom's consumer surplus is $2 on that unit. Total consumer surplus is $75.

    Topic: Consumer Surplus

26. The producer surplus of Big Bun Burgers is $3 on that burger. Total producer surplus is $1,400.

    Topic: Producer Surplus

27. An increase in demand is a shift up and to the right. A graph would be similar to Figure 2.3, with the increase in demand shown as the movement from D_2 to D_1. An increase in demand might be caused by an increase in consumer income for normal goods, a decrease in consumer income for inferior goods, an increase in the price of a substitute good, a decrease in the price of a complementary good, an increase in population, an increase in tastes (desire) for the good, or an expectation of higher future prices for the good.

    Topic: What Shifts the Demand Curve?

28. A decrease in supply is a shift up and to the left. A graph would be similar to Figure 2.6, with the decrease in supply shown as the movement from S_1 to S_2. A decrease in supply might be caused by a negative change in technology, an increase in input prices, an increased tax or a decreased subsidy, an expectation of higher future prices for the good, the exit of some producers of the good from the industry, and a higher opportunity cost of producing the good.

    Topic: What Shifts the Supply Curve?

29. The demand for an inferior good rises when consumer income falls. The terms "normal" and "inferior" just describe the relationship between consumer income and the demand for a good. Normal goods are positively related to consumer income. Inferior goods are negatively related to consumer income. These terms do not necessarily tell us anything about the quality of different goods.

    Topic: What Shifts the Demand Curve?

30. Whether two goods are complements or substitutes depends on how consumers use them. Different consumers do not necessarily use two goods in the same manner. For some people and in some uses, two goods may be complements, and for other people and in other uses, two goods may be substitutes. For example, for some people, sausage and pepperoni are substitutes on pizza. They prefer having only one of the substitutes (sausage or pepperoni) on the pizza. For other people, the more toppings, the better, and they would allow both sausage and pepperoni (complements) to be added to the pizza.

    Topic: What Shifts the Demand Curve?

3

Equilibrium

Why Learn about Equilibrium?

Interested student: It is nice that there is an equilibrium price and quantity in each market, but does it really matter?

Old professor: Sure it matters. It tells us how the price of anything from beer to human tissue is determined.

Interested student: Ok, but how does it matter in real life?

Old professor: Well, someday you might work for a business that depends on the price of its products. And certainly you will care about the wages you receive, because that is the price of your labor. Also, you may vote in an election in which one political candidate thinks that a new policy can reduce the price of some important good. Understanding equilibrium will make you a better-informed voter in such an election.

Interested student: Sure that makes sense.

Old professor: Plus, Chapters 2 and 3 are fundamental to understanding economics, and you are a student taking an economics class.

Summary

The interaction of supply and demand leads to a market equilibrium. As shown in Figure 3.1, market equilibrium occurs where supply and demand intersect.

Figure 3.1

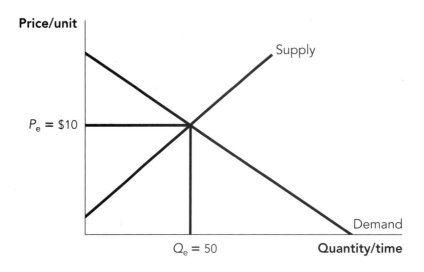

This intersection yields the **equilibrium price**, P_e = $10, and **equilibrium quantity**, Q_e = 50 units of the good.

The market equilibrium is stable, as shown in Figure 3.2, where the equilibrium is still at a price of $10 and a quantity of 50 units.

Figure 3.2

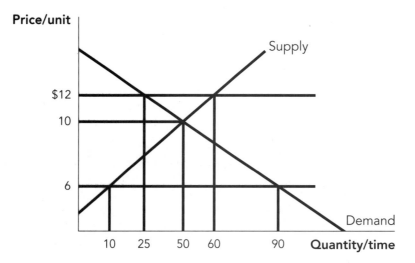

A price of $12 is above equilibrium. At $12, more of the product (60 units) is offered for sale than people want to purchase (25 units). Quantity supplied is greater than quantity demanded by 35 units, implying an excess quantity supplied, or **surplus**.

What will consumers and producers do about the excess quantity supplied? Producers who have rising inventories will start lowering prices below $12. Consumers who see that producers have extra product on hand will start offering prices below $12. Lower prices decrease quantity supplied and increase quantity demanded, moving the market toward equilibrium.

Similarly a price of $6 is below the equilibrium price. At $6, consumers want to buy more of the product (90 units) than producers want to sell (10 units). This time, quantity demanded is greater than quantity supplied by 80 units, implying an excess quantity demanded, or **shortage**.

What will consumers and producers do about the excess quantity demanded? Consumers, many of whom cannot get the item, will start offering prices above $6. Producers, who see their product flying off the shelf, will start asking prices above $6. Higher prices increase quantity supplied and decrease quantity demanded, again moving the market toward equilibrium.

So whether the price is above or below equilibrium, competitive pressures move price and quantity toward the market equilibrium. Only at the equilibrium does quantity supplied equal quantity demanded, implying no pressure from either consumers or producers to change price.

Gains from trade are maximized at the market equilibrium. This can be seen in Figure 3.3, where the 26th unit is worth slightly less than $12, say $11.99, to the consumer and costs the producer only slightly more than $8, say $8.01.

Figure 3.3

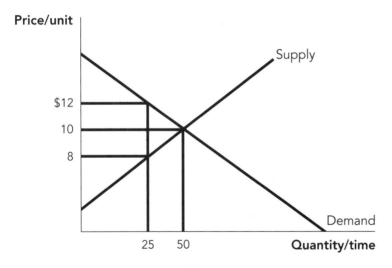

Any price between $11.99 and $8.01 makes both the buyer and seller better off. This is called an unexploited gain from trade. As long as the quantity is below the equilibrium quantity, there will be these unexploited gains from trade.

What if the quantity is above the market equilibrium of 50 units in Figure 3.3? In that case, the cost to producers of producing the unit is greater than what any consumer is willing to pay. So, while consumers are willing to consume the product at some specified price, that price is below the cost of producing the good. Producing such units would waste resources that would be better spent producing something consumers value more.

The free market's, maximizing gains from trade means three closely related things. First, the supply of goods is bought by buyers with the highest willingness to pay. Second, the supply of goods is sold by sellers with the lowest costs. Third, between buyers and sellers there are no unexploited gains from trade, nor any wasteful trades.

As shown in Figure 3.4, a change in demand causes a movement along the supply curve and a change in quantity supplied.

Figure 3.4

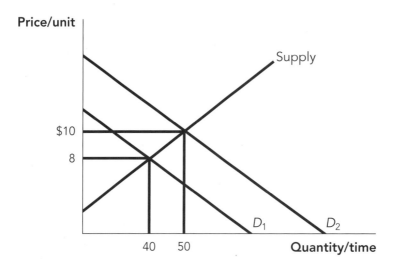

Originally with demand D_1, quantity supplied was 40 units. As demand increased to D_2, quantity moves along the supply curve and quantity supplied becomes 50 units.

For markets with upward-sloping supply curves and downward-sloping demand curves, an increase in demand increases equilibrium price and quantity. As shown in Figure 3.4, the movement of demand from D_1 to D_2 causes the equilibrium price to rise from $8 to $10 and the equilibrium quantity to rise from 40 to 50 units. If demand had decreased from D_2 to D_1 the reverse would have happened. The equilibrium price would have fallen from $10 to $8, and the equilibrium quantity would have fallen from 50 to 40 units.

Similarly, as shown in Figure 3.5, a decrease in supply causes a movement along the demand curve and a change in quantity demanded.

Originally with demand S_1, quantity demanded was 60 units. As supply decreased to D_2, quantity moves along the demand curve and quantity demanded becomes 35 units.

For markets with upward-sloping supply curves and downward-sloping demand curves, a decrease in supply increases equilibrium price and decreases equilibrium quantity. As shown in Figure 3.5, the movement of supply from S_1 to S_2 causes the equilibrium price to rise from $11 to $13 and the equilibrium quantity to fall from 60 to 35 units. If supply had increased from S_2 to S_1 the reverse would have happened. The equilibrium price would have fallen from $13 to $11, and the equilibrium quantity would have risen from 35 to 60 units.

Figure 3.5

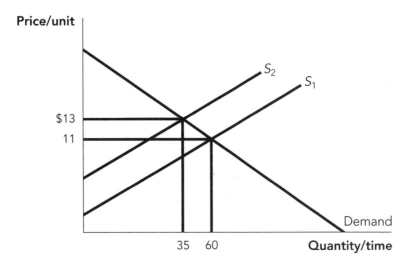

Key Terms

surplus a situation in which the quantity supplied is greater than the quantity demanded

shortage a situation in which the quantity demanded is greater than the quantity supplied

equilibrium price the price at which the quantity demanded is equal to the quantity supplied

equilibrium quantity the quantity at which the quantity demanded is equal to the quantity supplied

Traps, Hints, and Reminders

A surplus should not be confused with consumer or producer surplus, both of which were defined in Chapter 2. A surplus on a market is when quantity supplied is greater than quantity demanded. Consumer surplus is the maximum the consumer is willing to pay less market price. Producer surplus is market price less the minimum price at which the producer would sell.

A free market maximizes the gains from trade, or maximizes producer surplus plus consumer surplus.

A change in demand causes a movement along the supply curve and a change in quantity supplied. Similarly, a change in supply leads to a movement along the demand curve and a change in quantity demanded. The things that can cause changes in quantity demanded or supplied are different from the things that can cause demand and supply to change, as discussed in Chapter 2.

Also recall from Chapter 2 that changes in supply can be somewhat counterintuitive. An increase in supply is a shift to the right and down, while a decrease in supply is a shift up and to the left.

Practice Exercises: Learning by Doing

1. What is the market equilibrium? Draw supply and demand on the graph below. Note the equilibrium price and quantity.

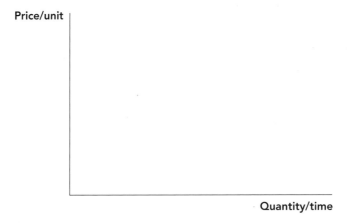

2. On the graphs below, draw a surplus and a shortage in a market.

3. Explain why the market equilibrium is a position the market will tend to. Why is it stable?

4. Explain how the market maximizes the gains from trade, or the sum of consumer and producer surplus.

5. Explain why the market will not produce beyond the equilibrium quantity.

6. In the graph below, draw an increase in supply. Explain what happens.

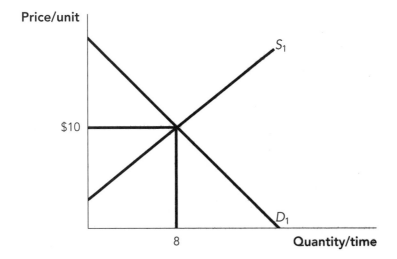

7. In the graph below, draw a decrease in demand. Explain what happens.

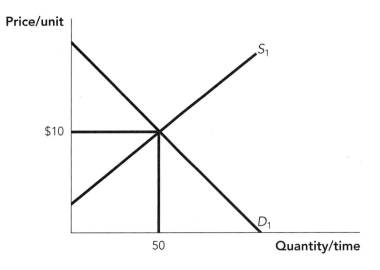

8. What are the three things implied by the free market's maximizing the gains from trade?

*9. In the last 10 years India and China became wealthier and oil prices increased. What is the best way to think about the rise in oil prices during that time? Was the rise in oil prices due to a rise in demand, a fall in demand, a rise in supply, or a fall in supply?[1]

---

[1]Questions marked with a ★ are also end-of-chapter questions.

Multiple-Choice Questions

1. In an equilibrium market
   a. quantity demanded equals quantity supplied.
   b. total surplus is minimized.
   c. the market price is unstable.
   d. All of the answers are correct.

2. If price is above the equilibrium price, some
   a. consumers will offer to pay a higher price to get the product.
   b. producers will ask a higher price of consumers to sell the product.
   c. producers will have excess supplies and thus start reducing price to get customers.
   d. All of the answers are correct.

3. If price is below the equilibrium price, some
   a. consumers will offer to pay a higher price to be sure to get the product.
   b. consumers will offer to pay a lower price because the product is so available.
   c. producers will have excess supplies and thus start reducing price to get customers.
   d. All of the answers are correct.

4. If price is below the equilibrium price, then
   a. every consumer who wants the product can get it.
   b. quantity supplied is greater than quantity demanded for the product.
   c. there is a shortage of the product.
   d. All of the answers are correct.

5. If price is above the equilibrium price, then
   a. every producer who wants to sell the product can do so.
   b. quantity supplied is greater than quantity demanded.
   c. there is a shortage of the product.
   d. All of the answers are correct.

Figure 3.6

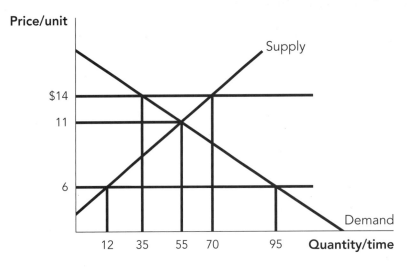

6. In Figure 3.6, the equilibrium price and quantity are
   a. $14 and 70 units.
   b. $11 and 55 units.
   c. $11 and 70 units.
   d. $6 and 12 units.

7. In Figure 3.6, at a price of $14, producers will want to sell
   a. 70 units.
   b. 55 units.
   c. 35 units.
   d. 12 units.

8. In Figure 3.6, at a price of $6, consumers will want to buy
   a. 12 units.
   b. 55 units.
   c. 70 units.
   d. 95 units.

9. In Figure 3.6, at a price of $14, there is an excess quantity
   a. demanded of 83 units.
   b. supplied of 83 units.
   c. demanded of 35 units.
   d. supplied of 35 units.

10. In Figure 3.6, at a price of $6, there is a

    a. shortage of 83 units.

    b. surplus of 83 units.

    c. shortage of 35 units.

    d. surplus of 35 units.

11. In a free market equilibrium,

    a. consumer plus producer surplus is maximized.

    b. gains from trade are maximized.

    c. no potential gains from trade are left unexploited.

    d. All of the answers are correct.

12. The market will not produce a quantity greater than equilibrium because

    a. there are unexploited gains from trade left.

    b. it is illegal.

    c. resources are wasted on production to the right of the equilibrium quantity.

    d. consumer plus producer surplus grows in that region.

13. The free market's maximizing gains from trade implies that

    a. the supply of goods is bought by buyers with the highest willingness to pay.

    b. the supply of goods is sold by sellers with the highest costs.

    c. between buyers and sellers there are unexploited gains from trade.

    d. All of the answers are correct.

14. The free market's maximizing gains from trade implies that

    a. the supply of goods is bought by buyers with the lowest willingness to pay.

    b. the supply of goods is sold by sellers with the lowest costs.

    c. between buyers and sellers there are wasteful trades.

    d. All of the answers are correct.

15. The free market's maximizing gains from trade implies that

    a. the supply of goods is bought by buyers with the lowest willingness to pay.

    b. the supply of goods is sold by sellers with the highest costs.

    c. between buyers and sellers there are no unexploited gains from trade, nor any wasteful trades.

    d. All of the answers are correct.

Figure 3.7

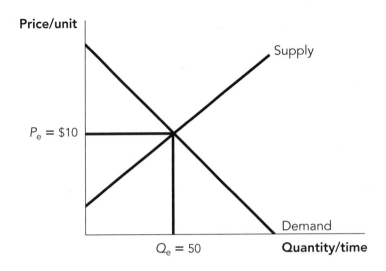

16. In Figure 3.7, if demand increases, then the equilibrium
    a. price and quantity fall.
    b. price and quantity rise.
    c. price falls and quantity rises.
    d. price rises and quantity falls.

17. In Figure 3.7, if supply decreases, then the equilibrium
    a. price and quantity fall.
    b. price and quantity rise.
    c. price falls and quantity rises.
    d. price rises and quantity falls.

18. In Figure 3.7, if the good is normal, and consumer income falls, then the equilibrium
    a. price and quantity fall.
    b. price and quantity rise.
    c. price falls and quantity rises.
    d. price rises and quantity falls.

19. In Figure 3.7, if there is a technological improvement in producing this good, then the equilibrium
    a. price and quantity fall.
    b. price and quantity rise.
    c. price falls and quantity rises.
    d. price rises and quantity falls.

20. In a free market equilibrium,

    a. quantity demanded is greater than quantity supplied.

    b. the sum of consumer and producer surplus is maximized.

    c. resources are wasted.

    d. there are unexploited gains from trade.

Short-Answer Questions

21. Describe market equilibrium.

22. What are the three things implied by the free market's maximizing gains from trade?

23. If the price in a market happens to be below equilibrium, what is the situation in the market? Describe what happens in the market in response to this situation.

24. What is the difference between a change in demand and a change in quantity demanded? What causes each to occur?

25. Graph an increase in demand in a market. Explain what happens to the market when this occurs.

26. Graph an increase in supply in a market. Explain what happens to the market when this occurs.

27. What is meant by trades that waste resources?

28. What is a shortage? What is a surplus?

29. If quantity is less than equilibrium quantity, why are there unexploited gains from trade?

30. What does the free market equilibrium maximize?

Answer Key

Answers to Practice Exercises: Learning by Doing

1. Market equilibrium is where supply and demand intersect. At the equilibrium price, quantity supplied equals quantity demanded. Draw a graph like Figure 3.1.

    Topic: Equilibrium and the Adjustment Process

2. Draw two graphs. Draw one graph like 3.2 with a price above equilibrium. Show how this leads to excess quantity supplied, that is, a surplus. Draw another graph with a price below equilibrium. Show how this leads to an excess quantity demanded, that is, a shortage.

    Topic: Equilibrium and the Adjustment Process

3. If price is above equilibrium, there is an excess quantity supplied. Producers have too much product on hand, and some will start selling at a lower price, moving the market toward equilibrium. If price is below equilibrium, there will be an excess quantity demanded. Not all consumers can get the good, and some will start offering a higher price to be sure to get the good. This also moves the market toward equilibrium. At the equilibrium price and quantity each producer sells all it wants and each consumer is able to buy all he or she wants. This makes the market equilibrium stable.

    Topic: Equilibrium and the Adjustment Process

4. The market maximizes gains from trade by allowing all producers (who want to sell) to sell at the going price and all consumers (who want to buy) to buy at the going price. This maximizes consumer surplus and producer surplus.

    Topic: Gains from Trade Are Maximized at the Equilibrium Price and Quantity

5. The market will not produce beyond the equilibrium, quantity because doing so would waste resources. Consumers will not value the product enough to make up for the costs to the producers of producing the product.

    Topic: Gains from Trade Are Maximized at the Equilibrium Price and Quantity

6. The new supply curve should be below and to the right of the old supply curve. The increase in supply leads to a movement along the demand curve. Quantity demanded increases, the new equilibrium price is lower, and quantity is larger.

    Topic: Shifting Demand and Supply Curves

7. The new demand curve should be below and to the left of the old demand curve. The decrease in demand leads to a movement along the supply curve. Quantity supplied falls, and the new equilibrium price and quantity are lower.

    Topic: Shifting Demand and Supply Curves

8. The supply of goods is bought by the buyers with the highest willingness to pay. The supply of goods is sold by sellers with the lowest costs. Between buyers and sellers there are no unexploited gains from trade, nor any wasteful trades.

   Topic: Gains from Trade Are Maximized at the Equilibrium Price and Quantity

9. India and China becoming richer in the last 10 years is best thought of as leading to an increase in the demand for oil that has led to some upward movements in the price of oil.

   Topic: Shifting Demand and Supply Curves

Answers to Multiple-Choice Questions

1. a, Topic: Equilibrium and the Adjustment Process

2. c, Topic: Equilibrium and the Adjustment Process

3. a, Topic: Equilibrium and the Adjustment Process

4. c, Topic: Equilibrium and the Adjustment Process

5. b, Topic: Equilibrium and the Adjustment Process

6. b, Topic: Equilibrium and the Adjustment Process

7. a, Topic: Equilibrium and the Adjustment Process

8. d, Topic: Equilibrium and the Adjustment Process

9. d, Topic: Equilibrium and the Adjustment Process

10. a, Topic: Equilibrium and the Adjustment Process

11. d, Topic: Gains from Trade Are Maximized at the Equilibrium Price and Quantity

12. c, Topic: Gains from Trade Are Maximized at the Equilibrium Price and Quantity

13. a, Topic: Gains from Trade Are Maximized at the Equilibrium Price and Quantity

14. b, Topic: Gains from Trade Are Maximized at the Equilibrium Price and Quantity

15. c, Topic: Gains from Trade Are Maximized at the Equilibrium Price and Quantity

16. b, Topic: Shifting Demand and Supply Curves

17. d, Topic: Shifting Demand and Supply Curves

18. a, Topic: Shifting Demand and Supply Curves

19. c, Topic: Shifting Demand and Supply Curves

20. b, Topic: Equilibrium and the Adjustment Process

Answers to Short-Answer Questions

21. The market equilibrium is where supply and demand intersect. This is also where, at one price, quantity demanded equals quantity supplied. At this point, the market has captured all gains from trade and maximized the sum of consumer and producer surplus. The equilibrium is stable because every consumer can buy all they want at the market price and every seller can sell all they want at the market price.

Topic: Equilibrium and the Adjustment Process

22. The supply of goods is bought by the buyers with the highest willingness to pay. The supply of goods is sold by sellers with the lowest costs. Between buyers and sellers there are no unexploited gains from trade, nor any wasteful trades.

Topic: Equilibrium and the Adjustment Process

23. When price is below the equilibrium price, quantity demanded is greater than quantity supplied, that is, there is a shortage. Not all consumers who want to consume at that price will be able to purchase the good. Some consumers will start offering higher prices to ensure that they can get the good. The higher price will cause quantity supplied to increase and quantity demanded to decrease, thus moving the market toward equilibrium.

Topic: Equilibrium and the Adjustment Process

24. A change in demand is a shift of the entire curve. Shifts in the entire curve are caused by the items discussed in Chapter 2, such as tastes and consumer income. A change in quantity demanded is a movement along the demand curve. A movement along the demand curve is caused by a shift in the supply curve or a change in price in the market.

Topic: Shifting Demand and Supply Curves

25. The new demand curve should be above and to the right of the initial demand curve. The equilibrium price and quantity increase.

Topic: Shifting Demand and Supply Curves

26. The new supply curve should be below and to the right of the initial supply curve. The equilibrium price falls and the equilibrium quantity rises.

Topic: Shifting Demand and Supply Curves

27. Exchanges beyond the equilibrium quantity are not made, because the cost to the producers of producing the product is greater than the value that consumers place on the product. Thus, if such trades were made, scarce resources would be wasted. A better use of these resources would be to produce something that consumers would value more. Thus if those units were produced and sold, the difference between the cost of producing them from the supply curve, and the value consumers place on them from the demand curve, would be wasted.

Topic: Gains from Trade Are Maximized at the Equilibrium Price and Quantity

28. A shortage is when quantity demanded is greater than quantity supplied, that is, there is excess quantity demanded. A surplus is when there is excess quantity supplied; that is, quantity supplied is greater than quantity demanded.

    Topic: Gains from Trade Are Maximized at the Equilibrium Price and Quantity

29. For each unit less than the market equilibrium quantity, some consumer values that unit more than it costs some producer to produce it. This is another way of saying that demand is above supply. Thus there is some price between the value the consumer places on the good and the producer's cost of producing the good that would make both consumer and producer better off. Those are the unexploited gains from trade when quantity is less than equilibrium quantity.

    Topic: Gains from Trade Are Maximized at the Equilibrium Price and Quantity

30. A free market equilibrium maximizes both the sum of producer and consumer surplus and gains from trade.

    Topic: Gains from Trade Are Maximized at the Equilibrium Price and Quantity

4

Elasticity and Its Applications

Why Learn about Elasticity?

Elasticity takes supply and demand and makes them practical. Rather than just saying, as we did in Chapter 3, if price changes, then the quantity changes, elasticity lets us answer the question—if we raise the price of our product, how much will the quantity demanded fall? For example, elasticity lets a city ask, if we raise bus fares, how much will bus ridership fall?

Who will be interested in elasticity?

> New entrepreneurs who want to decide what type of business to go into

> Legislators, government officials, and candidates at any level, who will be interested in determining the best price for services—whether it is bus service on the local level, car tags on the state level, or passports on the national level

> Businesspeople, particularly marketers, who want to decide what price to charge for their product

> Students of economics, of course, who will someday choose an occupation

Summary

Elasticity allows us to move from the theory of supply and demand to practical applications. Elasticity asks the questions—how much quantity is demanded or how much does supply change when something else changes?

Elasticity of demand measures how sensitive the quantity demanded is to a change in price. If the quantity demanded is very sensitive to a change in price we call it elastic. If the quantity demanded is not very sensitive to a change in price we call it inelastic.

As shown in Figure 4.1, a relatively flat demand curve is more elastic than a steeper demand curve at any given point. For a $1 price increase, the quantity demanded falls 6 units on the elastic, that is, a more responsive demand curve. For the same $1 price increase, the quantity demanded falls only 1 unit on the inelastic, that is, a relatively less responsive demand curve.

Figure 4.1

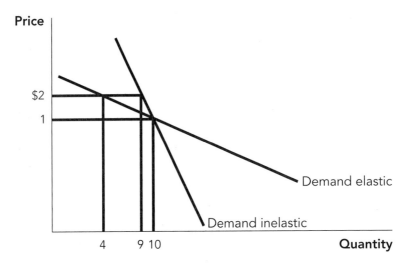

Goods that have fewer substitutes, are necessities, are categories of goods, and are a smaller part of consumers' budgets have more inelastic demands. Goods that have more substitutes are luxuries, are specific brands, and are a larger part of consumers' budgets have more elastic demands. The demand for any good is more inelastic in a shorter time frame than in a longer time frame.

Elasticity of demand is calculated as the percentage change in quantity demanded divided by the percentage change in price.

$$\text{Elasticity of demand} = E_D = \frac{\text{Percentage Change in Quantity Demanded}}{\text{Percentage Change in Price}}$$

$$= \frac{\%\Delta Q_{demanded}}{\%\Delta Price}$$

The symbol, delta, Δ, means change, and the resulting negative number is taken in absolute terms, that is, taken to be positive. Thus if the percentage change in price is 50% and the percentage change in quantity demanded is 100%, then the elasticity of demand = (100%/50%) = 2. Also, if the percentage change price is 50% and the percentage change in quantity demanded is 25%, then the elasticity of demand = (25%/50%) = 0.5 (or ½). Note that in these demand elasticity examples, either the percentage change in price or the percentage change in quantity must be negative. We are dropping the sign or taking the absolute values in our calculations.

Anytime the percentage change in quantity demanded is greater than the percentage change in price, then the elasticity of demand will be greater than 1 and called elastic.

Anytime the percentage change in quantity demanded is less than the percentage change in price, the elasticity of demand will be less than 1 and called inelastic. In the special case where the percentage change in quantity equals the percentage change in price, the elasticity of demand equals 1 and it is called unit elastic.

Elasticity also indicates the relationship between price and total revenue from selling the good. Total revenue is the price multiplied by the quantity. When demand is elastic, price and total revenue move in opposite directions. This is because when price goes up a little, the quantity demanded goes down a lot. As a result, total revenue declines because the price increase is more than offset by the decrease in the quantity demanded. When demand is inelastic, price and total revenue move in the same direction. This is because when price goes up a lot, the quantity demanded only goes down a little. Thus total revenue rises as the price increase is not completely offset by the decrease in the quantity demanded. For the case when demand is unit elastic, as price goes up, the quantity demanded goes down by the same proportion, and thus total revenue is unchanged. In other words, with unit elasticity, price and total revenue are unrelated because when price changes total revenue does not.

Consider the points on the demand curves we called elastic and inelastic in Figure 4.1. Total revenue is initially 1×10 units $= $10. When price rises to $2 on the relatively elastic demand curve, the quantity demanded falls to 4 units. Thus total revenue becomes 2×4 units $= $8 and as price rose on the relatively elastic demand curve, total revenue fell. When price rises to $2 on the relatively inelastic demand curve, the quantity demanded falls to 9 units. Thus total revenue becomes 2×9 units $= $18 and as price rose on the relatively inelastic demand curve, total revenue rose.

Of course the reverse is also true in each case. If price falls, then total revenue on an inelastic demand curve falls. If price falls, then total revenue rises on an elastic demand curve. The relationship between elasticity of demand and total revenue is summarized in the table below.

Absolute Value of Elasticity	Name	Price and Total Revenue
$E_D < 1$	Inelastic	move together
$E_D > 1$	Elastic	move opposite directions
$E_D = 1$	Unit Elastic	are unrelated

Elasticity of supply measures how sensitive the quantity supplied is to a change in price. As with elasticity of demand, a steeper supply curve is relatively more inelastic while a flatter supply curve is relatively more elastic.

Two extreme cases of elasticity of supply are shown in Figure 4.2.

In the left-hand graph of Figure 4.2 supply is perfectly elastic. In this case, price does not change when the quantity demanded changes. In the right-hand graph of Figure 4.2 supply is perfectly inelastic. In this case, quantity demanded does not change when price changes.

Supply is less elastic when it is difficult to increase production at unit costs; production uses up a large share of the market for inputs, for global supply, and in the

Figure 4.2

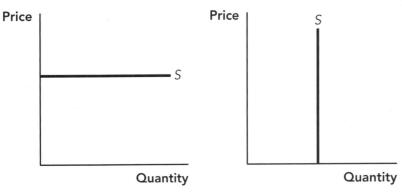

short run. Supply is more elastic when it is easy to increase production at unit costs; production uses up a small share of the market for inputs, for local supply, and in the long run.

Elasticity of supply is also calculated as percentage change in the quantity supplied divided by the percentage change in price, where delta, Δ, still means change.

$$\text{Elasticity of supply} = E_S = \frac{\text{Percentage Change in Quantity Supplied}}{\text{Percentage Change in Price}}$$

$$= \frac{\%\Delta Q_{Supplied}}{\%\Delta Price}$$

The resulting value is positive for the elasticity of supply, because when the price increases, so does the quantity. Thus if the percentage change in price is 100% and the percentage change in the quantity supplied is 300%, then elasticity of supply = (300%/100%) = 3. Also, if the percentage change in price is 80% and the percentage change in the quantity supplied is 20%, then the elasticity of supply = (20%/80%) = ¼ (or 0.25).

Elasticities can be used to predict changes in price from demand or supply shifts. If demand increases by 10%, the elasticity of demand, E_D, is ½ (or 0.5), and the elasticity of supply, E_S, is 2, then these numbers can be plugged into the following formula:

$$\text{Percentage change in Price from a shift in demand} = \frac{\text{Percentage Change in Demand}}{(E_D + E_S)}$$

Using these numbers would give 10/(2 + ½) or (10/2.5) = 4. Thus, in this example, we predict a 4% increase in price.

Similar formulas can be used to predict percentage change in price from a supply shift and percentage change in quantity from either a supply or demand shift, for instance:

$$\text{Percentage change in Price from a shift in supply} = -\frac{\text{Percentage Change in Supply}}{(E_D + E_S)}$$

Notice the equation above has a minus sign in front of the right-hand side.

Percentage change in Quantity from a shift in demand

$$= E_S \times \frac{\text{(Percentage Change in Demand)}}{(E_D + E_S)}$$

Percentage change in Quantity from a shift in supply

$$= E_D \times \frac{\text{(Percentage Change in Supply)}}{(E_D + E_S)}$$

Appendix 1: Using Excel to Calculate Elasticities

Percentage changes depend on one's point of reference. Thus we calculate elastiticities along a range of points based on the midpoint of the change. This is shown in the following formula:

$$\text{Elasticity of demand} = E_D = \frac{\dfrac{\text{Change in Quantity Demanded}}{\text{Average Quantity}}}{\dfrac{\text{Change in Price}}{\text{Average Price}}}$$

$$= \frac{\dfrac{Q_{before} - Q_{after}}{(Q_{before} + Q_{after})/2}}{\dfrac{P_{before} - P_{after}}{(P_{before} + P_{after})/2}}$$

For example, if at \$3 people buy 100 units of a product, and at \$1 people buy 200 units of a product, then:

$$E_D = \frac{\dfrac{Q_{before} - Q_{after}}{(Q_{before} + Q_{after})/2}}{\dfrac{P_{before} - P_{after}}{(P_{before} + P_{after})/2}} = \frac{\dfrac{100 - 200}{(100 + 200)/2}}{\dfrac{\$3 - \$1}{(\$3 + \$1)/2}} = \frac{\dfrac{100}{150}}{\dfrac{1}{1}} = 2/3 \text{ (or 0.67)}$$

Notice that we have dropped the minus sign. Also notice, as expected with a calculated elasticity of less than one, that when the price fell from \$3 to \$1, the total revenue also fell from \$300 to \$200.

A similar formula allows calculation of elasticity of supply over a range of points.

$$\text{Elasticity of supply} = E_S = \cfrac{\cfrac{\text{Change in Quantity Supplied}}{\text{Average Quantity}}}{\cfrac{\text{Change in Price}}{\text{Average Price}}}$$

$$= \cfrac{\cfrac{Q_{before} - Q_{after}}{(Q_{before} + Q_{after})/2}}{\cfrac{P_{before} - P_{after}}{(P_{before} + P_{after})/2}}$$

Appendix 2: Other Types of Elasticities

One can compute elasticities between any two variables that are related. Two other important variables are cross-price elasticity of demand and income elasticity.

Cross-price elasticity measures how sensitive the quantity demanded for one good is to the price of another good. It is calculated using the following formula where delta, Δ, still means change.

Cross-Price Elasticity of demand Good A

$$= \frac{\text{Percentage Change in Quantity Demanded of Good A}}{\text{Percentage Change in Price of Good B}}$$

$$= \frac{\%\Delta Q_{demanded\ of\ Good\ A}}{\%\Delta\ Price\ of\ Good\ B}$$

Or, if you have data on two different prices of good B, you would use the following midpoint formula for cross-price elasticity.

$$\cfrac{\cfrac{\text{Change in Quantity Demanded A}}{\text{Average Quantity of Good A}}}{\cfrac{\text{Change in Price B}}{\text{Average Price of Good B}}} = \cfrac{\cfrac{Q_{before\ A} - Q_{after\ A}}{(Q_{before\ A} + Q_{after\ A})/2}}{\cfrac{P_{before\ B} - P_{after\ B}}{(P_{before\ B} + P_{after\ B})/2}}$$

If the cross-price elasticity is > 0, then goods A and B are substitutes. If the cross-price elasticity is < 0, then goods A and B are complements.

Income elasticity measures how sensitive the quantity demanded of a good is to changes in consumer income. It is calculated using the following formula where delta, Δ, still stands for change.

$$\text{Income Elasticity of demand} = \frac{\text{Percentage Change in Quantity Demanded}}{\text{Percentage Change in Income}}$$

$$= \frac{\%\Delta Q_{demanded}}{\%\Delta Income}$$

Or, if you have data on two different consumer income levels, you would use the midpoint formula for income elasticity.

$$\frac{\dfrac{\text{Change in Quantity Demanded}}{\text{Average Quantity}}}{\dfrac{\text{Change in Income}}{\text{Average Income}}} = \frac{\dfrac{Q_{before} - Q_{after}}{(Q_{before} + Q_{after})/2}}{\dfrac{I_{before} - I_{after}}{(I_{before} + I_{after})/2}}$$

If the income elasticity is > 0, then the good is a normal good. If the income elasticity is < 0, then the good is inferior. Some economists define cases where income elasticity of demand is > 1 as luxury goods.

Key Terms

elasticity of demand a measure of how responsive the quantity demanded is to a change in price

elasticity of supply a measure of how responsive the quantity supplied is to a change in price

Traps, Hints, and Reminders

Remember with elasticity of demand take the absolute value or drop the sign. The meanings of elasticity of demand are all in terms of positive values.

All of the elasticities in this chapter follow one general formula. That is, percentage change in quantity demanded or supplied divided by percentage change in some other variable. The variable is in the denominator (that is, on the bottom), demand price, supply price, the cross-price, or price of another good or income, and gives the name to the elasticity (such as demand elasticity, supply elasticity, cross-price elasticity, or income elasticity).

When thinking about the relationship of price and total revenue, think of a string or even a steel rod if you like. A string or steel rod is relatively inelastic. If price and total revenue were tied together with a string or hooked together by a steel rod, then when price rises, total revenue also rises, and when price falls, total revenue also falls.

If you have data on two "price and quantity demanded" combinations, you can partly check your calculated elasticity of demand by checking to see if the relationship between price and total revenue is as it should be. For example, if you calculate a demand elasticity of ½ (or 0.5), but discover as price goes up in your data, total revenue goes down, you should know that you must have made a calculation error someplace. Thus you should recheck your calculations.

An increase in supply decreases price such that the predicted change in price, from a shift in supply, has a negative sign in front of the formula.

Practice Exercises: Learning by Doing

1. What does elasticity of demand measure? What does it tell us about the relationship between price and total revenue?

2. What factors tend to make demand more elastic?

3. What does elasticity of supply measure? What factors make supply more inelastic?

4. Why is either supply or demand more elastic on a flatter curve than on a steeper curve?

5. If when price decreases 10%, the quantity demanded increases 50%, then what is elasticity of demand? What does it tell us about price and total revenue?

6. Draw a perfectly inelastic supply curve in panel A below. Draw a perfectly elastic supply curve in panel B below. What are the implications of each?

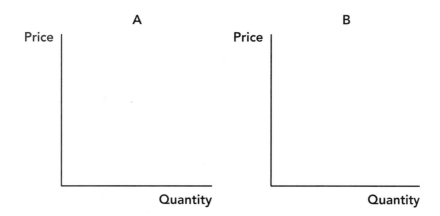

7. If the absolute value of the elasticity of demand is 0.4, the elasticity of supply is 2.1, and the demand increases by 50%, then by what percentage will price rise?

★**8.** A lot of American action movies are quests to eliminate a villain. If, in real life, villains are elastically supplied (like gun buyback programs), should we care whether the hero captures any particular villain? Why or why not?[1]

---

[1]Questions marked with a ★ are also end-of-chapter questions.

Appendix 1: Using Excel to Calculate Elasticities

9. If when price is $4, the quantity supplied is 100 units, and when price is $6, the quantity supplied is 200 units, then what is the elasticity of supply? Is this supply elastic or inelastic?

Appendix 2: Other Types of Elasticities

10. What are the meanings of income and cross-price elasticities?

11. When income is $30,000, people buy 1,000 units of a good, and when income rises to $50,000, people buy 500 units of the same good. Using the midpoint formula, calculate the income elasticity of this good. What kind of good is it?

Multiple-Choice Questions

1. A demand curve that is relatively responsive to price changes is
   a. more elastic.
   b. more inelastic.
   c. perfectly inelastic.
   d. more inferior.

2. A supply curve that is relatively less responsive to price changes is
   a. more elastic.
   b. more inelastic.
   c. perfectly elastic.
   d. less inferior.

3. Elasticity of demand measures
   a. the responsiveness of price to a change in the quantity demanded.
   b. the responsiveness of price to a change in the quantity supplied.
   c. the responsiveness of the quantity demanded to a change in price.
   d. the responsiveness of the quantity supplied to a change in price.

4. Elasticity of supply measures

    a. the responsiveness of price to a change in the quantity demanded.

    b. the responsiveness of price to a change in the quantity supplied.

    c. the responsiveness of the quantity demanded to a change in price.

    d. the responsiveness of the quantity supplied to a change in price.

5. A flatter supply curve is relatively more elastic than a steeper supply curve because

    a. price changes relatively more than the quantity supplied.

    b. the quantity supplied changes relatively more than price.

    c. the quantity demanded changes more than the quantity supplied.

    d. the quantity supplied is relatively insensitive to price changes.

6. A perfectly elastic supply curve is

    a. downward sloping.

    b. upward sloping.

    c. horizontal.

    d. vertical.

7. If the absolute value of elasticity of demand is 0.25 (or ¼), then

    a. demand is elastic.

    b. the quantity demanded is relatively insensitive to price changes.

    c. when price rises, total revenue falls.

    d. All of the answers are correct.

8. If elasticity of demand is 2.5, then

    a. demand is elastic.

    b. price and total revenue move in the opposite directions.

    c. the quantity demanded is relatively sensitive to price changes.

    d. All of the answers are correct.

9. If elasticity of demand is unit elastic, then

    a. price and total revenue move together.

    b. demand is elastic.

    c. total revenue does not change when price changes.

    d. All of the answers are correct.

10. Supply will be more elastic

    a. in a longer time frame.

    b. for raw materials.

    c. for global supply.

    d. All of the answers are correct.

11. Demand will be more inelastic

    a. in the short run.

    b. if the good is a small percentage of the consumer's budget.

    c. if the good has few substitutes.

    d. All of the answers are correct.

12. If when price rises by 5%, the quantity demanded falls by 10%, then the absolute value of elasticity of demand is

    a. 0.5 (or ½).

    b. 2.

    c. 15.

    d. 50.

13. If when price rises by 200%, the quantity supplied increases by 50%, then the elasticity of supply is

    a. 0.25 (or ¼).

    b. 4.

    c. 250.

    d. 10,000.

14. If the absolute value of the elasticity of demand for gasoline is 0.5 (or ½), the elasticity of supply is 1.5 (or ⅔), and demand increased 10%, then you would expect the price of gasoline to rise by

    a. 2%.

    b. 5%.

    c. 10%.

    d. None of the answers is correct.

15. If the elasticity of demand for cars is 0.2, the elasticity of supply is 0.8, and supply increases 15%, then you would expect the price of cars to fall by

    a. 1%.

    b. 4.33%.

    c. 15%.

    d. None of the answers is correct.

Multiple-Choice Questions: Appendixes

16. If cross-price elasticity is positive, then the two goods are

    a. substitutes.

    b. inferior.

    c. normal.

    d. complements.

17. If the income elasticity is negative then the good is

    a. elastic.

    b. inelastic.

    c. inferior.

    d. normal.

18. If when the price of butter is \$1, consumers buy 100 units of margarine, and when the price of butter is \$3, consumers buy 900 units of margarine, then the cross-price elasticity between butter and margarine is

    a. -3.2.

    b. -1.6.

    c. 1.6.

    d. 3.2.

19. If when peanut butter is \$5, firms supply 2,000 units, and when peanut butter is \$1, firms supply 1,000 units, then using the midpoint formula the elasticity of supply of peanut butter is

    a. 0 (zero).

    b. 0.5 (½).

    c. 1.

    d. 2.

20. If cross-price elasticity is negative, then the two goods are

    a. substitutes.

    b. inferior.

    c. normal

    d. complements.

Short-Answer Questions

21. What does elasticity of supply measure? What makes elasticity of supply more elastic?

22. What does demand elasticity tell us about the relationship between price and total revenue?

23. What is demand elasticity? Why is a relatively steeper demand curve more inelastic?

24. When price increases by 45% quantity demanded falls by 15%. What is the elasticity of demand? What must have happened to total revenue with this price change?

25. When price increases by 25% quantity supplied rises by 75%. What is the elasticity of supply? What is it called?

26. What factors make the elasticity of demand more inelastic?

27. In general, what are elasticities?

28. If the absolute value of the elasticity of demand for your product is 2.0, and the elasticity of supply is 3.0, then how would a 10% increase in supply influence your price?

Short-Answer Questions: Appendixes

29. What are the meanings of income and cross-price elasticities?

30. When the price of gasoline is $4, people buy 1,000 tires, and when the price of gasoline is $2, people buy 1500 tires. Using the midpoint formula, calculate the cross-price elasticity. What is the relationship between gasoline and tires?

Answer Key

Answers to Practice Exercises: Learning by Doing

1. Elasticity of demand measures how sensitive the quantity demanded is to a change in price. When demand is elastic, price and total revenue move in opposite directions. That is, when price rises, total revenue falls. When demand is inelastic, price and total revenue move together. That is, when price falls, total revenue falls too. When demand is unit elastic, price changes leave total revenue unchanged.

   Topic: The Elasticity of Demand

2. Goods with more substitutes are luxuries, are specific brands, are a larger part of consumers' budgets, and are more elastic demands. The demand for any good is more elastic in the long run.

   Topic: The Elasticity of Demand

3. Supply is less elastic when it is difficult to increase production at unit costs; production uses up a large share of the market for inputs, for global supply, and in the short run. Supply is more elastic when it is easy to increase production at unit costs; production uses up a small share of the market for inputs, for local supply and in the long run.

   Topic: The Elasticity of Supply

4. Elasticity of supply or demand is more elastic on a relatively flatter supply or demand curve, because a relatively flatter curve moves more on the quantity axis for a unit change along the price axis. In other words, for any given price increase, there is more change in quantity along a flatter demand or supply curve than along a steeper demand or supply curve.

   Topic: The Elasticity of Demand

5. Elasticity of demand is $\%\Delta Q_{demanded}/\%\Delta Price$ or in this case 50%/10%, which equals 5. So demand in this case is elastic, meaning as price falls, total revenue rises.

   Topic: The Elasticity of Demand

6. In panel A you should have drawn a vertical supply. In panel B you should have drawn a horizontal supply. The perfectly inelastic supply in panel A implies that the quantity supplied will not change no matter the price. The perfectly elastic supply in panel B implies price will not change no matter the quantity supplied.

   Topic: The Elasticity of Supply

7. Percentage change in Price from a shift in demand = Percentage Change in Demand divided by $(E_D + E_S)$. In this case, it would be 50/(0.4 + 2.1), which equals 20. So based on this data we would expect a 20% increase in price.

   Topic: Using Elasticities for Quick Predictions

8. Since the supply of villains is elastic, the capture of any villain raises the price of being a villain, and thus having a large effect on the quantity of villains. So, unless the particular villain is one immediately harming you, you should not care much whether the hero catches a particular villain. However, you should care that the hero catches some villains to make the cost of villainy higher, thus causing a large reduction in the quantity supplied of villains.

Topic: The Elasticity of Supply

9. Use the formula $E_S = (Q_{before} - Q_{after})/[(Q_{before} + Q_{after})/2]$ divided by $(P_{before} - P_{after})/[(P_{before} + P_{after})/2]$. Inserting the prices and quantities will give $E_S = (100 - 200)/[(100 + 200)/2]/(4 - 6)/[(4 + 6)/2]$, which equals $(-100/150)/(-2/5)$. The negative terms cancel out and you can reduce the fraction by multiplying the top and the bottom by 5/2 and you get 500/300 (or 5/3), or 1.67. This supply is elastic as quantity changes by a greater percentage than price.

Topic: Appendix 1: Using Excel to Calculate Elasticities

10. If the income elasticity is > 0, then the good is a normal good. If the income elasticity is < 0, then the good is inferior. Some economists define cases where income elasticity of demand is > 1 as a luxury good. If the cross-price elasticity is > 0, then goods A and B are substitutes. If the cross-price elasticity is < 0, then goods A and B are complements.

Topic: Appendix 2: Other Types of Elasticities

11. Elasticity of income $= (Q_{before} - Q_{after})/[(Q_{before} + Q_{after})/2]$ divided by $(I_{before} - I_{after})/[(I_{before} + I_{after})/2]$. Inserting the incomes and units of goods will give an Elasticity of income $= (1000 - 500)/[(1000 + 500)/2]/(30,000 - 50,000)/[(30,000 + 50,000)/2]$, which equals $(500/750)/(-20,000/40,000)$. You can reduce the fraction to $(50/75)/(-\frac{1}{2})$. You can further reduce the fraction by multiplying the top and the bottom by -2/1 and you get -100/75 (or -4/3), or -1.33. Since the income elasticity is negative, this good is an inferior good.

Topic: Appendix 2: Other Types of Elasticities

Answers to Multiple-Choice Questions

1. **a, Topic: The Elasticity of Demand**

2. **b, Topic: The Elasticity of Supply**

3. **c, Topic: The Elasticity of Demand**

4. **d, Topic: The Elasticity of Supply**

5. **b, Topic: The Elasticity of Supply**

6. **c, Topic: The Elasticity of Supply**

7. **b, Topic: The Elasticity of Demand**

8. **d, Topic: The Elasticity of Demand**

9. c, Topic: The Elasticity of Demand

10. a, Topic: The Elasticity of Supply

11. d, Topic: The Elasticity of Demand

12. b, Topic: The Elasticity of Demand

13. a, Topic: The Elasticity of Supply

14. b, Topic: Using Elasticities for Quick Predictions

15. c, Topic: Using Elasticities for Quick Predictions

16. a, Topic: Appendix 2: Other Types of Elasticities

17. c, Topic: Appendix 2: Other Types of Elasticities

18. c, Topic: Appendix 2: Other Types of Elasticities

19. b, Topic: Appendix 1: Using Excel to Calculate Elasticities

20. d, Topic: Appendix 2: Other Types of Elasticities

Answers to Short-Answer Questions

21. Elasticity of supply measures how sensitive the quantity supplied is to a change in price. As supply is more elastic, the easier it is to increase production at constant unit costs for manufactured goods in the long run. Elasticity of supply is more elastic if the industry hires a small share of its inputs, compared to the market for those inputs and for a local supply.

    Topic: The Elasticity of Supply

22. When demand is elastic, price and total revenue move in opposite directions. That is, when price rises, total revenue falls. When demand is inelastic, price and total revenue move together. That is, when price falls, total revenue falls too. When demand is unit elastic, price changes leave total revenue unchanged.

    Topic: The Elasticity of Demand

23. Elasticity of demand measures how sensitive the quantity demanded is to a change in price. Elasticity of demand is more inelastic along a relatively steeper demand curve, because a relatively steeper curve moves less along the quantity axis than along the price axis. In other words, for any given price increase, there is less change in quantity on a steeper demand curve than on a flatter demand curve, or quantity is less responsive to price on a steeper demand curve.

    Topic: The Elasticity of Demand

24. Elasticity of demand is $\%\Delta Q_{demanded}/\%\Delta Price$ or in this case 15%/45% which equals 0.33 (or 1/3). Total revenue must have risen as price rose and demand is inelastic.

    Topic: The Elasticity of Demand

25. Elasticity of supply is $\%\Delta Q_{demanded}/\%\Delta Price$ or in this case 75%/25% which equals 3. Supply is elastic in this case.

Topic: The Elasticity of Supply

26. Goods that have fewer substitutes, are necessities, are categories of goods, and are a smaller part of consumers' budgets have more inelastic demands. The demand for any good is more inelastic in a shorter time frame.

Topic: The Elasticity of Demand

27. Elasticities show the sensitivity of one good to changes in some other variable. In all of the elasticities in this chapter it is the sensitivity of the quantity demanded or supplied to some variable, particularly price. Thus elasticities tell us whether quantity changes by a larger percentage or a smaller percentage than some other variable that has changed.

Topic: The Elasticity of Demand

28. Percentage change in price from a shift in supply = -(Percentage Change in supply) divided by $(E_D + E_S)$. In this case it would be 10/(2+3) which equals -2. So based on this data we would expect a 2% decrease in price.

Topic: Using Elasticities for Quick Predictions

29. If the income elasticity is > 0, then the good is a normal good. If the income elasticity is < 0, then the good is inferior. Some economists define cases where income elasticity of demand is > 1 as luxury good. If the cross–price elasticity is > 0, then goods A and B are substitutes, If the cross-price elasticity is < 0, then goods A and B are complements.

Topic: Appendix 2: Other Types of Elasticities

30. Cross-price elasticity = $(Q_{before\ A} - Q_{after\ A})/[(Q_{before\ A} + Q_{after\ A})/2]$ divided by $(P_{before\ B} - P_{after\ B})/[(P_{before\ B} + P_{after\ B})/2]$ or (1000 − 1500)/[(1000 + 1500)/2]/(4 − 2)/[(4 + 2)/2] which equals (-500/1250)/(2/3). You can reduce the fraction to (-10/25)/(2/3). You can further reduce the fraction by multiplying the top and the bottom by 3/2 and thus you get -30/50 (or -3/5), or -0.6. Since the cross-price elasticity is negative, these goods are complements.

Topic: Appendix 2: Other Types of Elasticities

5

The Price System: Signals, Speculation, and Prediction

Why Learn about the Price System?

Typical Student: Will this be on the test?

Enthusiastic Professor: Of course it is likely to be covered on the test. It is very important material. This chapter is about the ideas associated with market equilibrium from Chapter 3.

Typical Student: Really? How is that?

Enthusiastic Professor: In this chapter, we learn what the price system does and how it does it. We learn that the ever-unpopular speculators serve economic functions. Understanding speculation is important to people who work in speculative markets and to people who might want to regulate such markets. We also discuss why central planning is unlikely to work. As a voter, you might not want to see the price system short-circuited by politicians, especially during a natural disaster when it might be needed the most. As a voter, you might want to know if central planning is a viable alternative to the price system.

Typical Student: I see your point. It sounds like this material will be on the test!

Summary

Through markets, much cooperation takes place in the world. The baker does not bake a loaf of bread because he knows you want bread. He bakes bread because he decides that baking a loaf of bread is the best use of his resources. By reacting to market signals and acting in his own self-interest, the baker also serves others.

The market connects everything. Your choice to buy a product says that it is worth more to you than any other product that you could buy for the same or lower price.

That is, it is worth more to you than any other product from any place in the world. Thus the market connects people around the world.

The market is like a computer because it processes huge amounts of information. It solves the **great economic problem** of how to allocate limited resources to best satisfy people's unlimited wants. The market works by using information and incentives.

However the market, unlike many computers, does not have a central processing unit (CPU). Market decisions are decentralized, and attempts to centrally plan markets fail due to lack of information and lack of incentives on the part of the planner.

A market price is an incentive, a signal, and a prediction. Market price signals whether people want more or less of a good. Market price gives people incentives to buy or sell the product based on a comparison of market price to the value people place on the item. Market price similarly gives firms an incentive to produce more or less of a good. Market price is a prediction of the value of a good. If the expected future value rises or falls, current market prices will also rise or fall.

Speculation is the attempt to profit from future changes in prices. Its function in the market is to smooth out price fluctuations. If a price of a product is expected to rise in the future, speculators will push the price up today by buying the item expected to be more valuable in the future. What this really means is that the price changes less than it would have without speculation. Speculators often buy and hold for future sales. As a result, speculation often allows for more of the product to be available in the future when it is expected to be relatively scarce. Similarly, if the price of a good is expected to fall in the future, speculators will push the price down today by selling the item expected to be less valuable in the future. By their actions, speculators can cause the future price not to rise or fall as much as it would have in the absence of speculation.

A **futures** contract is a standardized contract to buy or sell specific quantities of a commodity or financial instrument at a specified price with delivery set at a specified time in the future. A **prediction market** is a speculative market carefully designed so that prices can be interpreted as probabilities and used to make predictions. Prediction markets can be used to overcome information problems in large organizations.

Key Terms

great economic problem is to arrange our limited resources to satisfy as many of our infinite wants as possible

speculation an attempt to profit from future price changes

futures standardized contracts to buy or sell specified quantities of a commodity or financial instrument at a specified price, with delivery set at a specified time in the future

prediction market a speculative market designed so that prices can be interpreted as probabilities and used to make predictions

Traps, Hints, and Reminders

Speculation tends to smooth price fluctuations. Thus when speculation is barred, we expect more variance in prices over time.

The prices in predictions markets can be interpreted as the probabilities of an event happening.

Like a huge computer, the market processes a huge amount of information and solves a very complex problem, but unlike a computer, it does not have a central processing unit (CPU). The market is voluntary and undirected.

Practice Exercises: Learning by Doing

1. How does the market encourage cooperation? What type of cooperation does the market encourage?

2. How do markets link people around the world?

3. In what ways is the market system like a computer? In what ways is it not like a computer?

4. What is speculation? What is its function in the market?

5. What are prediction markets? How can they help organizations?

6. What is a market price? What functions do market prices serve?

7. What is a futures contract?

*8. You manage a department store in Florida and one winter day you read in the paper that orange juice futures have fallen dramatically in price. Should your store stock up more on sweaters than usual or should your store stock up more on Bermuda shorts?[1]

Multiple-Choice Questions

1. Free markets encourage
   a. cooperation.
   b. corruption.
   c. confrontation.
   d. All of the answers are correct.

2. The free market is
   a. centrally planned.
   b. voluntary.
   c. coercive.
   d. All of the answers are correct.

3. The free market is
   a. centrally planned.
   b. lacking in incentives.
   c. undirected.
   d. All of the answers are correct.

[1] Questions marked with a ★ are also end-of-chapter questions.

4. A free market's price is

   a. unfair.

   b. fair.

   c. the value of the good in its next-highest-valued use.

   d. determined by the number of hours the good takes to produce.

5. Free market prices are

   a. signals.

   b. predictions.

   c. incentives.

   d. All of the answers are correct.

6. By purchasing a product, a buyer is saying

   a. they would rather spend that money on this good than any other.

   b. they have no choice in the matter.

   c. their money is not worth much.

   d. their value of the good is less than the price.

7. The free market connects people

   a. locally.

   b. nationally.

   c. around the world.

   d. not at all.

8. Speculation is

   a. immoral.

   b. always illegal.

   c. attempting to profit from future price changes.

   d. All of the answers are correct.

9. If the price of oil is expected to rise in the future, speculators will

   a. buy more oil today, driving down its current price.

   b. buy less oil today, driving down its current price.

   c. buy less oil today, driving up its current price.

   d. buy more oil today, driving up its current price.

10. If the price of gold is expected to fall in the future, speculators will

   a. sell more gold today, driving down its current price.

   b. sell less gold today, driving down its current price.

   c. sell more gold today, driving up its current price.

   d. sell less gold today, driving up its current price.

11. Speculators

　　a. help the market send the correct signal.

　　b. reduce price fluctuations.

　　c. moderate the future price changes.

　　d. All of the answers are correct.

12. Without speculation

　　a. consumers would be better off.

　　b. prices would change more.

　　c. the free market would work more efficiently.

　　d. All of the answers are correct.

13. If the price of coffee is expected to rise in the future, speculation

　　a. increases the amount the price of coffee rises in the future.

　　b. has no effect on the increase in the price of coffee in the future.

　　c. decreases the amount the price of coffee rises in the future.

　　d. has an unpredictable effect on the change in the coffee price in the future.

14. Futures are

　　a. standardized contracts for the right to buy or sell at a set price and time in the future.

　　b. markets with prices that are probabilities that can be used to predict.

　　c. standardized contracts to buy or sell at a set price and time in the future.

　　d. products that do not yet exist.

15. Prediction markets

　　a. serve no economic function.

　　b. can be used to give decision makers in big organizations information only subordinates have.

　　c. are always correct in their predictions.

　　d. are only useful for betting on outcomes.

16. Prediction markets have

　　a. prices that can be interpreted as costs.

　　b. outputs that can be interpreted as probabilities.

　　c. prices that can be interpreted as probabilities.

　　d. outputs that can be interpreted as costs.

17. A problem with centrally planning an economy is that central planners lack

　　a. resources.

　　b. all the information the market has.

　　c. government power.

　　d. All of the answers are correct.

18. Central planning failed to work because central planners

    a. lack incentives to do what the public wants.

    b. had little control.

    c. had too much information.

    d. had too few resources.

19. The rose-growing worker in Kenya must know

    a. what the customer will do with the rose.

    b. why the customer wants the rose that time of year.

    c. nothing about the customer.

    d. everything about the customer.

20. The free market is

    a. voluntary.

    b. undirected.

    c. incentive driven.

    d. All of the answers are correct.

Short-Answer Questions

21. How does the free market promote cooperation?

22. How much must a producer of a product know about who will ultimately buy the product and what use they will put it to?

23. How is the market like and not like a large computer?

24. What is speculation?

25. Do speculators cause future prices to change more or less? Explain.

26. If silver speculators expect the price of silver to fall in the future what do they do today? What effects do their actions have?

27. What is a prediction market? How can organizations use them?

28. What are the roles of the free market price? How does it perform them?

29. Who does the free market link? How does it link them?

30. Who designed the free market? How does the market get people to produce what other people want?

Answer Key

Answers to Practice Exercises: Learning by Doing

1. The market encourages cooperation by rewarding people for doing what other people value. This cooperation is voluntary and undirected. Each person acts in their own self interest, but end up serving the interests of others.

   Topic: Markets Link the World

2. Markets link people around the world because whenever someone makes a decision to make a purchase, they are saying that they value one product over another. For example, someone may value coffee beans from Columbia over coffee beans from Jamaica or, for that matter, coffee beans from any other country. In addition, when making this decision, these purchasers are saying that they value those specific coffee beans over any other product that they might have bought, such as a shirt from China or a computer game from the United States. Thus every market decision is a choice both to spend money on one specific product at the exclusion of all other products around the world. It is also a decision to use the purchased product the way the purchaser wants to, and not in any other manner. The value of the products' next-highest-valued use is the market price of the product.

   Topic: Markets Link the World

3. The market is like a computer because it processes huge amounts of information. It solves the economic problem of how to allocate limited resources to best satisfy peoples' unlimited wants. The market works using information and incentives. However the market, unlike a computer, does not have a central processing unit (CPU). Market decisions are decentralized, and attempts to centrally plan markets fail due to lack of information and lack of incentives.

   Topic: Solving the Great Economic Problem

4. Speculation is the attempt to profit from future changes in prices. Its function in the market is to smooth out price fluctuations. If a price of a product is expected to rise in the future, speculators will push the price up today by buying the item expected to be more valuable in the future. This means that the price changes less than it would without speculation. Similarly, if a price of a good is expected to fall in the future, speculators will push the price down today by selling the item expected to be less valuable in the future. By their actions, speculators cause the future price not to rise or fall as much as it would have in the absence of speculation.

   Topic: Speculation

5. A prediction market is a speculative market that is carefully designed so that prices can be interpreted as probabilities and used to make predictions. They can be used to overcome information problems in large organizations.

   Topic: Prediction Markets

6. A market price is an incentive, a signal, and a prediction. Market price signals whether people want more or less of a good. Market price gives people incentives to buy or sell the product based on a comparison of market price to the value people place on the item themselves. Similarly, market price gives firms incentives to produce more or less of a good. Market price is a prediction of the value of a good. If the expected future value rises or falls, current market prices will also rise or fall.

   Topic: A Price Is a Signal Wrapped Up in an Incentive

7. A futures contract is a standardized contract to buy or sell specific quantities of a commodity or financial instrument at a specified price with delivery set at a specified time in the future.

   Topic: A Price Is a Signal Wrapped Up in an Incentive

8. The drop in the price of orange juice futures probably means a lack of freezes in Florida this winter and also, the possibility of spring and summer coming early. For those reasons, you should stock up Bermuda shorts more than usual.

   Topic: Signal Watching

Answers to Multiple-Choice Questions

1. **a, Topic: Markets Link the World**

2. **b, Topic: Markets Link the World**

3. **c, Topic: Markets Link the World**

4. **c, Topic: A Price Is a Signal Wrapped Up in an Incentive**

5. **d, Topic: A Price Is a Signal Wrapped Up in an Incentive**

6. **a, Topic: Solving the Great Economic Problem**

7. **c, Topic: Markets Link the World**

8. **c, Topic: Speculation**

9. **d, Topic: Speculation**

10. **a, Topic: Speculation**

11. **d, Topic: Speculation**

12. **b, Topic: Speculation**

13. **c, Topic: Speculation**

14. **c, Topic: A Price Is a Signal Wrapped Up in an Incentive**

15. **b, Topic: Prediction Markets**

16. **c, Topic: Prediction Markets**

17. **b, Topic: Solving the Great Economic Problem**

18. a, Topic: Solving the Great Economic Problem

19. c, Topic: Solving the Great Economic Problem

20. d, Topic: Markets Link the World

Answers to Short-Answer Questions

21. The market encourages cooperation by rewarding people for doing what other people value. This cooperation is voluntary and undirected. Each person acts in their own self interest, but, by doing so, also serve the interests of others.

    Topic: Markets Link the World

22. A producer ultimately does not have to know anything about why a customer wants a product or what they use it for. Market price will signal the producer and give them an incentive of what to produce. What the customer does with the product is not necessary for the producer to know. For example, the Kenyan rose grower need not understand Valentine's Day and why Americans' want so many roses in midwinter, or why Americans cannot grow the roses themselves. The price alone tells them to grow roses.

    Topic: Markets Link the World

23. The market is like a computer because it processes huge amounts of information. It solves the economic problem of how to allocate limited resources to best satisfy people's unlimited wants. The market works by using information and incentives. However, the market, unlike many computers, does not have a central processing unit (CPU). Market decisions are decentralized. Attempts to centrally plan markets fail due to lack of information and lack of incentives on the part of the planner.

    Topic: Solving the Great Economic Problem

24. Speculation is the attempt to profit from future changes in prices. Speculators buy things they expect to see increasing in price and sell things they expect to see decreasing in price.

    Topic: Speculation

25. The function of speculation in the market is to smooth out price fluctuations. If a price of a product is expected to rise in the future, speculators will push the price up today by buying the item expected to be more valuable in the future. This means that the price changes less than it would without speculation. Similarly, if a price of a good is expected to fall in the future, speculators will push the price down today by selling the item expected to be less valuable in the future. By their actions, speculators cause the future price not to rise or fall as much as it would have in the absence of speculation.

    Topic: Speculation

26. If silver speculators expect the price of silver to fall in the future, they will sell silver today. This will increase the current supply of silver and lower the price. In the future, the supply of silver will be reduced and prices will be higher. Thus

the price in the future will not fall as much as it would have without speculation. Overall, silver prices will not fluctuate as much as they would have without speculation.

Topic: Speculation

27. A prediction market is a speculative market carefully designed so that prices can be interpreted as probabilities and used to make predictions. They can be used to overcome information problems in large organizations.

Topic: Prediction Markets

28. A market price is an incentive, a signal, and a prediction. Market price signals whether people want more or less of a good. Market price gives people incentives to buy or sell the product by comparing the price to the value people place on the item. Market price is a prediction of the value of a good. If the expected future value rises or falls, current market prices will also rise or fall.

Topic: A Price Is a Signal Wrapped Up in an Incentive

29. The free market links everyone around the world. When any person decides to spend, it often impacts others around the world. The decision to buy your sweetheart a Valentine's Day rose impacts people in Kenya, Ecuador, Colombia, the Netherlands, and elsewhere.

Topic: Markets Link the World

30. No one designed the free market. It is voluntary and undirected. The market gets people to produce what other people want by incentives. The main incentive in the free market is the market price, that is, the opportunity cost or the next-highest-valued use of the resources.

Topic: A Price Is a Signal Wrapped Up in an Incentive

6

Price Ceilings

Why Learn about Price Ceilings?

Like elasticity from Chapter 4, price ceilings are an application of supply and demand. This is a practical application that is frequently discussed.

Who will be interested in price ceilings?

> Consumers who might think they will benefit from a price ceiling and be surprised to find out it is not necessarily so

> Businesspeople who need to understand the effects of potential government interference in their business

> Legislators, government officials, and candidates (at any level) who might be tempted by public pressure to enact a price ceiling when the price of some item rises quickly, but who might be surprised at how counterproductive price ceilings can be

> Students of economics, of course, both as students, voters, consumers, and people working in the market economy

Summary

A **price ceiling** is a maximum price allowed by law. Most interesting are effective or binding price ceilings. To be effective, a price ceiling must be below the equilibrium price. If Congress passed a law saying that soft drinks could not sell for more than $100 each, such a price ceiling would not bind the market and, as such, it would have no effects in the current economy. Binding price ceilings create five important effects:

shortages, reductions in product quality, wasteful waiting in line and other search costs, a loss of gains from trade, and a misallocation of resources.

That price ceilings cause shortages can be seen in Figure 6.1, where P_e and Q_e are the equilibrium price and quantity.

Figure 6.1

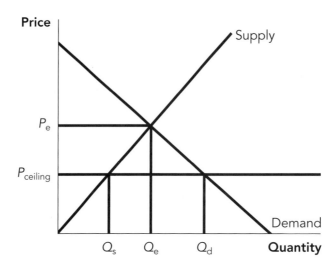

With the price ceiling below P_e people want to buy Q_d of the good but producers want to sell Q_s of the good. Thus there is a shortage of $Q_d - Q_s$ in the market.

Sellers have more customers than goods they want to sell at the ceiling price. One way they can react is to give the customer less. Another way to do this is to reduce quality. Making its product cheaper is a way the producer can bring its costs more in line with the price ceiling. For example, reductions in quality can be less meat on a price-controlled sandwich. A reduction in service, such as having the customer getting their own drink is another way to lower quality and costs.

Since, with a price ceiling, there are more people who want to buy goods than there are goods being offered for sale, price is not allocating the good. Somehow the good must still be allocated. If no other allocation scheme is used, then a "first-come, first-served" scheme will be used. Since not everyone who wants to consume at the ceiling price will get the good, some customers will start arriving early to make sure that they get the good. Thus we have people spending a valuable resource, that is, their time, to consume the product, yet the seller does not get the value of that time. So that resource is wasted. In addition, since there is a shortage, customers will not be sure who has the product in stock. Thus consumers will waste more resources in search of the product. The limit on these search costs are where the price ceiling plus the search cost equals a consumer's willingness to pay.

There are also lost gains from trade or deadweight losses with a price ceiling. This can be seen in Figure 6.2, where the equilibrium price is $10 and the price ceiling is $5.

With the $5 price ceiling, quantity demanded is 100 units and quantity supplied is 50 units, so the shortage, $Q_d - Q_s$, is 50. There are 50 units sold. So for every unit between 50 and the market equilibrium of 75, there are unexploited gains from trade. Put another way, for each unit between 50 and 75, consumers are willing to pay more than it would take to get producers to supply that unit. Thus area $A + B$ is the lost gains from trade or **deadweight loss** associated with the price ceiling of $5.

Figure 6.2

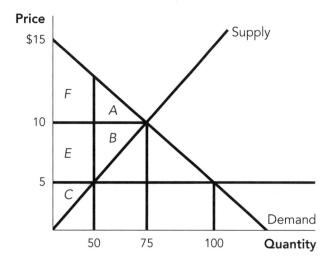

Finally, a price ceiling creates a misallocation of resources. With the price system, those that are willing to pay the market price get the item and those who are not willing to pay the market price forego the good. With the price ceiling, the buyer that is willing to pay the most may or may not get to consume the good. A price ceiling therefore encourages bribery, for example, by selling to friends first or by bypassing the means to purchase the good (for example, selling to someone "offline", when the only legal way the good can be purchased involves waiting in line).

If somehow, the consumers with the highest willingness to pay were able to get the good in Figure 6.2, then consumer surplus would be area *F* + *E* and producer surplus would be area *C*. But if people arrive randomly then the average value of ($5 + $15) /2 or $10 is the appropriate comparison and consumers only gain *E* rather than *F* + *E*. The loss of *F* is due to the misallocation of the good. An example of this would be someone in a warm state heating their pool with price controlled fuel, while someone in a cold state might not be able to buy enough fuel to heat their house.

Rent control is a regulation that prevents rents from rising to equilibrium levels. As with any other price ceiling, rent control creates a shortage. Rent control also leads to landlords not keeping up with the maintenance on their properties. Rent control leads to people wasting valuable resources searching for available properties. There are deadweight losses or lost gains from trade with rent control. Why? Because some people, who are looking to rent, are willing to pay more than some landlords charge, yet, with rent control, these potential renters are not able to rent. Finally, with rent control, resources are misallocated as fewer apartments are constructed and people often end up living in an apartment that is smaller or bigger than their optimal choice.

Rent controls and other price ceilings often start with a "freezing" of prices or rents due to public pressure about prices or rents rising too quickly. As we learned in Chapter 3, supply in a shorter time frame is relatively inelastic. So at first, there is not a huge impact on quantity supplied and the shortage is therefore not huge. But over time, the shortage grows as supply is more elastic in a longer time frame. Politicians who pass rent control or other price ceiling laws operate over short election cycles (from 2 to 6 years). So if they see "freezing" rents as a way to get reelected, then a politician may think that a price ceiling is worth implementing, even if the public does not care for price ceilings or rent controls.

Key Terms

price ceiling a maximum price allowed by law

deadweight loss the total of lost consumer and producer surplus when not all mutually profitable gains from trade are exploited. Price ceilings create a deadweight loss.

rent control a price ceiling on rental housing

Traps, Hints, and Reminders

To be effective, a price ceiling must be below the equilibrium price.

Rent control is just a price ceiling on a particular type of good, such as rental housing units.

Deadweight losses are the same thing as lost gains from trade.

Practice Exercises: Learning by Doing

1. What is a price ceiling? Why does a price control cause a shortage?

2. Why do price ceilings cause declines in the quality of goods?

3. How do people react to a shortage caused by a price ceiling? What is the limit on consumer's reaction?

4. In a graph, show the deadweight losses caused by a price ceiling when the good is somehow allocated to those consumers with the greatest willingness to pay. Why do these lost gains from trade occur?

5. How is a good with a price ceiling allocated? What problems can this cause?

6. What is rent control? What problems do rent controls cause?

7. Why might implementing a rent control be popular among politicians despite its long-term effects on the public?

8. Discuss some ways a firm can decrease quality in response to a price ceiling.

*9. If a government decides to make health insurance affordable by requiring all health insurance companies to cut their prices by 30 percent, what will probably happen to the number of people covered by health insurance?[1]

Multiple-Choice Questions

1. A price ceiling is
   a. the maximum a consumer is willing to pay for a good.
   b. a maximum price allowed by law.
   c. the maximum value of all the inputs used to produce the good.
   d. All of the answers are correct.

[1]Questions marked with a ★ are also end-of-chapter questions.

2. A price ceiling causes

   a. a shortage.

   b. a surplus.

   c. pressure on the producer to lower the price.

   d. pressure on consumers to offer lower prices.

3. An example of a price ceiling is

   a. farm price supports.

   b. the minimum wage.

   c. rent control.

   d. All of the answers are correct.

4. Price ceilings lead to

   a. wasted resources.

   b. consumers searching for product availability.

   c. consumers waiting in line to buy the product.

   d. All of the answers are correct.

5. With a price ceiling, if nothing else is set up the good will be allocated by

   a. income.

   b. price.

   c. a "first-come, first-served" scheme and waiting in line.

   d. All of the answers are correct.

Figure 6.3

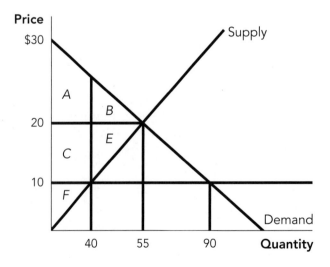

6. In Figure 6.3, a binding price ceiling would be

   a. $10.

   b. $20.

   c. $30.

   d. None of the answers is correct.

7. In Figure 6.3, the price ceiling quantity demanded is
   a. 40 units.
   b. 55 units.
   c. 90 units.
   d. None of the answers is correct.

8. In Figure 6.3, the price ceiling quantity supplied is
   a. 40 units.
   b. 55 units.
   c. 90 units.
   d. All of the answers are correct.

9. In Figure 6.3, the price ceiling causes a shortage of
   a. 15 units.
   b. 35 units.
   c. 50 units.
   d. None of the answers is correct.

10. In Figure 6.3, if those with the highest value of the good get to consume, then the deadweight loss associated with the price ceiling is area
   a. $A + B$.
   b. $B + E$.
   c. F.
   d. $A + C$.

11. In Figure 6.3, the price ceiling producer surplus is area
   a. $A + B$.
   b. $B + E$.
   c. F.
   d. $A + C$.

12. In Figure 6.3, if those with the highest value the good get to consume, then consumer surplus with the price ceiling is area
   a. $A + B$.
   b. C.
   c. F.
   d. $A + C$.

13. In Figure 6.3, if the product is randomly allocated so it is consumed by consumers with an average value for the product, then consumer surplus is area
   a. $A + B$.
   b. C.
   c. F.
   d. $A + C$.

14. In Figure 6.3, if the product is randomly allocated, the most resources that consumers would waste standing in line and searching for the good is area
    a. *A*.
    b. *B + E*.
    c. *C*.
    d. *F*.

15. In Figure 6.3, the extra loss in surplus due to random allocation compared to allocation to those with the highest value for the good is area
    a. *A*.
    b. *B + E*.
    c. *C*.
    d. *F*.

16. Rent controls
    a. cause shortages.
    b. create lost gains from trade.
    c. misallocate resources.
    d. All of the answers are correct.

17. The effects of rent controls are worse in the long run because
    a. the supply of rental units is more elastic in the long run.
    b. the supply of rental units is more inelastic in the long run.
    c. the demand for rental units is more elastic in the short run.
    d. the demand for rental units is unit elastic in the long run.

18. With a price ceiling,
    a. gains from trade are maximized.
    b. there are unexploited gains from trade.
    c. there are no trades made.
    d. the supply of goods is bought by the buyer with the highest willingness to pay.

19. With a price ceiling,
    a. the quality of the good improves.
    b. there is a surplus on the market.
    c. resources are misallocated.
    d. All of the answers are correct.

20. With a price ceiling, goods may be allocated by all except
    a. bribery.
    b. publically announced price alone.
    c. personal connections.
    d. a "first-come, first-served" scheme and waiting in line.

Short-Answer Questions

21. What is a price ceiling?

22. What is rent control? What problems do rent controls cause?

23. Show on a graph the effects a price ceiling has on price and quantity in the market. Why does a price ceiling have these effects?

24. In a graph, show the deadweight losses caused by a price ceiling when the good is allocated to the consumers who value the good the most. Why do these lost gains from trade occur?

25. In a graph, show the producer surplus with a price ceiling. Show what the consumer surplus would be if consumers with the highest value for the good get the product and if the product is allocated randomly. Show the additional losses associated with allocating the product randomly.

26. How do people react to a shortage caused by a price ceiling? In a graph, show the limit on the consumer's reaction.

27. How is a good with a price ceiling allocated? What problems can this cause?

28. Why might implementing a rent control be popular among politicians despite its long-term effects?

29. Why do price ceilings cause declines in the quality of goods?

30. Discuss some ways a firm can decrease quality in response to a price ceiling.

Answer Key

Answers to Practice Exercises: Learning by Doing

1. A price ceiling is a maximum price allowed by law. A price ceiling causes a shortage because when price is below equilibrium price more people want to buy at the price ceiling than are willing to sell at that price.

   Topic: Price Ceilings

2. A price ceiling reduces quality because, since firms can not raise price, they try to reduce costs. Thus a landlord may not maintain a property, a retail outlet may reduce service, or a soup company may put more broth and fewer noodles in the can.

   Topic: Reductions in Quality

3. People react to the shortages caused by price ceilings by searching for product availability and forming lines to make sure that they are capable of purchasing the product. The time spent waiting in line and searching for the good is not received by the seller of the good, and thus wasted. The limit on this behavior is willingness to pay. Consumers will not spend more on the good including the ceiling price, plus time waiting in line, and on search costs than their willingness to pay, as seen from the demand curve.

   Topic: Wasteful Lines and Other Search Costs

4. Draw a graph like Figure 6.2 and mark out the area $A + B$. These deadweight losses happen because there are unexploited gains from trade. That is, there are units consumers would be happy to pay more for than it would take to get producers to sell them. But these trades are prohibited because they are at prices above the price ceiling.

   Topic: Lost Gains from Trade

5. If there is a price ceiling, it is not clear how the good will be allocated. It is possible that bribes or other under the table payments will take place to get the good to those who want it the most. On the other hand, the good may be allocated on a first-come, first-served basis and that leads to wasted resources, due to people searching for product availability and waiting in line to buy the product. If the good is not allocated to those consumers with the greatest willingness to pay, the deadweight loss is even greater.

   Topic: Wasteful Lines and Other Search Costs, and Lost Gains from Trade

6. Rent control is a regulation that prevents rents from rising to equilibrium levels. Like any price ceiling, rent control causes a shortage of rental units, a reduction in quality, resources wasted on searching for an apartment, waiting in line, a misallocation of apartments and other resources, and deadweight losses or lost gains from trade.

Topic: Rent Regulation

7. Because the supply of rental units is more elastic in a longer time frame than in a shorter time frame, politicians may find rent control has a small effect in their election-cycle time, even though the bad effects become clear in the longer term. This may lead to politicians voting for rent controls even though they know that the long-term effects will be negative.

Topic: Arguments for Price Controls

8. In reaction to a price ceiling a firm can reduce quality in a number of ways. For example, a rental property owner can spend less on maintaining the property. Or a producer of a food item can put less food in a bag of chips or a can of green beans. A service firm can reduce the service you receive by eliminating specific services. Without full service, you would have to use the self-checkout station at the grocery store or pump your own gas at a gas station.

Topic: Reductions in Quality

9. Since the government is likely forcing the price below the equilibrium price, this is the same as price ceiling below the equilibrium price. This will likely lead to the number of people with health insurance to decline.

Topic: Price Ceilings

Answers to Multiple-Choice Questions

1. b, Topic: Price Ceilings

2. a, Topic: Shortages

3. c, Topic: Price Ceilings

4. d, Topic: Wasteful Lines and Other Search Costs

5. c, Topic: Wasteful Lines and Other Search Costs

6. a, Topic: Price Ceilings

7. c, Topic: Price Ceilings

8. a, Topic: Price Ceilings

9. c, Topic: Price Ceilings

10. b, Topic: Wasteful Lines and Other Search Costs

11. c, Topic: Wasteful Lines and Other Search Costs

12. d, Topic: Lost Gains from Trade

13. b, Topic: Advanced Material: The Loss from Random Allocation

14. c, Topic: Advanced Material: The Loss from Random Allocation

15. a, Topic: Advanced Material: The Loss from Random Allocation

16. d, Topic: Rent Regulation

17. **a, Topic: Rent Regulation**

18. **b, Topic: Price Ceilings**

19. **c, Topic: Price Ceilings**

20. **b, Topic: Price Ceilings**

Answers to Short-Answer Questions

21. A price ceiling is a maximum price allowed by law.

    Topic: Price Ceilings

22. Rent control is a regulation that prevents rents from rising to equilibrium levels. Like any price ceiling, rent control causes a shortage of rental units, a reduction in quality, resources wasted on searching for an apartment and waiting in line, deadweight losses or lost gains from trade, and a misallocation of apartments and other resources.

    Topic: Rent Regulation

23. Draw a graph like Figure 6.1 showing a price ceiling below equilibrium and a shortage in the market. The shortage happens because at the ceiling price people want to buy more of the good than producers are willing to sell.

    Topic: Price Ceilings

24. Draw a graph like Figure 6.2 and mark out the area $A + B$. These deadweight losses happen because there are unexploited gains from trade. That is, there are units consumers would be willing to pay more for than it would take to get producers to sell them, but these trades are prohibited because they are at prices above the price ceiling.

    Topic: Lost Gains from Trade

25. Draw a graph like Figure 6.2. Point out that area C is the producer surplus. Point out that area $F + E$ is consumer surplus, if the good is somehow allocated to those most willing to pay for it. Point out that area E is the consumer surplus, if the good is randomly allocated, and area F is the extra loss due to the misallocation of the good.

    Topic: Advanced Material: The Loss from Random Allocation

26. People react to the shortages caused by price ceilings by searching for product availability and forming lines to make sure that they are able to purchase the product. The time spent waiting in line and searching for the good is not received by the seller of the good, and thus wasted. The limit on this behavior is willingness to pay. Consumers will not spend more on the good, including the ceiling price, plus time waiting in line, and on search costs than their willingness to pay, as seen from the demand curve. Draw a graph like Figure 6.2 and show that area E is the limit on the consumers' willingness to waste resources to get the good if the good is allocated randomly.

    Topic: Lost Gains from Trade

27. If there is a price ceiling, it is not clear how the good will be allocated. It is possible that the bribes or other under-the-table payments will develop to get the good to those who want it the most. On the other hand, the good may be allocated on a first-come, first-served basis that leads to wasted resources due to people searching for product availability or waiting in line to buy the product.

Topic: Misallocation of Resources

28. Because the supply of rental units is more elastic in a long time frame than in a short time frame, politicians may that find rent control has a small effect in their election-cycle time, even though the bad effects become clear in the longer term. This may lead to politicians voting for rent controls even thought they know that the long-term effects will be negative.

Topic: Rent Controls

29. A price ceiling reduces quality because, since firms can not raise price, they try to reduce costs.

Topic: Reductions in Quality

30. In reaction to a price ceiling, a firm can reduce quality a number of ways. A rental property owner can spend less on maintaining the property. A producer of a food item can put less food in a bag of chips or a can of green beans. A service firm can reduce the service you receive by eliminating specific services. Without full service, you would have to use the self-checkout station at the grocery store or pump your own gas at a gas station.

Topic: Reductions in Quality

7

Price Floors, Taxes, and Subsidies

Why Learn about Price Floors, Taxes, and Subsidies?

Interested Student: Why another chapter on price floors? I thought we studied them last chapter.

Young Professor: Actually, we studied price ceilings last chapter. Certainly price floors are similar to price ceilings. Last chapter introduced us to government interference in the market. Chapter 7 discusses some additional types of government interference in the market. We learn about price floors, taxes, and subsidies and how they affect the market outcome.

Interested Student: So will the people interested in this chapter be similar to the people that were interested in price ceilings?

Young Professor: Yes, producers, consumers, and politicians will be interested in the effects that such policies would have on markets. Politicians will want to know how much a market would be affected if they tax it, subsidize production in it, or legislate a price floor in it. Producers and consumers will want to know what they would be facing if the government interferes in their production or consumption.

Interested Student: That makes a lot of sense. Now I can see why they would all be interested!

Summary

A **price floor** is a minimum price allowed by law. Most interesting are effective or binding price floors. To be effective, a price floor must be above the equilibrium price.

Binding price floors have four important effects: surpluses, a loss of gains from trade, wasteful increases in quality, and a misallocation of resources.

The effects of a price floor can be seen in Figure 7.1, where P_e and Q_e are the equilibrium price and quantity.

Figure 7.1

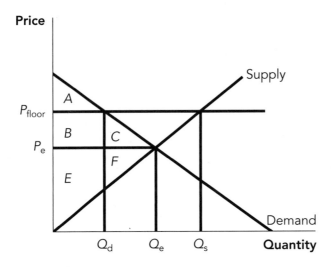

With the price floor above P_e, producers want to sell Q_s of the good, but consumers only want to buy Q_d. Thus there is a surplus of $Q_s - Q_d$ in the market.

Sellers have more of the good they want to sell at the price floor and not enough customers. Each firm is competing to attract customers and they can react by giving the customer more. One way to do this is to raise quality. This is a waste in resources because this higher quality is only used to attract customers who would be willing to buy at the current price and quality. The lost gains from trade or deadweight losses are area $C + F$. Finally, a price floor creates a misallocation of resources. With the price system, those that are willing to accept the market price get to sell the item, and those who are not willing to accept the market price forego selling the item. With the price ceiling, the sellers that are willing to sell at the lowest price may or may not get to sell the item.

Deadweight losses and lost gains from trade can also be caused by a commodity tax on a market, as can be seen from Figure 7.2, where a $5 per unit tax is imposed on the market.

The pre-tax equilibrium was a price of $12 and a quantity exchanged of 100 units. Notice that pre-tax, consumer surplus is the area $A + B + C + E$, producer surplus is the area $F + G + H$ and total surplus is $A + B + C + E + F + G + H$.

After the tax in Figure 7.2, the new equilibrium price of $15 is paid by the consumers and the new equilibrium quantity is 90 units. Additionally since $5 of that $15 price must be paid to the government in the form of a tax, the post-tax price received by sellers is $10. Thus the tax per unit is the amount paid by consumers, $15, less the amount received by sellers, $10, or $15 − $10 = $5 as originally specified. The tax is sometimes called a wedge between what the buyer pays and the seller receives for the product.

Further notice that the amount of exchange fell. The reason people were buying and firms were selling those units between 90 and 100 is because they gained from buying and selling them. Thus by reducing exchange, the tax creates a deadweight loss of area $E + G$.

Figure 7.2

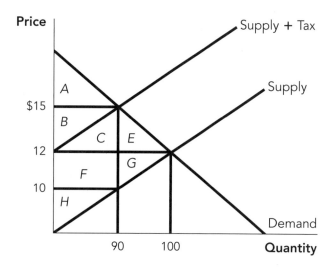

The amount of the tax is the vertical distance between the two supply curves, $5 in this example, and it is paid on the equilibrium quantity exchanged post-tax of 90 units. Thus the amount of tax paid is $450 or area $B + C + F$. Consumers pay the difference between the original equilibrium price and the post-tax equilibrium price, $15 − $12, or $3 times the 90 units which is $270 of the tax or area $B + C$. Producers pay the other part of the tax $450 − $270 or $2 × 90 units both of which equal $180 or area F.

We can also see the deadweight loss or lost gains from trade by comparing the pre-tax total surplus area $A + B + C + E + F + G + H$ to the post-tax situation. Post-tax consumer surplus is area A, producer surplus is area H and the amount of the tax paid is area $B + C + F$. That means post-tax total surplus is $A + B + C + F + H$. Pre-tax total surplus $A + B + C + E + F + G + H$ less post-tax total surplus ($A + B + C + F + H$) gives the deadweight loss of $E + G$.

This also illustrates two other points about commodity taxes. One point is that who pays the tax does not depend on who writes the check to the government. In our example, the $5 commodity tax was imposed on producers, yet even though they wrote the $450 check to the government they paid less than half the tax, $180. Had we modeled the $5 tax as a tax on demanders in this exact same market we would have come to exactly the same new equilibrium price and quantity of $15 and 90 units. We would also have the exact same distribution of the burden of the tax, $270 paid by consumers and $180 paid by producers.

The second point is that who pays the tax depends on relative elasticities of supply and demand. The general rule is the less elastic side of the market pays more of the tax. Thus in our case, in Figure 7.2, supply must be slightly more elastic than demand as demanders paid slightly more of the tax.

A subsidy is the negative of a tax. Rather than taking money from someone as with a tax, with a subsidy the government gives someone money. Thus the case of a subsidy is very similar to that of a tax.

Who gets the subsidy does not depend on who receives the check from the government. Who benefits from the subsidy does depend on the relative elasticities of demand and supply. Subsidies must be paid for by taxpayers and they create deadweight losses by increasing exchange beyond the unsubsidized equilibrium and causing resources to be wasted.

A minimum wage raises wages but reduces exchange in the market and thus decreases employment of low-wage workers. A low-wage subsidy would raise wages and increase the exchange in the low-wage-worker market and thus increase the employment of low wage workers. For this reason some economists prefer a low-wage subsidy to a minimum wage, if the government is going to interfere in the low-wage labor market.

Key Terms

price floor a minimum price allowed by law

Traps, Hints, and Reminders

A subsidy is just the negative or opposite of a tax. In the tax case, the government is making people pay taxes and receiving the money. In the subsidy case the government is giving people money and taxpayers must pay for this.

With a tax, the consumer pays the difference between the old price and the new price on each unit.

With a tax, the part of the tax not paid by consumers is necessarily paid by sellers or producers.

Practice Exercises: Learning by Doing

1. What is a price floor? What effects does a price floor have?

2. Draw a price floor and show the surplus in the market and deadweight losses that a price floor causes.

3. Why does a price floor, with an accompanying surplus in a market, lead to quality increases? In what sense are price floors wasteful?

4. What are the three truths about a commodity tax on a market that are emphasized in the chapter?

5. Draw the situation of a commodity tax on a market and show the amount of the tax, the portion consumers pay, the portion producers pay, and the loss of gains from trade.

6. For the figure below, calculate the tax paid, the part paid by consumers, the part paid by producers, and the deadweight loss.

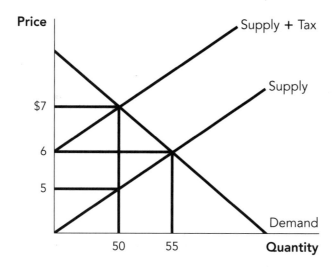

7. How does the effect of a commodity tax change, if the tax is charged to buyers of the good rather than sellers?

8. For a commodity with an elasticity of supply of 2 and an elasticity of demand of 0.5, who will receive the larger benefit from the commodity subsidy?

9. Why might a subsidy of the wages of low-wage workers be a better policy than a minimum wage?

*10. How do businesses change their behavior, when the minimum wage rises? How does this behavior change impact teenagers?[1]

Multiple-Choice Questions

1. A price floor is

  a. the maximum a consumer is willing to pay for a good.

  b. a maximum price allowed by law.

  c. the minimum a consumer is willing to pay for a good.

  d. a minimum price allowed by law.

2. A price floor causes

  a. surpluses.

  b. deadweight lost gains from trade.

  c. misallocation of resources.

  d. All of the answers are correct.

3. An example of a price floor is

  a. gasoline price controls.

  b. the minimum wage.

  c. rent control.

  d. All of the answers are correct.

---

[1] Questions marked with a ★ are also end–of–chapter questions.

Figure 7.3

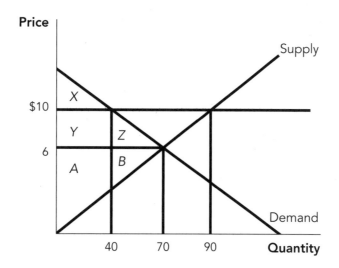

4. In Figure 7.3, with the price floor, the amount of the shortage is

  a. 20 units.

  b. 50 units.

  c. 90 units.

  d. None of the answers is correct.

5. In Figure 7.3, with the price floor, the deadweight lost gains from trade are area

  a. X.

  b. Z + B.

  c. A + B.

  d. Y.

6. If the government is to interfere in the low-wage labor market, some economists like a low-wage subsidy rather than a minimum wage because a low-wage subsidy

  a. raises low-wage worker employment, while a minimum wage lowers it.

  b. lowers low-wage worker employment, while a minimum wage raises it.

  c. raises low-wage worker wages, while a minimum wage lowers them.

  d. lowers low-wage worker wages, while a minimum wage raises them.

Figure 7.4

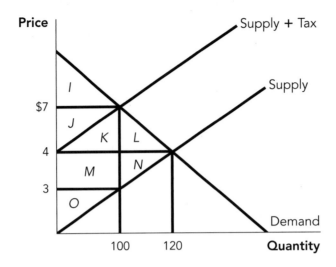

7. In Figure 7.4, after the commodity tax, the price the consumer pays for the product is
   a. $3.
   b. $4.
   c. $7.
   d. None of the answers is correct.

8. In Figure 7.4, with the commodity tax, the government tax revenue is area
   a. $J + K + M$.
   b. $L + N$.
   c. $J + K$.
   d. M.

9. In Figure 7.4, with the commodity tax, the government tax revenue is
   a. $100.
   b. $300.
   c. $400.
   d. None of the answers is correct.

10. In Figure 7.4, the part of the commodity tax paid by consumers is area
    a. $J + K + M$.
    b. $L + N$.
    c. $J + K$.
    d. M.

11. In Figure 7.4, the part of the commodity tax paid by consumers is
    a. $100.
    b. $300.
    c. $400.
    d. None of the answers is correct.

12. In Figure 7.4, the part of the commodity tax paid by producers is area

a. $J + K + M$.

b. $L + N$.

c. $J + K$.

d. M.

13. In Figure 7.4, the part of the commodity tax paid by producers is

a. $100.

b. $300.

c. $400.

d. None of the answers is correct.

14. In Figure 7.4, the deadweight loss due to the commodity tax is area

a. $J + K + M$.

b. $L + N$.

c. $J + K$.

d. M.

15. If the elasticity of supply of water is less than the elasticity of demand for water, then the benefits of a per unit subsidy of water would

a. be split roughly evenly between buyers and sellers.

b. go mainly to buyers.

c. go mainly by sellers.

d. go mainly to the government.

16. With a commodity subsidy,

a. who benefits depends on who gets the check from the government.

b. who benefits depends on the relative elasticities of supply and demand.

c. there are no deadweight losses.

d. All of the answers are correct.

17. With a commodity tax,

a. who pays the tax does not depend on who writes the check to the government.

b. who pays depends on the relative elasticities of supply and demand.

c. the government gets revenue, and the tax causes deadweight losses.

d. All of the answers are correct.

18. A minimum wage

a. increases unemployment of low-wage workers.

b. creates extra gains from trade.

c. creates a shortage of workers.

d. All of the answers are correct.

19. Since the demand elasticity of cigarettes is much lower than the elasticity of supply, a tax on cigarettes is

    a. split roughly evenly between buyers and sellers.

    b. paid mainly by buyers.

    c. paid mainly by sellers.

    d. not very effective at raising revenue.

20. A price floor

    a. causes wasteful increases in quality.

    b. creates a shortage.

    c. increases gains from trade.

    d. leads to a better allocation of resources.

Short-Answer Questions

21. What is a price floor? What effects does a price floor have?

22. In Figure 7.5 below, show the surplus and the lost gains from trade caused by the price floor.

Figure 7.5

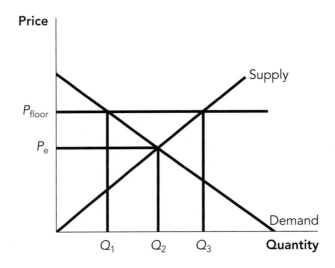

23. Why does a surplus lead to quality increases? In what sense are they wasteful?

24. What must be true if the impact of a cigarette tax increase is borne more by the buyers?

25. If the absolute value of demand elasticity for cars is 0.33, and supply elasticity of cars is 1, will buyers or sellers pay more of a commodity tax? Explain.

26. In Figure 7.6 below, show the amount of the tax, the part paid by consumers, the part paid by producers, and the deadweight loss.

Figure 7.6

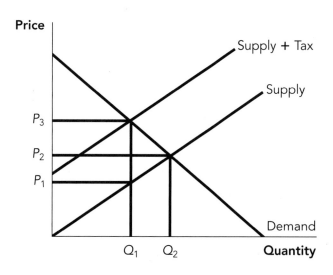

27. What are the facts about commodity subsidies emphasized in the book?

28. Why might a low-wage subsidy be a better policy to increase low-wage workers wages than a minimum wage?

29. How does the effect of a commodity tax change, if the tax is charged to buyers of the good rather than sellers?

30. Based on Figure 7.7 below, calculate the tax paid, the part paid by consumers, the part paid by producers, and the deadweight loss.

Figure 7.7

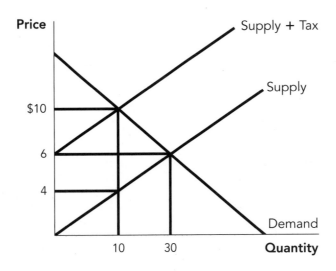

Answer Key

Answers to Practice Exercises: Learning by Doing

1. A price floor is a minimum price allowed by law. Binding price floors have four important effects: surpluses in the market, a loss of gains from trade, wasteful increases in quality and a misallocation of resources.

   Topic: Price Floors

2. Draw a graph like Figure 7.1, with a price floor above equilibrium. Show that $Q_s > Q_d$ and mark in your graph the deadweight loss which is $C + F$ in Figure 7.1.

   Topic: Surpluses

3. Firms do not have enough customers for their product. There would be enough customers to thoroughly buy each product that producers wish to sell at a lower price, but the price floor prohibits that. Thus, the firm competes with other firms for customers by raising quality. This is wasteful in two ways. First customers would like to consume the product without the quality increases at a lower price. Second, all businesses will react by raising quality so all businesses will have higher costs but all businesses together cannot attract more customers.

   Topic: Wasteful Increases in Quality

4. Who pays the tax does not depend on who writes the check to the government. Who pays the tax does depend on the relative elasticities of demand and supply. Commodity taxation raises revenue and creates lost gains from trade (deadweight losses).

   Topic: Commodity Taxes

5. Draw a graph like 7.2. Show that the tax is the difference between what consumers pay and producers receive times the post-tax quantity or $B + C + F$ the way Figure 7.2 is labeled. Show that consumers pay the increase in price paid times the post-tax quantity, $B + C$ the way Figure 7.2 is labeled. Show that producers pay the rest of the tax or area F in Figure 7.2. Show the lost gains from trade as the area between the supply and demand curve and between the original and new quantity or area $E + G$ as Figure 7.2 is labeled.

   Topic: Who Ultimately Pays the Tax Does Not Depend on Who Writes the Check

6. The tax paid is $2 on 50 units or $100. Consumers pay the difference between the old market price and the new market price times the number of units or $1 times 50 units or $50. The producer pays the rest or $100–$50 which equals $50. The loss of gains from trade is the areas of the triangle between the old and new quantity and supply and demand, or height $\times$ base/2 or ($2 $\times$ 5)/2 which equals $5.

   Topic: Who Ultimately Pays the Tax Does Not Depend on Who Writes the Check

7. There is no difference in the effects of a commodity tax whether it is levied on the buyers or the sellers. If the same tax is modeled as affecting demand or supply, you get exactly the same price, same quantity exchanged, same tax paid, same proportion of the tax paid by the consumer and producers and the same deadweight loss.

Topic: Subsidies

8. Since the elasticity of supply is greater than elasticity of demand most of the benefit of the subsidy will go to buyers.

Topic: Who Ultimately Pays the Tax Depends on the Relative Elasticities of Supply and Demand

9. A minimum wage increases the wage of low-wage workers, but reduces the number of low wage workers hired. A low-wage subsidy would raise the wages of low wage workers and at the same time increase the number of low-wage workers employed. So both policies raise low-wage workers wages, but the subsidy increases employment while the minimum wage decreases employment among low-wage workers. Of course one draw back of the wage subsidy is that taxpayers would have to pay for the subsidy.

Topic: Wage Subsidies

10. A rise in the minimum wage would cause U.S. businesses to substitute away from low skilled labor and toward more skilled labor and capital. As low-skilled labor becomes relatively more expensive, businesses will try use less of it and will try to use more of the now relatively less expensive skilled labor and capital. Unskilled teenagers are likely to find it harder to find jobs and teenage unemployment is likely to rise.

Topic: Price Floors

Answers to Multiple-Choice Questions

1. d, Topic: Price Floors

2. d, Topic: Surpluses

3. b, Topic: Price Floors

4. b, Topic: Surpluses

5. b, Topic: Lost Gains from Trade

6. a, Topic: Wage Subsidies

7. c, Topic: A Commodity Tax Raises Revenue and Creates Lost Gains from Trade (Deadweight Loss)

8. a, Topic: A Commodity Tax Raises Revenue and Creates Lost Gains from Trade (Deadweight Loss)

9. c, Topic: A Commodity Tax Raises Revenue and Creates Lost Gains from Trade (Deadweight Loss)

10. c, Topic: A Commodity Tax Raises Revenue and Creates Lost Gains from Trade (Deadweight Loss)

11. b, Topic: A Commodity Tax Raises Revenue and Creates Lost Gains from Trade (Deadweight Loss)

12. d, Topic: A Commodity Tax Raises Revenue and Creates Lost Gains from Trade (Deadweight Loss)

13. a, Topic: A Commodity Tax Raises Revenue and Creates Lost Gains from Trade (Deadweight Loss)

14. b, Topic: A Commodity Tax Raises Revenue and Creates Lost Gains from Trade (Deadweight Loss)

15. c, Topic: Who Ultimately Pays the Tax Depends on the Relative Elasticities of Supply and Demand

16. b, Topic: Subsidies

17. d, Topic: Commodity Taxes

18. a, Topic: Surpluses

19. b, Topic: Who Pays the Cigarette Tax?

20. a. Topic: Price Floors

Answers to Short-Answer Questions

21. A price floor is a minimum price allowed by law. Binding price floors have four important effects: surpluses in the market, a loss of gains from trade, wasteful increases in quality, and a misallocation of resources.

    Topic: Price Floors

22. Mark the distance $Q_3 - Q_1$ to show the surplus. Mark the area between Q_2 and Q_1 and supply and demand as the deadweight loss.

    Topic: Surpluses

23. Firms do not have enough customers for their product. There would be enough customers to buy all of the product producers wish to sell at a lower price, but the price floor prohibits that. Thus, the firm competes with other firms for customers by raising quality. This is wasteful in two ways. First, customers would like to consume the product without the quality increases at a lower price. Second, all businesses will react by raising quality, so all businesses will have higher costs, but all businesses together cannot attract more customers.

    Topic: Wasteful Increases in Quality

24. We know that supply must be more elastic than demand, or $|E_s|/|E_d| > 1$. When supply is more elastic, it means the producers can more readily move to another market, so the tax burden falls more on the buyers with a demand less elastic than the supply.

    Topic: Who Ultimately Pays the Tax Depends on the Relative Elasticities of Supply and Demand

25. Since demand is less elastic than supply, more of the burden of this tax will fall on car buyers than car sellers.

   Topic: Who Ultimately Pays the Tax Depends on the Relative Elasticities of Supply and Demand

26. The amount of the tax should be marked as the area $(P_3 - P_1) \times Q_1$. The part paid by consumers is $(P_3 - P_2) \times Q_1$. The part paid by producers is $(P_2 - P_1) \times Q_1$. The deadweight loss is the triangle between Q_1 and Q_2 and the supply and demand curves.

   Topic: A Commodity Tax Raises Revenue and Creates Lost Gains from Trade (Deadweight Loss)

27. Who gets the subsidy does not depend on who receives the check from the government. Who benefits from the subsidy does depend on the relative elasticities of demand and supply. Subsidies must be paid for by taxpayers, and they create deadweight losses by increasing exchange.

   Topic: Who Ultimately Pays the Tax Does Not Depend on Who Writes the Check

28. A minimum wage increases the wage of low-wage workers but reduces the number of low-wage workers hired. A low-wage subsidy would raise the wages of low-wage workers and at the same time increase the number of low-wage workers employed. So both policies raise low wages, but the subsidy increases employment while the minimum wage decreases employment among low-wage workers. Of course, one drawback of the low-wage subsidy is that taxpayers would have to pay for the subsidy.

   Topic: Wages Subsidies

29. There is no difference in the effects of a commodity tax whether it is put on the buyers or the sellers. If the same tax is modeled as affecting demand or supply, you get exactly the same price, same quantity exchanged, same tax paid, same proportion of the tax paid by the consumer and producers, and the same deadweight loss.

   Topic: Subsidies

30. The tax paid is 6×10 units or $60. The consumers pay 4×10 units or $40, where $4 comes from the difference between the post-tax price of $10 and the pre-tax price of $6. The producers pay the rest of the tax $60 − $40 or $20. The deadweight loss is the reduction in exchange 20 units times the tax $6 divided by 2 or $20 \times \$6/2$ which equals $60.

   Topic: A Commodity Tax Raises Revenue and Creates Lost Gains from Trade (Deadweight Loss)

8

International Trade

Why Learn about International Trade?

As the authors say in the introductory paragraph to this chapter, asking why you should learn about international trade is a very good question. After all, trade is trade. Trade between two people is the same whether they happen to live on the same side of an artificial line drawn on a map or whether they happen to live on opposite sides of that line. So, as the authors say, this is a chapter on the economics of trade and the politics of international trade.

However, almost everyone should care about this topic because we all trade with people in our own country and other countries. So, who will be interested in international trade?

> Consumers who must make purchases, that is, trade with businesses or other people, or else become self-sufficient and make their own goods

> Businesspeople, who are generally on the other side (that is, the selling side) of trading with consumers

> Legislators, government officials, and candidates (at any level), who will be under pressure to regulate trade, would want to have a better understanding of how to proceed and what the effects of regulation will be

> Students of economics, of course, as consumers or potentially businesspeople

Summary

The economics of trade does not vary, whether it is between two parties within a country or two parties in different countries. Trade takes place when both sides expect to gain. There are, however, political issues associated with trade between two parties in different countries.

Trade allows people to specialize in production and take advantage of division of knowledge and economies of scale. Division of knowledge is important as it allows people to specialize. The farmer need only know about farming, the attorney need only know about the law, and the chef need only know about cooking. Division of knowledge allows each individual to know more about their one specific area. Without specialization, one person running a restaurant would have to know enough about farming to grow crops, know enough about the law to set up the business enterprise, and know enough about food preparation to be the chef.

Economies of scale are cost per unit savings that come with the size of an enterprise. Division of knowledge allows enterprises to grow larger and take advantage of economies of scale. The farmer-attorney-chef person described above would not be growing enough wheat to take advantage of combine threshers, but a farmer that specializes in growing wheat to sell to others, could realize such economies of scale.

One has a **comparative advantage** in producing those goods that can be produced at the lowest opportunity cost. This concept can be contrasted with **absolute advantage,** which is when one can produce goods using fewer resources than other producers. Everyone will have a comparative advantage in something, even if they do not have an absolute advantage in any one good. This applies to people individually and the people of a country. Exploiting comparative advantage can be summed up as it was in the text as "sell what you can make at low cost and buy what you can make only at high cost."

Comparative and absolute advantage can be shown with the simple example in Table 8.1, where Jill can produce either pizzas or sandwiches using less of the labor input.

Table 8.1

	Labor units required to produce. . .		Opportunity cost of. . .	
	1 Pizza	**1 Sandwich**	**1 Pizza**	**1 Sandwich**
Jack	2	6	0.33 Sandwiches	3 Pizza
Jill	1	2	0.5 Sandwiches	2 Pizza

Thus Jill has an absolute advantage in producing both goods as she can produce each good with few labor units. Jack does not have an absolute advantage in either good. Still Jack and Jill can trade based on comparative advantage. Notice that Jack has a lower opportunity cost of producing pizzas. He gives up only one-third of a sandwich to produce a pizza while Jill gives up half a sandwich. On the other hand, Jill has a comparative advantage in producing subs. She gives up only 2 pizzas per sandwich produced, while Jack's opportunity cost is 3 pizzas per sandwich.

If Jack and Jill each worked an 8-hour day, then we can see the benefits of free trade in Table 8.2, where the production amounts are based on labor units required from Table 8.1.

Table 8.2 Gains from Free Trade

		Pizzas		Sandwiches	
		Production	Consumption	Production	Consumption
No trade with	Jack	1 (2 hours)	1	1 (6 hours)	1
an 8-hour day	Jill	4 (4 hours)	4	2 (4 hours)	2
		Production	Consumption	Production	Consumption
Trade with an	Jack	4 (8 hours)	1.5	0	1
8-hour day	Jill	2 (2 hours)	4.5	3 (6 hours)	2

With no trade, Jack can produce and consume 1 pizza and 1 sandwich, while Jill can produce and consume 4 pizzas and 2 sandwiches. But remember from Table 8.1, Jack has a comparative advantage in producing pizzas, while Jill has a comparative advantage in producing sandwiches. So in our example, if Jack specializes in pizza and Jill moves toward producing more sandwiches, Jack plus Jill's total production of pizza can rise from 5 to 6 pizzas, while they are jointly able to maintain their production of sandwiches at 3. Thus in our example, Jill can trade 1 sandwich for 2.5 pizzas from Jack and both increase their consumption of pizzas by one-half pizza, while maintaining the same consumption of sandwiches. Remember, an example like this showing gains from trade can be constructed for the people of two countries just as it was for two people here.

Gains from free trade can also be seen graphically in Figure 8.1, where $5 and 100 units are the equilibrium price and quantity if there is no trade.

With no trade, consumer surplus is area A, producer surplus is area $B + F$, and total surplus is area $A + B + F$. Once this market is opened up for free trade, then con-

Figure 8.1

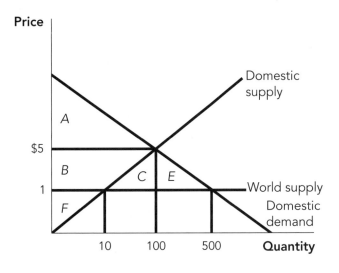

sumers can buy at the world price of $1. Then consumer surplus is $A + B + C + E$, producer surplus is F, and total surplus is $A + B + C + E + F$. Thus total surplus has grown by area $C + E$ or there are gains from trade of $C + E$.

Conversely, we can see what happens if the government imposes some type of protection on this market. **Protectionism** is an economic policy of restraining trade through **quotas**, **tariffs**, or other regulations that burden foreign producers but not domestic producers. A trade quota is a quantity restriction where imports greater than the quota amount are forbidden. A tariff is a tax on imports.

In Figure 8.1, if the government imposed a quota or tariff large enough that none of the good was imported and price returned to the no-trade equilibrium, where domestic supply equals domestic demand, there will be lost gains from trade. As in the no-trade situation discussed above, consumer surplus is area A, producer surplus is area $B + F$, and total surplus is $A + B + F$. The gains from opening up the market to free trade, area $C + E$, are lost due to the protection. Area E is a consumption loss due to domestic consumers losing consumption they formerly had. Area C is an efficiency loss due to relatively inefficient domestic producers replacing relatively efficient foreign producers in supplying this good to the domestic market.

The losses due to protectionism can also be described in terms of the conditions from Chapter 3, concerning why a free market is efficient. With the protection, the good is no longer sold by suppliers with the lowest costs. Since there are lost gains from trade with the protection, the sum of consumer plus producer surplus is no longer maximized.

Protectionism, in general, raises the price of imported goods by reducing supply in the domestic market. This leads to an increase in price of the domestic substitutes for the foreign good too, as the supply of the good, domestic plus foreign, will be reduced.

There are other issues associated with international trade. One concern is the effect on wages. Wages depend on productivity and by encouraging workers to move to relatively productive industries. International trade between two countries can cause wages in both countries to rise. With international trade, jobs are lost in some industries, but jobs grow in other industries. Keeping jobs via protectionism is very expensive and retraining displaced workers or somehow compensating workers who lost their jobs would be a better policy. Child labor is related to the income of the people of a country, as is free trade. So free trade, rather than restrictions on free trade, is a better policy to reduce child labor around the world. Some people argue for protection of certain strategic or national defense industries. Every industry will argue that they are strategic or important for national defense and if protected they will eventually become inefficient due to reduced competition.

Decreases in transportation costs, integration of world markets, and increased speed of communication has made the world seem smaller. This trend is sometimes called *globalization*. Some people think this is new or bad, but the world has only recently become as globalized as it was prior to World War I. To give up globalization is to give up the gains from international trade.

Key Terms

economies of scale costs per unit fall with increases in production

absolute advantage the ability to produce the same good using fewer inputs than another producer

comparative advantage the ability to produce a good at a lower opportunity cost than another producer

protectionism the economic policy of restraining trade through quotas, tariffs, or other regulations that burden foreign producers but not domestic producers

trade quota a restriction on the quantity of goods that can be imported: Imports greater than the quota amount are forbidden or heavily taxed

tariff a tax on imports

Traps, Hints, and Reminders

Trade takes place, whether it occurs between individuals in a country or individuals in different countries, when both individuals expect to benefit.

One has a comparative advantage when one can produce at lower opportunity costs than other producers.

A tariff is simply a tax, so it has many of the effects on a market that any other tax would.

Practice Exercises: Learning by Doing

1. How is the economics of international trade different from trade between two people within a country?

2. What are division of knowledge and economies of scale? What is their role in trade?

3. What is comparative advantage? How does comparative advantage differ from absolute advantage?

4. Fill in the opportunity costs in the table below. Who has the comparative advantage and what is it for? Who has the absolute advantage and what is it for?

	Labor units required to produce. . .		Opportunity cost of. . .	
	1 Barrel of Oil	1 Movie	1 Barrel of Oil	1 Movie
United States	1	2		
Canada	2	8		

5. In the graph below, mark out (that is, set boundaries to) the losses associated with protecting the market to such an extent that there is no trade. Calculate the value of the deadweight loss associated with the protection.

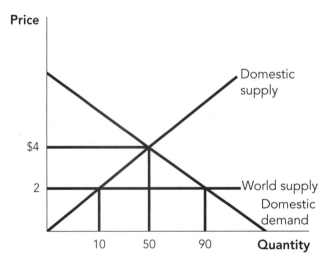

6. What is protectionism? What is a tariff? What is a quota?

7. What does specialization and trade lead to for individuals and the people of countries that trade?

*8. The Japanese people currently pay about four times the world price for rice. If Japan removed its trade barriers so that Japanese consumers could buy rice at the world price, who would be better off: Japanese consumers or Japanese rice farmers? If we added all the gains and losses to the Japanese, would there be a net gain or net loss? Who would lobby for reducing trade barriers? Explain why. Who would lobby against reducing trade barriers? Explain why.[1]

Multiple-Choice Questions

1. You have a comparative advantage in producing goods you can produce
   a. more of.
   b. at the lowest opportunity cost.
   c. using fewer inputs.
   d. All of the answers are correct.

2. You have an absolute advantage in producing goods you can produce
   a. more of.
   b. at the lowest opportunity cost.
   c. using fewer inputs.
   d. All of the answers are correct.

3. Everyone must necessarily have
   a. a comparative advantage.
   b. an absolute advantage.
   c. a tariff.
   d. All of the answers are correct.

[1]Questions marked with a ★ are also end-of-chapter questions.

Table 8.3

| | Labor units required to produce. . . | | Opportunity cost of. . . | |
	1 Computer	1 Camera	1 Computer	1 Camera
United States	3	5		
Japan	2	2		

4. According to the data in Table 8.3, the opportunity cost of a computer in the United States is

   a. 0.6 cameras.

   b. 1 camera.

   c. 1.67 cameras

   d. None of the answers is correct.

5. According to the data in Table 8.3, the opportunity cost of a camera in Japan is

   a. 0.6 computers.

   b. 1 computer.

   c. 1.67 computers.

   d. None of the answers is correct.

6. According to the data in Table 8.3, Japan has an absolute advantage in

   a. producing cameras.

   b. producing computers.

   c. producing both goods.

   d. producing neither good.

7. According to the data in Table 8.3, the United States has a comparative advantage in

   a. producing cameras.

   b. producing computers.

   c. producing both goods.

   d. producing neither good.

8. According to the data in Table 8.3, Japan has a comparative advantage in

   a. producing cameras.

   b. producing computers.

   c. producing both goods.

   d. producing neither good.

Figure 8.2

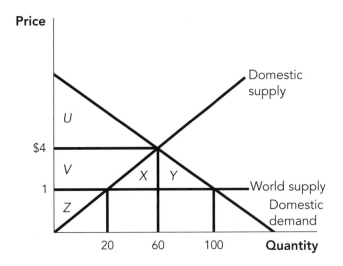

9. In Figure 8.2, with no international trade, consumer surplus is area
   a. *U.*
   b. *U + V + X + Z.*
   c. *V + Z.*
   d. *Z.*

10. In Figure 8.2, with no international trade, producer surplus is area
    a. *U.*
    b. *U + V + X + Y.*
    c. *V + Z.*
    d. *Z.*

11. In Figure 8.2, with international trade, consumer surplus is area
    a. *U.*
    b. *U + V + X + Y.*
    c. *X + Y.*
    d. *Z.*

12. In Figure 8.2, with international trade, producer surplus is area
    a. *U.*
    b. *U + V + X + Y.*
    c. *X + Y.*
    d. *Z.*

13. In Figure 8.2, the gain from international trade is area
    a. *U.*
    b. *U + V + X + Y.*
    c. *X + Y.*
    d. *Z.*

14. In Figure 8.2, if the market was protected to such an extent that all international trade stopped, then the deadweight loss would be
    a. $3.
    b. $60.
    c. $120.
    d. $240.

15. A tax on imports is called
    a. a comparative advantage.
    b. a tariff.
    c. an absolute advantage.
    d. a quota.

16. A restriction on the amount of imports to less than they would be with free trade is called
    a. a comparative advantage.
    b. a tariff.
    c. an absolute advantage.
    d. a trade quota.

17. Free international trade
    a. necessarily reduces wages in the high-wage country.
    b. potentially increases wages in both countries because workers are encouraged to enter into more productive lines of work.
    c. potentially lowers wages in the low-wage country.
    d. increases child labor.

18. Economies of scale occur
    a. due to government aid.
    b. as firm size increases.
    c. due to protectionism.
    d. All of the answers are correct.

19. Trade can take place because of
    a. specialization.
    b. economies of scale.
    c. division of knowledge.
    d. All of the answers are correct.

20. Among the winners with a tariff on cars are

    a. domestic producers of cars.

    b. domestic consumers of cars.

    c. the economy as a whole.

    d. All of the answers are correct.

Short-Answer Questions

21. How is the economics of international trade different from trade between two people within a country?

22. What are division of knowledge and economies of scale? What is their role in trade?

23. What is comparative advantage? How does it differ from absolute advantage?

24. Fill in the table below and state who has absolute and comparative advantages in what good.

	Labor Units Required to Produce. . .		Opportunity cost of. . .	
	1 salad	1 hamburger	1 salad	1 hamburger
Bonnie	1	5		
Clyde	3	3		

25. Refer to the graph below. What area shows the losses associated with protecting the market to such an extent that there is no trade? Calculate the value of the deadweight loss associated with the protection.

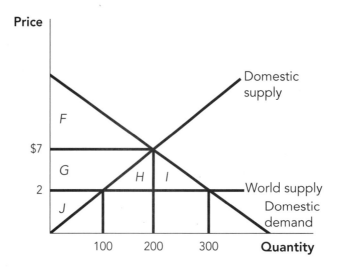

26. In the graph in Question 25, explain the sources of the lost gains from trade due to the protection eliminating any international trade.

27. What is protectionism? What is a tariff? What is a quota?

28. If protectionism makes a foreign good more expensive, what happens to the price of the domestic version of the good? Why?

29. What does specialization and trade lead to for individuals and the people of countries that trade?

30. Who are the winners and losers with a tariff?

Answer Key

Answers to Practice Exercises: Learning by Doing

1. The economics of trade does not vary whether it is between two parties within a country or two parties in different countries. Two parties trade when each expects to be made better off by the trade.

   Topic: Division of Knowledge; Economies of Scale and Creating Competition

2. Division of knowledge is important as it allows people to specialize. The farmer need only know about farming, the attorney need only know about the law, and the chef need only know about cooking. Division of knowledge allows each individual to know more about their specific area than if to operate a restaurant one person had to grow the crops, know enough law to set up the business enterprise, and finally know enough about food preparation to be the chef. Economies of scale are cost per unit savings that come with the size of an enterprise. Division of knowledge allows enterprises to grow larger and take advantage of economies of scale. The farmer-attorney-chef scenario described above would not be growing enough wheat to take advantage of combine threshers, but a specialist farmer that grows wheat to sell to others, can realize such economies of scale and produce at lower per unit costs. Trade allows people to specialize in production and take advantage of division of knowledge and economies of scale.

   Topics: Division of Knowledge; Economies of Scale and Creating Competition

3. One has a comparative advantage in producing those goods that one can produce for the lowest opportunity cost. This concept can be contrasted with absolute advantage, that is, when one can produce using fewer resources than other producers. Everyone will have a comparative advantage in something, even if they do not have an absolute advantage in any one good. This applies to people individually and all the people of a country. Exploiting comparative advantage can be summed up as it was in the text as "sell what you can make at low cost and buy what you can make only at high cost."

   Topic: Comparative Advantage

4. The table below contains the filled-in boxes.

	Labor units required to produce. . .		Opportunity cost of. . .	
	1 Barrel of Oil	1 Movie	1 Barrel of Oil	1 Movie
United States	1	2	.5 movies	2 barrel
Canada	2	8	.25 movies	4 barrels

The people of the United States have an absolute advantage in both oil and movie production as they can produce each with fewer labor inputs. But looking at the opportunity costs, we can see that the people of the United States have a lower opportunity cost of producing movies and thus a comparative advantage in producing movies. The people of Canada have a lower opportunity cost of producing oil and thus a comparative advantage in producing oil.

Topic: Comparative Advantage

5. The losses associated with protection, eliminating all international trade in this market, are marked in the graph below.

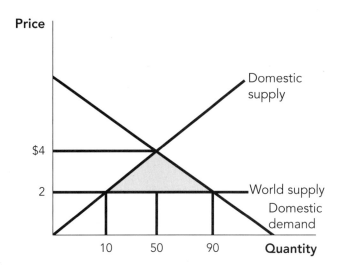

The amount of the area is $2 \times 80/2$ or $80 in deadweight loss.

Topic: The Costs of Protectionism

6. Protectionism is an economic policy of restraining trade through quotas, tariffs, or other regulations that burden foreign producers but not domestic producers. A tariff is a tax on imports. A trade quota is a quantity restriction where imports greater than the quota amount are forbidden.

Topic: Analyzing Trade with Supply and Demand

7. Trade between individuals and countries can lead to gains by both sides. Trade only takes place when both sides expect to gain. Also since wages depend on productivity, by encouraging workers to move to relatively productive industries, international trade can cause wages in both countries to rise. With international trade, jobs are lost in some industries, but jobs grow in other industries. Child labor is related to the income of the people of a country, as is free trade. So free trade can increase incomes in poorer countries and thereby reduce child labor.

Topics: Trade and Jobs; Child Labor

8. Japanese rice consumers would be better off by the removal of all Japanese barriers to rice trade. The gains of Japanese rice consumers would be greater than the losses of Japanese rice farmers, meaning that there would be a net gain from removing all barriers to rice trade in Japan. But since the costs to the farmers are concentrated on a relatively few farmers and the benefits are spread across a larger number of consumers, the farmers are likely to spend more money lobbying against this policy change than consumers would spend lobbying for it.

Topic: Winners and Losers from Trade

Answers to Multiple-Choice Questions

1. b, Topic: Comparative Advantage

2. c, Topic: Comparative Advantage

3. a, Topic: Comparative Advantage

4. a, Topic: Comparative Advantage

5. b, Topic: Comparative Advantage

6. c, Topic: Comparative Advantage

7. b, Topic: Comparative Advantage

8. a, Topic: Comparative Advantage

9. a, Topic: Analyzing Trade with Supply and Demand

10. c, Topic: Analyzing Trade with Supply and Demand

11. b, Topic: Analyzing Trade with Supply and Demand

12. d, Topic: Analyzing Trade with Supply and Demand

13. c, Topic: Analyzing Trade with Supply and Demand

14. c, Topic: The Costs of Protectionism

15. b, Topic: The Costs of Protectionism

16. d, Topic: The Costs of Protectionism

17. b, Topic: Comparative Advantage

18. b, Topic: Economies of Scale and Creating Competition

19. d, Topics: Division of Knowledge; Economies of Scale and Creating Competition

20. a, Topic: Winners and Losers from Trade

Answers to Short-Answer Questions

21. The economics of trade does not vary whether it is between two parties within a country or two parties in different countries. Two parties trade when each expects to be made better off by the trade.

   Topics: Division of Knowledge; Economies of Scale and Creating Competition

22. Division of knowledge is important as it allows people to specialize. The farmer need only know about farming, the attorney need only know about the law, and the chef need only know about cooking. Division of knowledge allows each individual to know more about their area than if to operate a restaurant one person grows the crops, knows enough law to set up the business enterprise, and finally knows enough about food preparation to be the chef. Economies of scale are cost per unit savings that come with the size of an enterprise. Division of knowledge allows enterprises to grow larger and take advantage of economies of scale. The farmer-attorney-chef scenario described above would not grow enough wheat to take advantage of combine threshers, but a specialist farmer that grows wheat to sell to others, can realize such economies of scale and produce at lower per unit costs. Trade allows people to specialize in production and take advantage of division of knowledge and economies of scale.

   Topics: Division of Knowledge; Economies of Scale and Creating Competition

23. One has a comparative advantage in producing those goods that one can produce for the lowest opportunity cost. This concept can be contrasted with absolute advantage, that is, when one can produce using fewer resources than other producers. Everyone will have a comparative advantage in something, even if they do not have an absolute advantage in any one good. This applies to both people individually and the people of a country. Exploiting comparative advantage can be summed up as it was in the text as "sell what you can make at low cost and buy what you can make only at high cost."

   Topic: Comparative Advantage

24. The table below contains the filled-in boxes.

	Labor Units Required to Produce. . .		Opportunity cost of. . .	
	1 salad	1 hamburger	1 salad	1 hamburger
Bonnie	1	5	0.2 hamburger	5 salad
Clyde	3	3	1 hamburger	1 salad

   Bonnie has a comparative and absolute advantage in producing salads. Clyde has a comparative and absolute advantage in producing hamburgers.

   Topic: Comparative Advantage

25. The deadweight loss would be $H + I$, which has have a value of $5 \times 200/2$ or $500.

Topic: The Costs of Protectionism

26. Area H is a loss of efficiency due to less efficient domestic producers replacing relatively efficient foreign producers in the market. Area I is a consumption loss due to exchanges that previously took place being pushed out of the market due to the protectionist policy.

Topic: The Costs of Protectionism

27. Protectionism is an economic policy of restraining trade through quotas, tariffs, or other regulations that burden foreign producers but not domestic producers. A tariff is a tax on imports. A trade quota is a quantity restriction where imports greater than the quota amount are forbidden.

Topic: The Costs of Protectionism

28. Protectionism, in general, raises the price of imported goods by reducing supply in the domestic market. This will lead to an increase in price of the domestic substitutes for the foreign good too, as the supply of the good, domestic plus foreign, will be reduced.

Topic: The Costs of Protectionism

29. Trade between individuals and countries can lead to gains by both sides. Trade only takes place when both sides expect to gain. Also, since wages depend on productivity, by encouraging workers to move to relatively productive industries, international trade can cause wages in both countries to rise. With international trade, jobs are lost in some industries, but jobs grow in other industries. Child labor is related to the income of the people of a country as is free trade. So free trade can increase incomes in poorer countries and thereby reduce child labor.

Topics: Trade and Jobs; Child Labor

30. The winners with a tariff include domestic workers and firms that produce the product. They get to produce more and their surplus goes up. Another winner is the government that collects the tariff revenue. The losers include consumers who pay more and consume less. Thus, their surplus falls. The economy as a whole loses because what the winner gains is smaller than what the losers lose.

Topic: Trade and Globalization

9

Externalities: When Prices Send the Wrong Signals

Why Learn about Externalities?

Interested Student: What is this about prices sending the wrong signal? I thought we learned that the market produces the best output and maximizes total surplus. Wouldn't that imply that the market price is the best price, too?

Old Professor: Yes, we did learn that the market, when it works, leads to the best possible economic outcome.

Interested Student: When the market works?

Old Professor: Right, under certain specific circumstances the market does not produce the best possible outcome. Externalities are one example of such a situation. Think about a car. In general, it will get you where you want to go. However, under certain circumstances, like when there is very deep snow, a car will not be able to get you there.

Interested Student: So I guess this makes externalities pretty important?

Old Professor: Exactly. And many externalities you see in the world may affect how you vote. In addition, politicians will be very interested in this topic to make a case for some actions on their parts.

Summary

In the past several chapters we have seen that the free market maximizes total surplus. This is the case when all costs are private costs. A **private cost** is a cost paid by the consumer or producer.

An **external cost** is a cost paid by people other than the consumer or producer trading in the market. **Social cost** is the cost to everyone: the private cost plus external cost. When there are external costs, social costs are different than private costs. **Social surplus** is consumer surplus plus producer surplus plus everyone else's surplus. When there are external costs, social surplus is greater than the total of consumer surplus plus producer surplus.

These ideas are shown in Figure 9.1, where social costs are private costs or supply plus social costs.

Figure 9.1

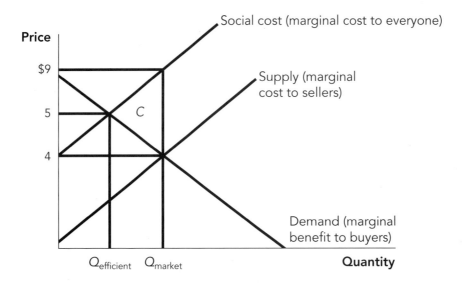

The **efficient quantity** is the quantity that maximizes social surplus. The efficient quantity is determined by the point where social costs equal demand. The market quantity, where supply or private costs equal demand, is larger than the efficient quantity, showing that, if left alone, the market may produce too much of this good.

The deadweight loss associated with the market quantity is area *C*. In this area, private costs are less than demand, but social costs are greater than demand. Thus for any unit produced past the efficient quantity, the costs to society are greater than any consumer's willingness to pay. In Figure 9.1, the last unit exchanged has a social cost of $9 but a benefit of only $4, so the deadweight loss is $5.

There can also be external benefits from a product. An **external benefit** is a benefit received by people other than the consumers and producers trading in the market. When there are external benefits, social benefits are greater than private benefits, and social surplus is greater than the total of consumer surplus plus producer surplus.

The case of an external benefit is shown in Figure 9.2, where this time the efficient quantity is greater than the market quantity.

This is because the individuals who buy the product do not receive the external benefit and thus undervalue the product from society's point of view. For example, the next unit past the market quantity will cost a bit more than $4 to produce, say $4.01. Consumers of the good value it at less than $4 so it may not be produced even though society values it at something a bit under $9, say $8.99. This is true of every unit up

Figure 9.2

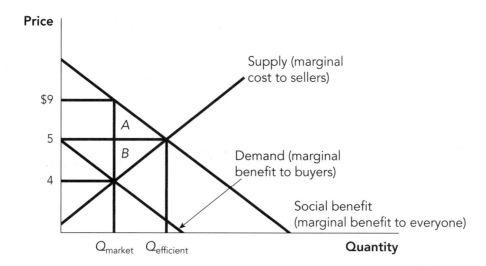

to the efficient output, where social benefits equal supply. Thus the areas *A* + *B* are deadweight losses if only the market quantity is produced.

There are a number of potential solutions to the problems of external costs and benefits in a market. There are conditions under which private solutions are likely. There are also possible government solutions.

The **Coase theorem** shows that if transaction costs are low and property rights are well defined, private bargains will ensure that the market solution is efficient even when there are externalities. **Transaction costs** are all the costs necessary to reach an agreement. Thus under these conditions the market will produce the efficient output and maximize social surplus even if there is an externality. For example, if the right to clean air is well defined and transaction costs are low, breathers and polluters will bargain and agree to the socially optimal amount of air pollution.

Of course, at times the conditions required by the Coase theorem—well defined property rights and low transaction cost—will not exist. In such cases a government solution may improve on the market result. The simplest government solution is an optimal tax or subsidy. An optimal tax in the case of an external cost can lead to private costs equaling social costs and thus the market will produce the efficient quantity and maximize social surplus. Similarly, in the case of an external benefit an optimal subsidy can make consumers realize the social benefits and lead to the market producing the efficient quantity and maximizing social surplus.

Another government solution is command and control. This is when the government tells the market how much to produce. Command and control is not very likely to produce the efficient quantity and maximize social surplus. Tradable allowances are a type of command and control policy that may be more efficient. In such a policy the government sets limits, say on pollution, but allows the producers to trade any amount as long as they are below their limit. By allowing trade, the command and solution control is reached in the lowest-cost manner, as those firms where reductions in pollution are expensive will buy allocations from firms who can reduce emissions more cheaply.

Key Terms

private cost a cost paid by the consumer or the producer

external cost a cost paid by people other than the consumer or the producer trading in the market

social cost the cost to everyone: the private cost plus the external cost

social surplus consumer surplus plus producer surplus plus everyone else's surplus

efficient equilibrium the price and quantity that maximizes social surplus

efficient quantity the quantity that maximizes social surplus

the Pigouvian tax a tax on a good with external costs

external benefit a benefit received by people other than the consumers or producers trading in the market

externalities external costs or external benefits, costs or benefits that fall on bystanders

the Pigouvian subsidy a subsidy on a good with external benefits

the Coase theorem posits that if transaction costs are low and property rights are clearly defined, private bargains will ensure that the market equilibrium is efficient even when there are externalities

transaction costs all the costs necessary to reach an agreement

Traps, Hints, and Reminders

Costs should be counted regardless of who bears them.

Benefits should be counted regardless of who receives them.

Remember from Chapter 7 that it does not matter if a tax or a subsidy is modeled as impacting supply or demand. You get the same result in either case.

Practice Exercises: Learning by Doing

1. What are private costs and benefits?

a cost paid by the consumer to the producer. A private benefit is one recieved by a producer or consumer of a product. Private costs + benefits do not affect anyone not involved in the transaction

2. What are external benefits and costs? What are social costs?

External cost is a cost paid by people other than the consumer or producer. External benefit is one recieved by someone other than the consumer or producer. Social costs are a cost to everyone; the private cost plus the external cost.

3. What is social surplus? How does social surplus differ from the total of consumer plus producer surplus?

Social surplus is consumer surplus plus producer surplus plus everyone else's surplus. When there are external costs, or benefits, social surplus is different than the total of consumer plus producer surplus.

4. Draw a graph showing the effects of an external cost on a market.

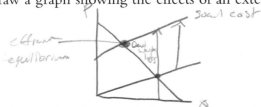

5. In the graph below, mark the market quantity, the efficient quantity, and the deadweight loss associated with the market quantity.

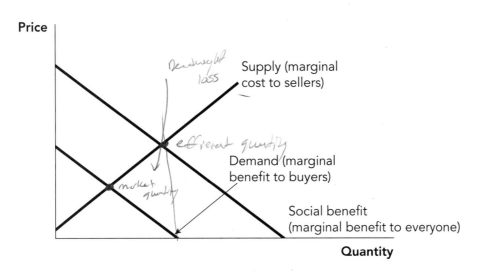

6. Discuss the conditions required for a private solution to externalities.

The Coase theorem which states that if transaction costs are low & property rights are clearly defined, private buyers will ensure that the market equilibrium is efficient even when there are externalities

7. Discuss the possible government solutions to externalities.

The most simple is an optimal tax or subsidy

A tax when an external cost can lead to a private cost equaling social costs + thus the market can produce the efficient quantity - max. social surplus.

a subsidy can make consumers realize the social benefits & lead to the market producing the efficient quantity max. social surplus.

command & control is not likely to produce the efficient quantity & max. social surplus

8. Explain why there is a deadweight loss in the case of an external cost.

w/ an EC at any quantity produced past the efficient output private costs are less than demand, but social costs are greater than demand. So, for any unit produced past efficient quantity, the costs to society are greater than any consumers' willingness to pay. Thus, these units are wasted resources that are deadweight loss to society

*9. Considering what we have learned about externalities, should human-caused global warming be completely stopped? Explain using the language of social benefits and social costs.[1]

Multiple-Choice Questions

1. Social surplus includes

  a. consumer surplus.

  b. producer surplus.

  c. everyone else's surplus.

  d. All of the answers are correct.

2. Social cost is

  a. private cost plus private benefit.

  b. private cost plus external cost.

  c. government cost plus social benefit.

  d. government cost plus external cost.

3. A private cost is paid by

  a. consumers or producers.

  b. everyone other than consumers and producers of the good.

  c. some private persons not engaged in the trade.

  d. the government.

4. The efficient output with an external cost is where

  a. social costs equal demand.

  b. social surplus is maximized.

  c. social costs equal the marginal benefit to buyers.

  d. All of the answers are correct.

[1]Questions marked with a ★ are also end-of-chapter questions.

5. The market output with an external cost is where

    a. social costs equal demand.

    b. supply equals demand.

    c. social costs equal the marginal benefit to buyers.

    d. All of the answers are correct.

Figure 9.3

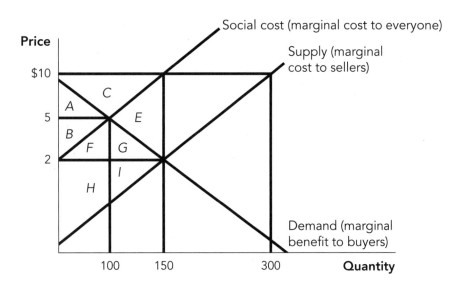

6. In Figure 9.3, the market output is

    a. 100 units.

    b. 150 units.

    c. 300 units.

    d. None of the answers is correct.

7. In Figure 9.3, the efficient output is

    a. 100 units.

    b. 150 units.

    c. 300 units.

    d. None of the answers is correct.

8. In Figure 9.3, the deadweight loss associated with the market output is area

    a. *A.*

    b. *F* + *G.*

    c. *E.*

    d. *M.*

9. In Figure 9.3, the area of the deadweight loss measures
   a. $50.
   b. $200.
   c. $400.
   d. None of the answers is correct.

10. In Figure 9.3, the value of wasted resource's on the last unit produced to get to the market output is
    a. $2.
    b. $8.
    c. $10.
    d. None of the answers is correct.

11. In Figure 9.3, a way to get the market to the efficient solution would be
    a. an optimal tax.
    b. an optimal subsidy.
    c. government taking over ownership of the market.
    d. All of the answers are correct.

Figure 9.4

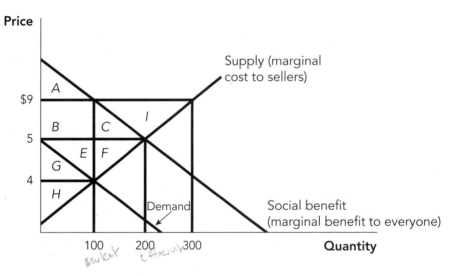

12. Figure 9.4 shows the case of a(n)
    a. external cost.
    b. external benefit.
    c. price discriminator.
    d. price ceiling.

13. In Figure 9.4, the market output is

    a. 100.

    b. 200.

    c. 300.

    d. None of the answers is correct.

14. In Figure 9.4, the efficient output is

    a. 100.

    b. 200.

    c. 300.

    d. None of the answers is correct.

15. In Figure 9.4, the deadweight loss at the market output is area

    a. $A + B$.

    b. $E + F$.

    c. $C + F$.

    d. I.

16. In Figure 9.4, the deadweight loss measures

    a. $100.

    b. $250.

    c. $500.

    d. None of the answers is correct.

17. For there to be private solutions to externalities, there must be

    a. low transaction costs.

    b. untradable allowances.

    c. undefined property rights.

    d. All of the answers are correct.

18. For there to be private solutions to externalities, there must be

    a. large transaction costs.

    b. tradable allowances.

    c. well-defined property rights.

    d. All of the answers are correct.

19. When the government tells a market how much to produce of something, this is called

    a. command and control.

    b. an optimal tax.

    c. an optimal subsidy.

    d. the Coase theorem.

20. A way that the government can encourage producers to lower pollution reduction cost is to

a. use the Coase theorem.

b. make the individual firm allowances tradable.

c. ban trade in the allowances.

d. have a government ceiling price on the allowances.

Short-Answer Questions

21. What are private costs and benefits? Who pays or receives them?

22. What are external benefits and costs? What are social costs? Who pays them?

23. What is social surplus? How does social surplus differ from the total of consumer plus producer surplus?

24. Draw a graph showing the effects of an external benefit on a market.

25. On the graph below, mark the market output, the efficient output, and the deadweight loss associated with market output.

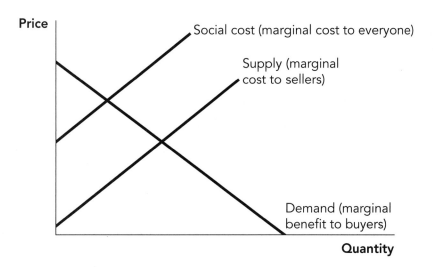

26. On the graph above, if the market is 200 units and efficient output is 150 units, and the price with the market output is $50, and the price where the market output hits the social cost curve is $60, then how much is the deadweight loss?

27. What is the Coase theorem? What conditions does it require?

28. Discuss the possible government solutions to externalities.

29. Explain why there is a deadweight loss in the case of an external cost.

30. What is gained by allowing trade in the pollution allowances given by the government to firms in a command and control attempt to adjust for external costs?

Answer Key

Answers to Practice Exercises: Learning by Doing

1. A private cost is one paid by the consumer or producer of a product. A private benefit is one received by the consumer or producer of a product. Private costs and benefits do not affect anyone not involved in the transaction.

   Topic: External Costs, External Benefits, and Efficiency

2. An external cost is a cost paid by people other than the consumer or producer trading in the market. An external benefit is a benefit received by people other than the consumer or producer trading in the market. Social cost is the cost to everyone: the private cost plus external cost.

   Topic: External Costs, External Benefits, and Efficiency

3. Social surplus is consumer surplus plus producer surplus plus everyone else's surplus. When there are external costs or benefits, social surplus is different than the total of consumer plus producer surplus.

   Topic: External Costs, External Benefits, and Efficiency

4. Draw a graph like Figure 9.1. Show that the social costs are greater than supply or private costs. Show that the market quantity is where private or supply costs equal demand and that the efficient output is where social cost equals demand. Point out that the market output is greater than the efficient output. Mark the deadweight loss, which is area *C* in Figure 9.1.

   Topic: External Costs, External Benefits, and Efficiency

5. Show the market quantity where demand intersects supply. Show that the efficient quantity is where social benefit intersects supply. Note that the market quantity is less than the efficient quantity. Mark the deadweight loss as in Figure 9.2.

   Topic: External Benefits

6. The Coase theorem shows that if transaction costs are low and property rights are well defined, private bargains will ensure that the market solution is efficient even when there are externalities. Transaction costs are all the costs necessary to reach an agreement. Thus under these conditions the market will produce the efficient output and maximize social surplus even if there is an externality.

   Topic: Private Solutions to Externality Problems

7. The simplest government solution is an optimal tax or subsidy. An optimal tax in the case of an external cost can lead to private costs equaling social costs, and thus the market can produce the efficient quantity, thereby maximizing social surplus. Similarly, in the case of an external benefit an optimal subsidy can make consumers realize the social benefits and lead to the market producing the efficient quantity maximizing social surplus. Another government solution is command and control. That is government telling the market how much to produce. Command and control is not very likely to produce the efficient quantity and maximize social surplus.

   Topic: Government Solutions to Externality Problems

8. With an external cost, at any quantity produced past the efficient output, private costs are less than demand, but social costs are greater than demand. Thus for any unit produced past the efficient quantity, the costs to society are greater than any consumer's willingness to pay. Thus those units involve wasted resources that are a deadweight loss for society.

Topic: External Costs, External Benefits, and Efficiency

9. Human-caused global warming should only be completely stopped, if the marginal cost of stopping human-caused global warming is zero. The efficient equilibrium for an externality is where marginal social costs equal marginal social benefit. Stopping the last units of human-caused global warming is likely to have a high marginal cost and a relatively low marginal social benefit. Thus human-caused global warming probably should not be completely stopped.

Topic: External Costs, External Benefits, and Efficiency

Answers to Multiple-Choice Questions

1. **d, Topic: External Costs, External Benefits, and Efficiency**
2. **b, Topic: External Costs, External Benefits, and Efficiency**
3. **a, Topic: External Costs, External Benefits, and Efficiency**
4. **d, Topic: External Costs, External Benefits, and Efficiency**
5. **b, Topic: External Costs, External Benefits, and Efficiency**
6. **b, Topic: External Costs, External Benefits, and Efficiency**
7. **a, Topic: External Costs, External Benefits, and Efficiency**
8. **c, Topic: External Costs, External Benefits, and Efficiency**
9. **b, Topic: External Costs, External Benefits, and Efficiency**
10. **b, Topic: External Costs, External Benefits, and Efficiency**
11. **a, Topic: External Costs, External Benefits, and Efficiency**
12. **b, Topic: External Benefits**
13. **a, Topic: External Benefits**
14. **b, Topic: External Benefits**
15. **c, Topic: External Benefits**
16. **b, Topic: External Benefits**
17. **a, Topic: Private Solutions to Externality Problems**
18. **c, Topic: Private Solutions to Externality Problems**
19. **a, Topic: Goverment Solutions to Externality Problems**
20. **b, Topic: Goverment Solutions to Externality Problems**

Answers to Short-Answer Questions

21. A private cost is one paid by the consumer or producer of a product. A private benefit is one received by the consumer or producer of a product. Private costs and benefits are paid or received only by producers and consumers of the good exchanged.

Topic: External Costs, External Benefits, and Efficiency

22. An external cost is a cost paid by people other than the consumer or producer trading in the market. An external benefit is a benefit received by people other than the consumer or producer trading in the market. Social cost is the cost to everyone: the private cost plus external cost.

Topic: External Costs, External Benefits, and Efficiency

23. Social surplus is consumer surplus plus producer surplus plus everyone else's surplus. When there are external costs or benefits, social surplus is greater than the total of consumer plus producer surplus.

Topic: External Costs, External Benefits, and Efficiency

24. Draw a graph like Figure 9.2. Show that the social benefits are greater than demand or private benefits. Show that the market quantity is where supply equals demand or private benefits and that the efficient output is where supply equals social benefits. Point out that the market output is less than the efficient output. Mark the deadweight loss as area $A + B$ in Figure 9.2.

Topic: External Benefits

25. On the graph show the market quantity where demand equals supply. Show that the efficient quantity is where social costs equal demand. Note that the market quantity is greater than the efficient quantity. Mark the deadweight loss as in Figure 9.1.

Topic: External Costs, External Benefits, and Efficiency

26. The deadweight loss measures 50 units times $10 divided by 2, or $250.

Topic: External Costs, External Benefits, and Efficiency

27. The Coase theorem shows that if transaction costs are low and property rights are well defined, private bargains will ensure that the market solution is efficient even when there are externalities. Transaction costs are all the costs necessary to reach an agreement. Thus under these conditions the market will produce the efficient output and maximize social surplus even if there is an externality.

Topic: Private Solutions to Externality Problems

28. The simplest government solution is an optimal tax or subsidy. An optimal tax in the case of an external cost can lead to private costs equaling social costs, and thus the market can produce the efficient quantity maximizing social surplus. Similarly, in the case of an external benefit an optimal subsidy can make consumers realize the social benefits and lead to the market producing the efficient quantity maximizing social surplus. Another government solution is command

and control. That is, the government tells the market how much to produce. Command and control is not very likely to produce the efficient quantity and maximize social surplus.

Topic: Government Solutions to Externality Problems

29. With an external cost, at any quantity produced past the efficient output, private costs are less than demand, but social costs are greater than demand. Thus for any unit produced past the efficient quantity, the costs to society are greater than any consumer's willingness to pay. Thus those units involve wasted resources which are a deadweight loss for society.

Topic: External Costs, External Benefits, and Efficiency

30. Tradable allowances are a type of command and control policy that may be more efficient. With such a policy the government sets limits say on pollution, but allows the producers to trade any amount as long as they are below their limit. By allowing trade, the command and solution control level of pollution is reached in the lowest-cost manner, as those firms where reductions are expensive will buy allocations from firms who can reduce emissions more cheaply.

Topic: Tradable Allowances

10

Profits, Prices, and Costs under Competition

Why Learn about Competition?

Sometimes profit is a controversial word. As we have seen in prior chapters on price ceilings and floors, price too can be controversial. In this chapter the authors cover profits, prices, and costs under competition. Specifically, we learn about the function of profit and how competition and profit work together.

Who will be interested in competition?

> Business owners and managers who are interested in costs, pricing, and profit

> Legislators, government officials, and candidates, plus voters, who may be surprised that profit has a function and what that function is

> Students of economics, of course, both as students and voters

Summary

If the demand increases for a product, the industry producing it grows. If the demand decreases for a product, the industry producing it shrinks. The signal for this increase or decrease in production is profit. Profit is defined as:

$$\text{Profit} = \text{Total Revenue} - \text{Total Cost}$$

$$\text{or Profit} = TR - TC.$$

To find the profit maximizing output or quantity for a firm, it is convenient to look at the revenue from selling one more of the product compared to the cost of producing one more of the product. The revenue from selling one more unit of the product is called the firm's **marginal revenue**, MR. More formally, MR is the change in total revenue, TR, when output changes or $\Delta TR/\Delta Q$. The cost of producing one more unit of the good is called the firm's **marginal cost**, MC. More formally, MC is the change in total cost, TC, when output changes or $\Delta TC/\Delta Q$.

To maximize profit, a firm will produce any unit where $MR > MC$. Any unit where $MR > MC$ adds to profit. Any unit where $MR < MC$ reduces profit. Thus the profit maximizing firm produces all units where $MR > MC$ and stops expanding output when $MR = MC$.

For a competitive firm, price, P, equals MR. This is because a competitive firm can sell all it wants at the market price without changing price.

MC for each firm in a competitive industry will equal the same price and thus each firm in a competitive industry will have the same level or value of MC. That is not the same MC curve, but each firm will move along its MC curve until MC equals P so that MC of each firm is the same value. This is the mechanism that minimizes total cost of production in the industry. The logic is that if firm 1 has an MC of \$10 and firm 2 has an MC of \$6, then by having firm 1 produce one less unit of the good (saving \$10) and having firm 2 produce one more of the good (at a cost of \$6), reduces total cost of production by \$10 − \$6 or \$4, while industry output does not change.

Fixed costs are those that do not vary with output. You should enter industries where producer surplus less fixed cost is greater than zero. This is the same thing as saying that you should enter an industry when profit is greater than zero.

Average cost, AC, is total cost divided by output, $AC = TC/Q$. Total revenue is price times quantity, $P \times Q$. Since profit, as defined above, is $TR - TC$ and firms enter industries with profit greater than zero, then firms enter when $TR - TC > 0$ or when $TR > TC$. In addition, $TR > TC = P \times Q > TC$ and thus firms also enter if $P \times Q / Q > TC/Q$ or when $P > AC$.

TC can be broken down into fixed cost, FC, and variable cost, VC. Variable costs are the costs that change with output. Variable cost is also the marginal cost for each unit produced that is added together or the sum of the marginal cost of each unit produced. This means that average cost can be expressed as follows:

$$AC = TC/Q = (VC/Q) + (FC/Q)$$

Also, profit can be calculated from average cost and price as follows:

$$\text{Profit} = (P - AC) \times Q$$

As fixed costs are spread over more and more units of production, the average fixed costs decline and AC also declines. For many industries, AC eventually becomes flat or begins to rise.

Some of the ideas discussed above are shown in Figure 10.1.

At P_1 the firm will produce Q_1, where price $= MC$. However notice that AC is greater than P at Q_1 so that a competitive firm would lose money as $P < AC$ at that quantity. At P_2 the firm will produce Q_2. At this quantity AC equals P and the firm is making a zero or normal profit. At P_3 the firm will produce Q_3 and makes a profit as $P > AC$ at that quantity.

Figure 10.1

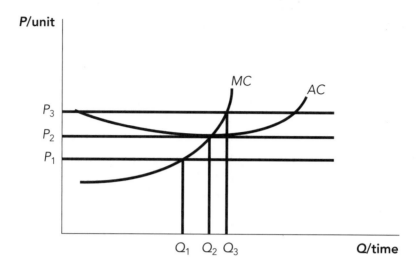

A **sunk cost** is a cost that cannot be recovered. Because the cost cannot be recovered, sunk costs do not affect the decision of a firm to exit an industry. A firm will exit if $P - AC < 0$ or producer surplus less recoverable costs is less than zero. When there is uncertainty, the entry and exit decisions become related to lifetime profits rather than profits today. Thus a firm may not exit when price is below AC, if the firm expects price to rise in the future.

The industry supply curve is all the MC curves of all the firms in (or potentially in) the industry. As price rises, more firms will start producing, resulting in the industry supply curve becoming more elastic than the MC curves of individual firms.

The **long run** is the time it takes for substantial investment and entry to occur. The **short run** is when there cannot be entry.

In many industries, the AC is U-shaped in the long run (at first declining and then later rising). For other industries, the AC is flat or constant over a range of output. In the constant cost case, an increase in demand leads to a temporary increase in price and profits. The increase in profits induces others to enter into business. The entrants are able to produce at the same AC of firms already in the industry leading to a flat or constant AC. An industry where AC is declining over the relevant range of output is a special case that is sometimes associated with the clustering of firms in an industry in a geographical area.

The dynamics of competition illustrates the **elimination principle** that says above normal profits are eliminated by entry into the industry and below normal profits (or losses) are eliminated by exit from the industry. Joseph Schumpeter famously described the dynamics of competition as "creative destruction."

Key Terms

total revenue, TR, price times quantity sold: $TR = P \times Q$

total cost, TC, the cost of producing a given quantity of output

marginal revenue, MR, the change in total revenue from selling an additional unit. $MR = \Delta TR/\Delta Q$. For a firm in a competitive industry $MR = $ Price

marginal cost, MC, the change in total cost from producing an additional unit

fixed costs, FC, costs that do not vary with output

average cost, AC, the cost per unit, that is, the total costs of producing Q units divided by Q, $AC = TC/Q$

variable costs, VC, costs that do vary with output

short run the time period before entry occurs

long run the time it takes for substantial new investment and entry to occur

elimination principle above normal profits are eliminated by entry and below normal profits are eliminated by exit

zero profits also called normal profits, occur when $P = AC$, at this price the firm is covering all of its costs including enough to pay labor and capital their ordinary opportunity costs

invisible hand property #1 even though no actor in a market economy intends to do so, in a free market $P = MC_1 = MC_2 = \ldots MC_N$ and as a result the total costs of production are minimized

invisible hand property #2 entry and exit decisions not only work to eliminate profits, they work to ensure that labor and capital move across industries to optimally balance production so that the greatest use is made of our limited resources

increasing cost industry an industry in which industry costs increase with greater output; shown with an upward sloped supply curve

constant cost industry an industry in which industry costs do not change with greater output; shown with a flat supply curve

decreasing cost industry an industry in which industry costs decrease with an increase in output; shown with a downward sloped supply curve

Traps, Hints, and Reminders

In the models used in this chapter production equals sales. If $P > AC$, then the firm makes a profit.

When all firms set $P = MC$, industry total costs are minimized for industry output. Since sunk costs cannot be recaptured, they do not affect the exit decision.

Entry will drive above-normal profits out of a competitive industry and exit will drive below-normal profits (or losses) out of a competitive industry.

Practice Exercises: Learning by Doing

1. What is profit? How does a competitive firm maximize profit?

2. In the table below, how can you tell this firm is in a competitive industry?

Production/Sales	Marginal Revenue	Marginal Cost	Change in Profit
2	$10	$6	
3	$10	$8	
4	$10	$10	
5	$10	$12	
6	$10	$14	

What is the firm's profit maximizing output? Fill in the change in the profit column in the table.

3. Why does each firm in a competitive industry have the same level of marginal cost?

4. In the long run, why must a firm in a competitive industry produce at the lowest point of the average total cost curve?

5. Suppose the competitive firm is making a short-run positive profit. Draw an average marginal cost graph showing the competitive firm's profit and profit output.

6. What are the entry and exit criteria for a firm?

7. What is the elimination principle?

*8. We mentioned that carpet manufacturing looks like a decreasing-cost industry. In American homes, carpets are much less popular than they were in the 1960s and 1970s, when wall-to-wall carpeting was fashionable in homes. Suppose that carpeting became even less popular than it is today. What would this fall in demand probably do to the price of carpet in the long run?[1]

Multiple-Choice Questions

1. A competitive firm maximizes profit where
   a. total revenue equals total cost.
   b. price equals average cost.
   c. price equals marginal cost.
   d. All of the answers are correct.

2. For a competitive firm, marginal revenue equals price because
   a. firm demand is downward sloping.
   b. the firm need not lower price to sell more of its product.
   c. marginal costs are falling.
   d. average costs are increasing.

3. When all of the firms in a competitive industry have the same level of MC,
   a. the total cost of production for the industry is minimized.
   b. the marginal cost of production for the industry is minimized.
   c. the average cost of production for the industry is maximized.
   d. None of the answers is correct.

[1]Questions marked with a ★ are also end-of-chapter questions.

4. In competition when price is greater than average cost

    a. there will be entry in the industry in the long run.

    b. the firm is making a profit.

    c. price will fall in the long run.

    d. All of the answers are correct.

5. There will be entry in an industry when

    a. profit is less than zero.

    b. producer surplus less fixed cost is positive.

    c. sunk costs are positive.

    d. All of the answers are correct.

Use the following graph to answer Questions 6 through 9.

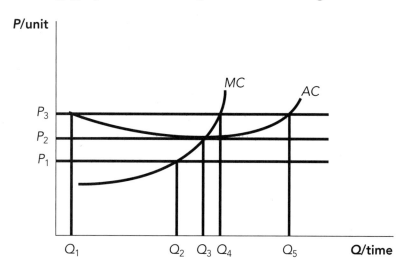

6. In the preceding graph, at P_3 the firm will produce

    a. Q_1.

    b. Q_4.

    c. Q_5.

    d. None of the answers is correct.

7. In the preceding graph, at P_1 the firm would be

    a. making a normal profit.

    b. making an above-normal profit.

    c. losing money.

    d. expecting entry into its industry.

8. In the preceding graph, at P_3 the industry will see
   a. entry of new firms in the long run.
   b. exit of some firms in the long run.
   c. each firm making a zero profit.
   d. price remaining the same over the long run.

9. In the preceding graph, in the long run we would expect the price to be
   a. P_1.
   b. P_2.
   c. P_3.
   d. None of the answers is correct.

10. Fixed costs are those that
    a. do not vary with output.
    b. do not change in the long run.
    c. are determined by the government.
    d. All of the answers are correct.

11. Average cost is
    a. TC/Q.
    b. $AVC + AFC$.
    c. $VC/Q + FC/Q$.
    d. All of the answers are correct.

12. If marginal cost is above average cost, then average cost is
    a. at its minimum.
    b. at its maximum.
    c. falling.
    d. rising.

13. Sunk costs
    a. can be recaptured and do not affect a firm's exit decision.
    b. cannot be recaptured and do not affect a firm's exit decision.
    c. can be recaptured and do affect a firm's exit decision.
    d. cannot be recaptured and do affect a firm's exit decision.

14. The short run is
    a. less than a year.
    b. when all factors of production are fixed.
    c. the period before entry occurs.
    d. All of the answers are correct.

Use the following table to answer Questions 15 through 18.

Production or Sales	Marginal Revenue	Marginal Cost	Variable Cost	Fixed Cost	Average Cost	Profit
1	$6	$2	$2	$2	$4	$2
2	$6	$3	$5	$2	$3.5	$5
3	$6	$5	—	—	—	—

15. Based on the data in the preceding table, fixed cost at three units of output is

   a. $2.

   b. $4.

   c. $5.

   d. $10.

16. Based on the data in the preceding table, variable cost at three units of output is

   a. $2.

   b. $4.

   c. $6.

   d. $10.

17. Based on the data in the preceding table, average cost at three units of output is

   a. $4.

   b. $5.

   c. $6.

   d. $10.

18. Based on the data in the preceding table, profit at three units of output is

   a. $4.

   b. $5.

   c. $6.

   d. $10.

19. Marginal cost

   a. rises when average cost falls.

   b. is costs divided by output.

   c. intersects average cost at average cost's minimum.

   d. All of the answers are correct.

20. A decreasing cost industry is one where

   a. total cost falls as output rises.

   b. the supply curve is downward sloped.

   c. fixed cost falls as output rises.

   d. All of the answers are correct.

Short-Answer Questions

21. What are the implications of $P = MC$ in competition? What causes these implications?

22. What quantity does a competitive firm produce to maximize profit?

23. Fill in the third row on the table below for a competitive firm.

Production or Sales	Marginal Revenue	Marginal Cost	Variable Cost	Fixed Cost	Average Cost	Profit
1	$7	$2	$2	$2	$4	$3
2	$7	$3	$5	$2	$3.5	$7
3	—	$4	—	—	—	—

24. In the graph below mark the competitive firm's profit maximizing quantity. At that quantity, what profit does the firm make?

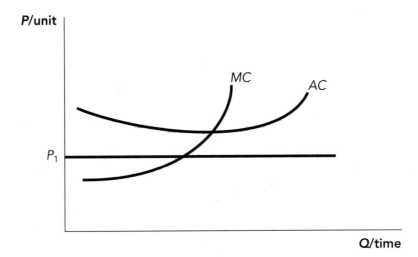

25. When will a firm enter an industry? When will it exit an industry?

26. What is creative destruction? Why is it important?

27. How is an industry's supply curve found?

28. How are the long run and short run different? How long is the short run?

29. What are the relationships between marginal cost and average cost?

30. What is the elimination principle?

Answer Key

Answers to Practice Exercises: Learning by Doing

1. A firm's profit is total revenue less total cost. This difference is maximized when the firm sells all units where marginal revenue is greater than marginal cost. Thus the firm produces where marginal revenue equals marginal cost. Since a competitive firm does not perceptibly affect price by producing more, price equals marginal revenue. Thus a competitive firm maximizes profit where price equals marginal cost.

   Topic: What Price to Set?

2. You can tell the industry is competitive because as the firm's output/sales change, its marginal revenue does not change and thus marginal revenue equals price. The profit maximizing output for the firm is 4 units of output where marginal cost equals marginal revenue and the change in profit is zero. The table is filled in below.

   Topic: What Quantity to Produce?

Production/Sales	Marginal Revenue	Marginal Cost	Change in Profit
2	$10	$6	$4
3	$10	$8	$2
4	$10	$10	$0
5	$10	$12	−$2
6	$10	$14	−$4

3. Each firm in a competitive industry has the same level of MC because each firm faces the same price. So even if competitive firms have different MC curves, they will move along the curve until they get to where $MC = P$ and thus MC will be the same for each firm.

   Topic: Invisible Hand Property #1: The $P = MC$ Decision and the Minimization of the Total Costs of Production

4. If one firm in a competitive industry is producing at an output where Price = MC but greater than average total cost, then it is making a positive profit. The above normal profit attracts new entry into the market, driving the price down until Price = $MC = ATC$, which is the lowest point of the average total cost curve.

   Topic: Invisible Hand Property #1: The $P = MC$ Decision and the Minimization of the Total Costs of Production

5. Draw a graph such as the one below.
  Label the profit maximizing output of $Q\star$, where MC = Price and the area
  of profit (that is, A + B + C).

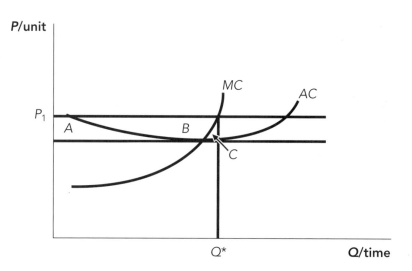

Topic: Profits and the Average Cost Curve

6. A firm should enter an industry if the firm expects to make a positive profit (profit > 0). A firm will exit an industry when it expects persistent negative profits (profit < 0).

Topic: When to Enter and Exit an Industry

7. The elimination principle is that above-normal profits in an industry are eliminated by entry and below-normal profits (or losses) in an industry are eliminated by exit.

Topic: Invisible Hand Property #2: The Balance of Industries and Entry, Exit, and the Elimination Principle

8. If the carpet industry is indeed a decreasing cost industry, a decrease in demand in the future will lead to an increase in price of carpet. A decreasing cost industry is one that has a downward sloping supply curve. Thus decreases in quantity will lead to higher a market price.

Topic: A Special Case: The Decreasing Cost Industry

Answers to Multiple-Choice Questions

1. c, Topic: What Price to Set?

2. b, Topic: What Quantity to Produce?

3. a, Topic: Invisible Hand Property #1: The *P=MC* Decision and the Minimization of the Total Costs of Production

4. d, Topic: When to Enter and Exit an Industry

5. b, Topic: When to Enter and Exit an Industry

6. **b, Topic: What Quantity to Produce?**

7. **c, Topic: Profits and the Average Cost Curve**

8. **a, Topic: Profits and the Average Cost Curve**

9. **b, Topic: When to Enter and Exit an Industry**

10. **a, Topic: Profits and the Average Cost Curve**

11. **d, Topic: Profits and the Average Cost Curve**

12. **d, Topic: Profits and the Average Cost Curve**

13. **b, Topic: Profits and the Average Cost Curve**

14. **c, Topic: Entry, Exit, and Industry Supply Curves**

15. **a, Topic: Profits and the Average Cost Curve**

16. **d, Topic: Profits and the Average Cost Curve**

17. **a, Topic: Profits and the Average Cost Curve**

18. **c, Topic: Profits and the Average Cost Curve**

19. **c, Topic: What Quantity to Produce?**

20. **b, Topic: Entry, Exit, and Industry Supply Curves**

Answers to Short Answer Questions

21. The implications of $P = MC$ in competition are that each firm is maximizing profit and has the same level of MC because each firm faces the same price (and industry production costs are minimized). Even if competitive firms have different MC curves, they will move along them until they get to where $MC = P$ and thus MC will be the same for each firm and firms with a lower MC will replace those with higher MC lowering industry total cost to its minimum. For example, if firm 1 has a MC of $20 and firm 2 has a MC of $10, then by having firm 1 produce one less unit of the good (saving $20) and having firm 2 produce one more of the good (at a cost of $10), total cost of production is reduced by $20 − $10 (or $10) while industry output does not change. Profit is increased by each unit where $P > MC$, so by producing all those units and getting to where $P = MC$ each firm maximizes profits.

   Topic: Invisible Hand Property #1: The $P=MC$ Decision and the Minimization of the Total Costs of Production

22. A firm's profit is total revenue less total cost. This difference is maximized when the firm sells all units where marginal revenue is greater than marginal cost. Thus the firm produces where marginal revenue equals marginal cost.

   Topic: What Quantity to Produce?

23. The completed table is below.

Production or Sales	Marginal Revenue	Marginal Cost	Variable Cost	Fixed Cost	Average Cost	Profit
1	$7	$2	$2	$2	$4	$3
2	$7	$3	$5	$2	$3.5	$7
3	$7	$4	$9	$2	$3.67	$10

24. The completed figure is below.

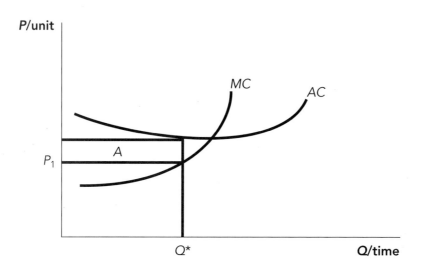

Output is labeled $Q^\star$, and since P is less than AC, this firm would be losing money equal to area A.

Topic: Profits and the Average Cost Curve

25. A firm should enter an industry if that firm expects to make a positive profit, profit > 0. A firm will exit an industry when it expects persistent negative profits, profit < 0.

Topic: When to Enter and Exit an Industry

26. Creative destruction is the idea that firms going out of business (that is, destruction) leads to the new firms and products coming in the market (that is, creative). This is as Schumpeter point that competition and "entry and exit" pushes cost down to the minimum of the average cost.

Topic: Creative Destruction

27. A competitive industry's supply curve is found by adding up or summing the MC of each of the firms in the industry at various prices. The industry will generally be upward sloping as a higher price leads to greater production.

Topic: Entry, Exit, and Industry Supply Curves

28. The short run is the time period before entry occurs. The long run is the time it takes for substantial new investment and entry to occur. The short run has no set time. As the definition of the long run implies, it depends on how long it takes to make a substantial investment and expand production of the particular product. The amount of time it takes to be considered a long run varies from industry to industry.

Topic: Entry, Exit, and Industry Supply Curves

29. MC intersects AC at its minimum. Further, when MC is above AC, AC must be rising and when MC is below AC, AC must be falling.

Topic: Profits and the Average Cost Curve

30. The elimination principle is when above-normal profits in an industry are eliminated by entry and below-normal profits or losses in an industry are eliminated by exit.

Topic: Invisible Hand Property #2: The Balance of Industries and Entry, Exit, and the Elimination Principle

11

Monopoly

Why Learn about Monopoly?

Interested Student: Wow, monopoly, everyone knows that there are a lot of monopolies caused by businesses and they are bad, right?

Patient Professor: Some of that is true, but as you will see it is a little more complicated than that.

Interested Student: Really, how so?

Patient Professor: For one thing, some monopolies are established by the government. Some may be a political payoff, but some may be granted to encourage innovators in an industry like the drug industry that discovers life-saving drugs. Also, there is the matter of why a monopoly is bad and what to do if something should be done about particular monopolies.

Interested Student: I guess I see what you are talking about.

Patient Professor: I hope so. An informed voter or policy maker needs to understand the concept of a monopoly and also understand if anything needs to be done about the monopolies that they might encounter.

Summary

This chapter covers **monopoly**. **Market power** is defined as the ability to raise price above average cost without fear that other firms will enter the industry.

The chapter shows how to find a monopoly's **marginal revenue (MR)** given its demand curve. When the monopolist's demand is linear and downward sloping, its marginal revenue is linear, downward sloping and twice as steep as its demand. Marginal revenue for a change in output can be calculated from prices and quantities. For example, if at a price of $10, a firm sells 5 units, then its total revenue at 5 units is $50. If when the firm drops its price to $9, it sells 6 units, then the firm's total revenue at 6 units is $54. In this example, the marginal revenue from selling the 6th unit is $54 − $50 or $4.

The chapter further shows how to determine the *monopoly output* and *monopoly price*. As shown in Figure 11.1, the monopoly output, Q_m, is that quantity below the intersection of marginal revenue and **marginal costs (MC)**, that is, $MR = MC$.

Figure 11.1

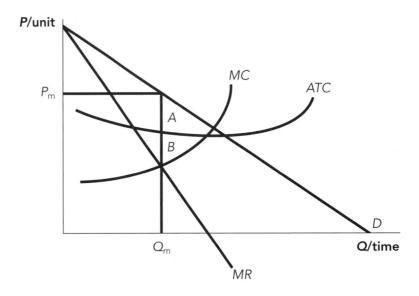

The monopoly price, P_m, is that price on the monopolist's demand curve above where $MR = MC$. Put another way, it is the price people are willing to pay for the monopoly quantity, Q_m.

One way to measure the cost of a monopoly is to measure the *deadweight loss* associated with that monopoly. The deadweight loss associated with a monopoly is the reduction in *total surplus*, that is, consumer plus producer surplus compared to the competitive outcome or where marginal costs equals demand or where $MC = D$. In Figure 11.1, the deadweight loss is area *A* plus area *B* (or *A* + *B*).

Chapter 11 also shows how to find the *monopoly profit* given the average total cost curve. The monopolist's profit is the difference between average revenue or price, P_m, and *ATC* at Q_m multiplied by the monopoly quantity, Q_m. In Figure 11.2, this is the rectangle bounded by points P_m, *A*, *C*, and *B*.

After covering the mechanics of monopoly, the issue of whether a particular monopoly is good or bad is taken up. Again, with a monopoly, one problem is that there is a deadweight loss or a reduction of total surplus below what it would be in a competitive market. However, with some types of monopolies the story is not so simple and there can be trade-offs involved.

For example, *patent monopolies* for a new drug or medical device involve a trade-off between deadweight loss and innovation. Without the prospect of monopoly profits, the new drug or medical device may not be developed. In this type of situation, societies often choose to grant the monopoly, that is, the patent, and accept the deadweight loss to get the innovation.

Figure 11.2

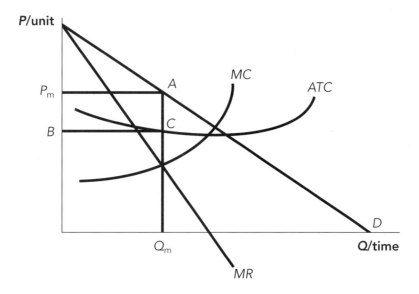

Natural monopoly involves a trade-off between economies of scale and dead-weight losses. Regulation of natural monopolies may offer a partial escape from this trade-off, but other issues such as product quality may arise.

Many, maybe most, monopolies are neither patent nor natural monopolies. That is, they neither encourage innovation nor take advantage of economies of scale. They are usually created to transfer wealth to politically powerful elites. In such cases, the economic solution is to open the market to competition.

Key Terms

market power the power to raise price above average cost without fear that other firms will enter the market

monopoly a firm with market power

marginal revenue, MR, the change in total revenue from selling an additional unit

marginal cost, MC, the change in total cost from producing an additional unit. To maximize profit, a firm increases output until $MR = MC$

natural monopoly said to exist when a single firm can supply the entire market at a lower cost than two or more firms

barriers to entry factors that increase the cost to new firms of entering an industry

Traps, Hints, and Reminders

Profit Maximization

A firm maximizes its profit by increasing output until marginal revenue, MR, equals marginal cost, MC. In competition price, P, equals MR while for monopoly $MR < P$.

Marginal Revenue Shortcut

When demand is a downward-sloping straight line, marginal revenue, *MR*, is also a downward sloping straight line, but is twice as steep as demand.

Relationship of Monopoly Marginal Revenue to Demand

Monopoly marginal revenue is below demand because the monopoly perceives that to sell more it must lower the price on all units sold.

Calculating Total Revenue

Total revenue is price times quantity, so if at a price of $1 you sell 50 units, your total revenue is $50.

Calculating Marginal Revenue

Marginal revenue for a particular price change can be calculated by subtracting the total revenue from the first price from the total revenue from the second price. For example, if at a price of $2 the total revenue is $100, and at a price of $1 the total revenue is $110, then the marginal revenue is calculated by reducing the price from $2 to $1 is $110 − $100, which = $10.

Markup Over Cost

Remember that the more inelastic demand, the more the monopolist can markup price above average total costs.

Practice Exercises: Learning by Doing

1. Draw the marginal revenue, *MR*, curve on the graph below.

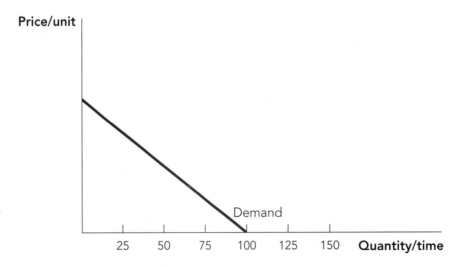

2. If demand equals $Q = 50 - 10P$, then the following price and quantities are possibilities.

P	Q
0	50
$1.00	40
$2.00	30
$2.10	29
$3.00	20
$3.90	11
$4.00	10
$5.00	0

a. At a price of $4, what is the total revenue?

b. At a price of $3.90, what is the total revenue?

c. What is the marginal revenue from lowering the price from $4 to $3.90?

d. At a price of $2.10, what is the total revenue?

e. At a price of $2, what is the total revenue?

f. What is the marginal revenue from lowering the price from $2.10 to $2?

3. In the graph below, show the monopoly price and quantity.

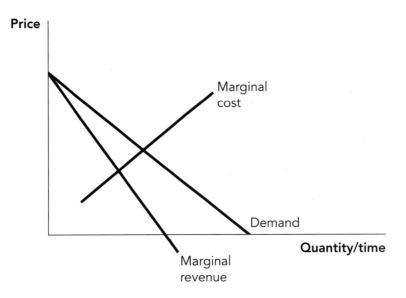

4. On the graph above, show the deadweight loss associated with a monopoly.

5. On the graph above, draw in an average total cost such that the monopolist is making an economic profit.

6. On the graph above, show the economic profit the monopolist is making based on the *ATC* curve you drew for Question 5.

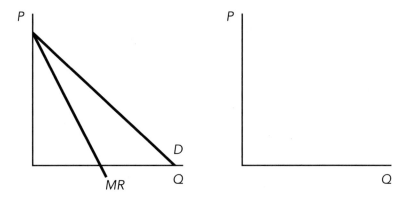

7. On the graph above, on the right draw a demand/marginal revenue combination, where the monopolist will have a greater ability to raise price above *MC* than the monopolist on the left.

*8. Common sense might say that a monopolist would produce more output than a competitive firm facing the same marginal cost. After all, if you are making a profit, you would want to sell as much as you can, correct? What is wrong with this line of reasoning? Why do monopolistic industries sell less than the competitive industries?[1]

Multiple-Choice Questions

1. Market power is
   a. the ability to raise price above average cost without fear that other firms will enter the industry.
   b. the ability to raise average costs without fear that other firms will enter the industry.
   c. the ability to influence government intervention in your industry.
   d. the ability to raise marginal costs without fear that the other firms will enter the industry.

---

[1] Questions marked with a ★ are also end-of-chapter questions.

Figure 11.3

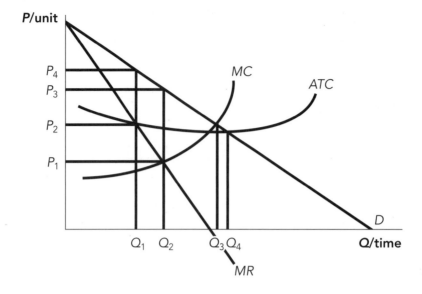

2. In Figure 11.3, the monopoly output is

a. Q_1.

b. Q_2.

c. Q_3.

d. Q_4.

3. In Figure 11.3, the monopolist will charge

a. P_1.

b. P_2.

c. P_3.

d. P_4.

4. In Figure 11.3, the firm is

a. losing money.

b. making a normal profit.

c. breaking even.

d. making an economic profit.

5. In Figure 11.3, an economist would want to

a. allow entry and encourage competition.

b. accept the deadweight loss to get economies of scale.

c. remove the patent if it is an industry with many potential innovations.

d. All of the answers are correct.

Figure 11.4

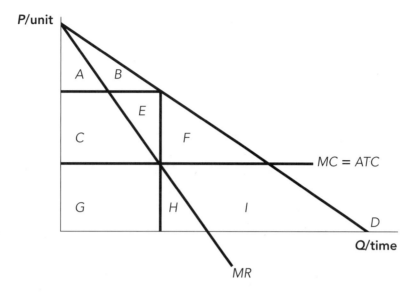

6. In Figure 11.4, the deadweight loss of monopoly is area
   a. *A + B.*
   b. *C + E.*
   c. *F.*
   d. *G + H + I.*

7. In Figure 11.4, the monopoly makes economic profits of area
   a. *A + B.*
   b. *C + E.*
   c. *F.*
   d. *G + H + I.*

8. A patent monopoly involves a trade-off between
   a. innovation and economies of scale.
   b. deadweight losses and economies of scale.
   c. deadweight losses and innovation.
   d. deadweight losses and market power.

9. A natural monopoly involves a trade-off between
   a. innovation and economies of scale.
   b. deadweight losses and economies of scale.
   c. deadweight losses and innovation.
   d. deadweight losses and market power.

10. An economic problem with a monopoly is that
    a. there is a loss in total surplus compared to competition.
    b. monopolists produce too much of their product.
    c. monopolists produce where marginal cost equals marginal revenue.
    d. the monopolist charges a price where marginal revenue equals marginal cost.

11. The solution economists offer for the monopoly problem is
    a. government takeover of the market.
    b. government banning production of the good.
    c. opening the industry up to competition.
    d. government production of the good.

12. A natural monopoly is characterized by
    a. marginal costs rising with quantity.
    b. average total costs falling as quantity increases.
    c. small fixed costs.
    d. All of the answers are correct.

13. A drug can often be priced well above cost because of
    a. market power.
    b. the "you can't take it with you" effect.
    c. the "other people's money" effect.
    d. All of the answers are correct.

14. The ability of the monopolist to markup price above costs is greater
    a. when there is more inelastic demand.
    b. when there is more elastic demand.
    c. when demand is unitary elastic.
    d. over a longer time period.

15. The deadweight loss associated with a monopoly is
    a. the reduction in gains from trade due to deviations from competitive markets.
    b. the economic profits a monopoly makes.
    c. the total of producer and consumer surplus.
    d. the difference between monopoly price and marginal cost.

16. A monopolist recognizes that its *MR* is below demand because
    a. its total cost increases with outputs.
    b. it can charge whatever it wants for its product.
    c. it must lower price on all units sold to sell more of its product.
    d. it will make a profit at any output.

17. The economic reason for governments to grant patent monopolies is to

    a. encourage innovation.

    b. reward campaign donors.

    c. capture economies of scale.

    d. increase total surplus.

18. If at a price of $20 a firm sells 100 units, and at a price of $19 a firm sells 101 units, then its marginal revenue from selling the 101st unit is

    a. $2000.

    b. $1919.

    c. $81.

    d. −$81.

19. The deadweight loss associated with a monopoly is viewed as bad by economists because it is captured by

    a. the government.

    b. consumers.

    c. the monopolist.

    d. no one.

20. If a natural monopolist is forced to produce the competitive optimal quantity, it will

    a. lose money.

    b. make a normal profit.

    c. break even.

    d. make an economic profit.

Short-Answer Questions

    21. What is market power?

    22. Why is the monopolist's marginal revenue curve below its demand curve?

23. What is the problem that economists find with a monopoly?

24. Draw the situation of a monopoly, mark the profit maximizing output and price, and show the deadweight loss due to a monopoly.

25. What do economists suggest as a solution to solve the problem of a regular monopoly?

26. Why might society want to accept a natural monopoly despite the deadweight loss associated with a natural monopoly? How can the problems with a natural monopoly be overcome in part?

27. Why might society accept a patent monopoly despite the deadweight loss associated with a patent monopoly?

28. Under what conditions can a monopolist raise price more over marginal cost?

29. Why might a manufacturer of a drug that is part of the treatment for a life threatening disease have the ability to markup its price much higher than costs?

30. If at a price of $30 a firm sells 10 units, and at a price of $25 a firm sells 11 units, then what would the firm's marginal revenue be after lowering the price from $30 to $25?

Answer Key

Answers to Practice Exercises: Learning by Doing

1. Draw a straight line from where the demand curve intersects the price axis and 50 on the quantity axis.

   Topic: How a Firm Uses Market Power to Maximize Profit

2. **a.** $4 times 10 units equals a total revenue of $40.00.

   b. $3.90 times 11 units equals a total revenue of $42.90.

   c. The marginal revenue from reducing the price from $4 to $3.90 is $42.90 − $40 or $2.90.

   d. $2.10 times 29 units equals a total revenue of $60.90.

   e. $2 times 30 units equals a total revenue of $60.00.

   f. The marginal revenue from reducing the price from $2.10 to $2 is $60 − $60.90 or -0.90 (that is, minus 90 cents).

   Topic: How a Firm Uses Market Power to Maximize Profit

3. Draw in the quantity where $MC = MR$. Then go up to the demand curve above that point and draw in that price.

   Topic: How a Firm Uses Market Power to Maximize Profit

4. Mark the area defined by $MC = D$, $MC = MR$, and $P_m = D$.

   Topic: The Elasticity of Demand and the Monopoly Markup

5. Draw in an ATC curve such that ATC is below the monopoly price at the Q where $MC = MR$.

   Topic: The Elasticity of Demand and the Monopoly Markup

6. Mark the area between monopoly price and ATC from the origin to monopoly output.

   Topic: The Elasticity of Demand and the Monopoly Markup

7. In the right-hand graph draw steeper demand and marginal revenue curves than those in the graph on the left.

   Topic: The Elasticity of Demand and the Monopoly Markup

8. A monopolist wants to maximize profit. The monopolist realizes that to sell more of a product it must lower its price on every unit sold. Thus monopolists realize that their marginal revenue curve (MR) is below their demand curve. Any unit sold whose MR is less than marginal cost (MC) reduces profits. Thus the monopolist stops selling more once $MR = MC$. This is at a lower Q than where $MC =$ supply or where a competitive firm will produce because the monopolist perceives its MR curve as below its demand curve.

   Topic: How a Firm Uses Market Power to Maximize Profit

Answers to Multiple-Choice Questions

1. a, Topic: Market Power
2. b, Topic: How a Firm Uses Market Power to Maximize Profit
3. c, Topic: How a Firm Uses Market Power to Maximize Profit
4. d, Topic: How a Firm Uses Market Power to Maximize Profit
5. a, Topic: The Costs of Monopoly
6. c, Topic: The Costs of Monopoly
7. b, Topic: How a Firm Uses Market Power to Maximize Profit
8. c, Topic: Monopoly and Incentives for Research and Development
9. b, Topic: Economies of Scale and the Regulation of Monopoly
10. a, Topic: How a Firm Uses Market Power to Maximize Profit
11. c, Topic: How a Firm Uses Market Power to Maximize Profit
12. b, Topic: Monopoly and Incentives for Research and Development
13. d, Topic: Market Power
14. a, Topic: The Elasticity of Demand and the Monopoly Markup
15. a, Topic: The Costs of Monopoly
16. c, Topic: How a Firm Uses Market Power to Maximize Profit
17. a, Topic: Monopoly and Incentives for Research and Development
18. d, Topic: How a Firm Uses Market Power to Maximize Profit
19. d, Topic: The Costs of Monopoly
20. a, Topic: Economies of Scale and the Regulation of Monopoly

Answers to Short-Answer Questions

21. Market power is the ability to raise price above average cost without fear that other firms will enter the market.

    Topic: Market Power

22. The monopolist recognizes that to sell more of its product it must lower price on all units sold. The marginal revenue is the price the extra unit sells for less the lower revenue from reducing the price on the units previously sold. Thus its marginal revenue is the total of the extra revenue from selling more.

    Topic: How a Firm Uses Market Power to Maximize Profit

23. The problem with a monopoly is that the gains from trade are reduced compared to competitive markets. That is, the total surplus under a monopoly is less than it would be with a competitive market.

    Topic: The Costs of Monopoly

24. On a graph with price/unit on the vertical axis and quantity/time on the horizontal axis, draw a downward-sloping demand and marginal revenue curves and a regular MC curve. Mark the quantity below where $MC = MR$ and the price on the demand curve above where $MC = MR$. Then mark the deadweight loss as the area set off by where $MC = MR$, $D = P$, and $MC = D$.

Topic: How a Firm Uses Market Power to Maximize Profit

25. Economists suggest that the market be opened up to more competition.

Topic: The Costs of Monopoly

26. Natural monopoly involves a trade-off between the deadweight loss and economies of scale. Society might accept the deadweight loss to get the economies of scale. Society can, in part, overcome the natural monopoly trade-off between deadweight loss and economies of scale by regulating the natural monopoly price to where $ATC = D$. This means that after reaching the monopoly quantity, the firm no longer must lower the price to sell more of its product.

Topic: Economies of Scale and the Regulation of Monopoly

27. A patent monopoly involves a trade-off between the deadweight loss and innovation. Society might accept the deadweight loss to get innovation in the product or new products.

Topic: Monopoly and Incentives for Research and Development

28. A monopolist can raise its price more above the average cost the more inelastic the demand for its product.

Topic: The Elasticity of Demand and the Monopoly Markup

29. The drug manufacturer's demand will be very inelastic due to both the "other people's money" effect and the "you can't take it with you" effect. That is, insured consumers will not be as sensitive to price because they are not paying and someone with a life-threatening disease will not be very sensitive to price.

Topic: Market Power

30. $-\$25$ (minus $25). $30 times 10 units is $300. $25 times 11 units is $275. $275–$300 $= -\$25$ (minus $25).

Topic: How a Firm Uses Market Power to Maximize Profit

12

Price Discrimination

Why Learn about Price Discrimination?

Price discrimination is a topic in economics that leads to some surprising conclusions. This is a practical chapter that covers many interesting real-world situations that each of us frequently encounters.

Who will be interested in price discrimination?

> Consumers who may or may not want to avoid price discrimination schemes

> Legislators, government officials, and candidates (at any level) who will be interested in how much effort is required to try to impede price discrimination via legislation and how many scarce administrative resources they should use to try to stop price discrimination

> Businesspeople (particularly marketers) who set prices need to know whether or not their product is suitable for a price discrimination scheme

> Students of economics, of course, who will find this chapter includes many examples they encounter in the real world

Summary

Price discrimination is selling the same product at different prices to different customers. Here are just a few examples of price discrimination (this list is far from exhaustive):

> Student, military, and senior citizen discounts

> Time-of-day discounts, such as charging less for movie matinees or early dinners at restaurants

> Selling products in one country for more (or less) than you would sell them in other countries

If the demand curves are different, it is more profitable for a firm to set different prices in different markets than a single price that covers all markets. As seen in Figure 12.1, to maximize profit the monopolist should set a higher price in markets with more inelastic demand, where Q_i is the quantity produced for demanders with the relatively inelastic demand and Q_e is the quantity produced for the demanders with the relatively elastic demand. As predicted, the higher price is charged of the demanders with the relatively inelastic demand.

Figure 12.1

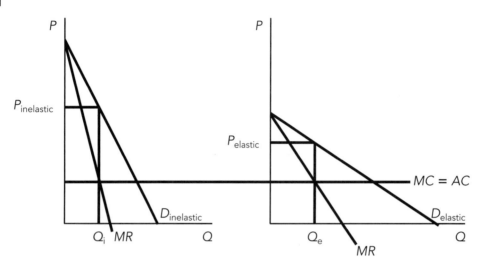

Arbitrage is taking advantage of price differences for the same good in different markets by buying low in one market and selling high in another market. Arbitrage makes it difficult for a firm to set different prices in different markets reducing the profit from price discrimination. Thus to price discriminate, a firm must be able to prevent arbitrage.

It is often easier to prevent arbitrage in services. If you go to a doctor or an attorney, you cannot generally sell the advice you received to someone else. With tangible goods, firms can sell differently marked goods to different segments of the market and try to track if the lower priced goods are being resold.

Perfect price discrimination is when each customer is charged his or her willingness to pay. This can be seen in Figure 12.2, where the perfect price discriminator charges the consumer who buys unit 1 exactly the maximum they are willing to pay.

Then the perfect price discriminator charges the consumer who buys unit 2 a slightly lower price, but still the most that consumer is willing to pay. The perfect price discriminator keeps lowering the price as it sells each additional unit until it sells unit $Q\star$ to the last consumer at the maximum price they are willing to pay which is MC.

As can be seen in Figure 12.3, the perfect price discriminator captures all the gains from trade, that is, they capture the shaded area.

Figure 12.2

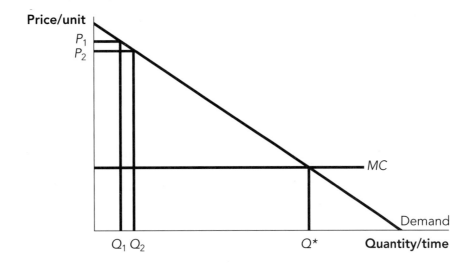

Figure 12.3

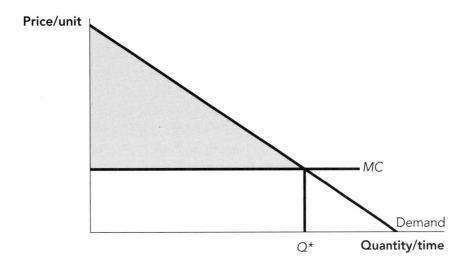

Since the perfect price discriminator captures all the gains from trade, they have an incentive to maximize those gains from trade, and unlike a single-price monopoly there are no deadweight losses. Put another way, the perfect price discriminator produces where marginal costs equal demand, $Q^\star$ in Figure 12.3. This is exactly the quantity that would be produced if this market were competitive.

Since they produce the competitive output, perfect price discriminators create no deadweight losses. A less-than-perfect price discriminator may also increase total surplus compared to a monopolist with a single price. Price discrimination is most likely to increase total surplus when it increases output and when there are large fixed costs of development. By increasing output, price discrimination spreads fixed costs over more customers.

Tying is a form of price discrimination in which one good, called the base good, is tied to a second good called the variable good. For example, printers are a base good and ink is a variable good. The variable good reveals the customer's intensity of use and thus willingness to pay. Thus a firm charges a low price for the base good and a high price for the variable good. Tying allows the firm to charge as many different prices as there are usage rates among customers.

Of course for tying to work as price discrimination, the firm must be able to prevent others from selling the variable good. That is, the base and variable goods must be actually tied in some manner. In the "printer-ink" example, sometimes the ink is tied to the printer by including a patented printer head on the ink cartridge.

Bundling is requiring that products be bought together in a bundle or package. A firm can sell some products either separately or together. For example, in Table 12.1 there are two customers and two channels.

Table 12.1 Maximum Willingness to Pay for TV Channels

	Maximum willingness to pay for ESPN	Maximum willingness to pay for AMC	Prices: ESPN=$50 AMC=$65 Revenue:	Bundle Price for ESPN and AMC = $70 Revenue:
Bill	$50	$20	$50 for ESPN	$70 for bundle
Mary	$10	$65	$65 for AMC	$70 for bundle
Company Revenues			$115	$140

The provider can either sell the channels separately to the two customers or the provider can bundle them. If the provider prices ESPN at $50 and AMC at $65, then only Bill buys ESPN and only Mary buys AMC, and company revenue is $115. However, if the provider bundles the channels and sells the bundle for $70, both will buy the bundle as Bill values the two channels at $70 and Mary values them at $85. In this example, bundling will increase company revenue to $140. (Note that if the provider priced ESPN at $10 and AMC at $20 to maximize sales, both customers would buy both channels, but company revenue would be even lower at $60.)

Bundling is a form of price discrimination because the company is basically charging Bill a low price for AMC and a high price for ESPN, while simultaneously charging Mary a low price for ESPN and a high price for AMC. As is often true in other cases of price discrimination, output is increased.

Key Terms

price discrimination selling the same product at different prices to different customers

arbitrage taking advantage of price differences for the same good in different markets by buying low in one market and selling high in another market

perfect price discrimination (PPD) when each customer is charged his or her maximum willingness to pay

tying a form of price discrimination in which one good, called the base good, is tied to a second good called the variable good

bundling requiring that products be bought together in a bundle or package

Traps, Hints, and Reminders

Remember that the price discriminator charges a higher price to the customers with a more inelastic demand.

Arbitrage, buying low in one market and selling at a higher price in another, is often legal. It was only illegal in the example in the book because Combivir was patent protected.

Tying does not mean the goods are always bought together. Generally they are bought together at the initial purchase, but the variable good is often bought alone later.

Bundling does imply the bundled goods are all purchased at the same time.

Perfect price discrimination (PPD) is perfect in the sense that each customer is charged exactly the maximum they are willing to pay for what they purchase.

Practice Exercises: Learning by Doing

1. What is price discrimination? Which customers does the price discriminator charge a higher price? Give some examples of price discrimination.

2. What is arbitrage? Why must a price discriminator prevent arbitrage?

3. What are the principles of price discrimination?

4. What is perfect price discrimination? Why does a perfect price discriminator not reduce the gains from trade? Is there a deadweight loss with perfect price discrimination?

5. On the graph below, show what the perfect price discriminator charges the first and last customer. Then show how much this firm produces and mark the gains from trade.

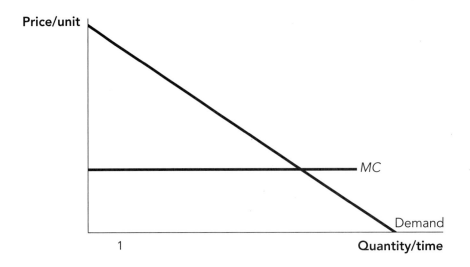

6. Are other types of price discrimination (other than perfect price discrimination) bad?

7. What is tying? What is bundling?

8. Complete the table below.

Maximum Willingness to Pay for Microsoft Word or Excel

	Maximum willingness to pay for Word	Maximum willingness to pay for Excel	Revenue (Prices: Word = $90; Excel = $80)	Revenue (Bundle Price: Word + Excel = $105)
Bill	$90	$40		
Mary	$25	$80		
Company Revenues	N/A	N/A		

*9. Who probably has more elastic demand for a Hertz rental car? Someone who reserves a car online weeks before a trip or someone who walks up to a Hertz counter immediately after their flight arrives in the airport? Who probably gets charged more?[1]

Multiple-Choice Questions

1. Price discrimination

    a. always reduces gains from trade.

    b. may increase gains from trade.

    c. always maximizes gains from trade.

    d. does not affect gains from trade.

2. Arbitrage

    a. may make price discrimination impossible.

    b. takes advantage of price differences for the same good in different markets by buying low in one market and selling high in another market.

    c. reduces the profits from price discrimination.

    d. All of the answers are correct.

3. A price discriminator charges a

    a. lower price to customers with a more inelastic demand.

    b. single price to all customers.

    c. lower price to customers with a more elastic demand.

    d. higher price to customers with a more elastic demand.

4. To succeed at price discrimination a firm must

    a. be competitive.

    b. prevent arbitrage.

    c. eliminate deadweight losses.

    d. prevent tying.

5. Price discrimination

    a. is selling the same product at different prices to different customers.

    b. is selling different quality goods to different customers at the same price.

    c. requires that customers be able to resell the product.

    d. requires that all customers have the same demand for the product.

[1]Questions marked with a ★ are also end-of-chapter questions.

6. Perfect price discriminators
   a. maximize gains from trade.
   b. reduce quantity sold in the market.
   c. charge all customers a very high price.
   d. restrict output compared to competition.

7. Perfect price discriminators
   a. reduce gains from trade.
   b. reduce quantity sold on the market.
   c. charge each customer the maximum they are willing to pay.
   d. restrict output compared to competition.

8. Perfect price discriminators
   a. maximize gains from trade.
   b. eliminate deadweight losses.
   c. increase output to the competitive quantity.
   d. All of the answers are correct.

Use the following graph to answer Questions 9 and 10.

Figure 12.4

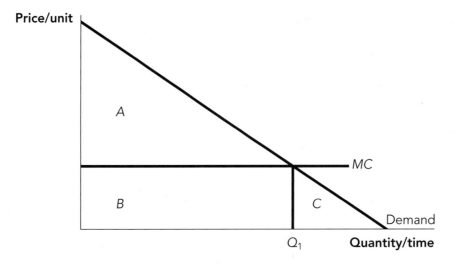

9. If the firm, in the preceding graph, is a perfect price discriminator, then the gains from trade will be area
   a. *A*.
   b. *B*.
   c. *C*.
   d. zero.

10. If the firm in the preceding graph, is a perfect price discriminator, then the deadweight loss associated with perfect price discrimination will be

    a. area *A*.

    b. area *B*.

    c. area *C*.

    d. zero.

11. Price discrimination is bad in economic terms, if

    a. output is increased.

    b. output stays the same or falls.

    c. there is arbitrage.

    d. the firm is able to prevent arbitrage.

12. With tying, the firm will sell _____ at a low price.

    a. the bundle of products

    b. the variable product

    c. the base product

    d. each individual product

13. Tying is a form of price discrimination because

    a. the base product price is set high.

    b. the variable product lets each customer reveal their own willingness to pay for the tied products.

    c. the variable product price is set low.

    d. the base product shows willingness to pay on the part of the customer.

14. When tying products, a firm must somehow be sure competitors cannot produce

    a. its base product.

    b. its bundle of products.

    c. its variable product.

    d. arbitrage.

Use the following table to answer Questions 15 through 18.

	Maximum willingness to pay for MTV	Maximum willingness to pay for FNC
Bill	$70	$20
Mary	$15	$80

15. In the preceding table, if the provider prices MTV at $70 and FNC at $80, then the firm will have a revenue of
   a. $0.
   b. $70.
   c. $150.
   d. $185.

16. In the preceding table, if the provider prices MTV at $70 and FNC at $80, then
   a. Mary will buy MTV but not FNC, and Bill will buy FNC but not MTV.
   b. both Mary and Bill will buy MTV and FNC.
   c. Mary will buy FNC but not MTV, and Bill will buy MTV but not FNC.
   d. neither Mary nor Bill will buy either channel.

17. In the preceding table, if the provider bundles MTV and FNC at a price of $90, then the firm will have revenue of
   a. $0.
   b. $90.
   c. $150.
   d. $180.

18. In the preceding table, if the provider bundles MTV and FNC at a price of $90, then
   a. Mary will buy the bundle but not Bill.
   b. Bill will buy the bundle but not Mary.
   c. Mary and Bill will both buy the bundle.
   d. neither Mary nor Bill will buy the bundle.

19. Bundling
   a. makes customers buy a low-quality product to get a high-quality one.
   b. reduces output and gains from trade.
   c. creates a deadweight loss.
   d. requires that products be bought together in a package or bundle.

20. Firms want to price discriminate because it

a. increases profits.

b. reduces deadweight losses.

c. maximizes gains from trade.

d. increases output.

Short-Answer Questions

21. What is price discrimination? When is it likely to increase total surplus?

22. What is arbitrage? What are its implications for price discrimination?

23. What are the principles of price discrimination?

24. What is perfect price discrimination? How is price determined under it? Draw a graph of perfect price discrimination and shade in the gains from trade.

25. Is perfect price discrimination bad in an economic sense?

26. What is tying? How does tying allow a firm to price discriminate?

27. Why do firms price discriminate?

28. Which customers will price discriminators charge the highest prices?

29. Complete the table below.

	Maximum willingness to pay for FNC	Maximum willingness to pay for MTV	Revenue (Prices: FNC = $80; MTV = $65)	Revenue (Bundle Price: FNC + MTV = $90)
Bill	$80	$20		
Mary	$25	$65		
Company Revenues	N/A	N/A		

30. What is bundling? How does bundling help a firm price discriminate?

Answer Key

Answers to Practice Exercises: Learning by Doing

1. Price discrimination is selling the same product at different prices to different customers. The price discriminator charges the customers with the more inelastic demand a higher price. Examples of possible price discrimination include senior and student discounts, lower air fares for those who book in advance (or stay a weekend), the difference between the price of hard cover and paperback books, and time-of-day discounts.

   Topic: Price Discrimination

2. Arbitrage is taking advantage of price differences for the same good in different markets by buying low in one market and selling high in another market. A price discriminator must prevent or limit arbitrage, otherwise the arbitrager will erode the profits from price discrimination and the price discriminator would just be selling its good for a low price.

   Topic: Price Discrimination

3. If the demand curves are different, it is more profitable to set different prices in different markets than to set a single price that covers all markets. To maximize profit the firm should set a higher price in the markets with more inelastic demands. Arbitrage makes it difficult to set different prices in different markets, thereby reducing the profit from price discrimination.

   Topic: Price Discrimination

4. Perfect price discrimination is when the firm is able to charge each customer their willingness to pay. A perfect price discriminator captures all gains from trade and thus increases them compared to a single-price monopoly. Since gains from trade are maximized there is no deadweight loss associated with perfect price discrimination.

   Topic: Price Discrimination Is Common

5. The firm charges the first customer the price on the demand curve above unit 1 on the graph and the last customer MC, as the last unit produced is where $MC = D$. The firm produces the quantity where $MC = D$. The gains from trade are the area under the demand curve and above MC. That area should be marked in some way.

   Topic: Price Discrimination Is Common

6. All types of price discrimination can increase gains from trade. While perfect price discrimination always maximizes gain, other types of price discrimination are not necessarily bad (from an economic point of view). Total surplus usually increases, as long as total output increases with the price discrimination. Also, when total output increases, fixed costs are spread out over more customers.

   Topic: Is Price Discrimination Bad?

7. Tying is a form of price discrimination in which one good, called the base good, is tied to a second good, called the variable good. Bundling is another type of price discrimination where the seller requires that products be bought together in a bundle or package.

Topic: Tying and Bundling

8. The table is filled in as follows:

Maximum Willingness to Pay for Microsoft Word or Excel

	Maximum willingness to pay for Word	Maximum willingness to pay for Excel	Revenue (Prices: Word = $90; Excel = $80)	Revenue (Bundle Price: Word + Excel = $105)
Bill	$90	$40	$90 for Word	$105
Mary	$25	$80	$80 for Excel	$105
Company Revenues			$170	$210

9. The person who reserves a car a few weeks in advance online probably has a more elastic demand. This person can search for the best price. Thus the person who walks up to the counter in the airport will likely pay the higher price.

Topic: Price Discrimination

Answers to Multiple-Choice Questions

1. b, Topic: Price Discrimination

2. d, Topic: Price Discrimination

3. c, Topic: Price Discrimination

4. b, Topic: Price Discrimination

5. a, Topic: Price Discrimination

6. a, Topic: Price Discrimination Is Common

7. c, Topic: Price Discrimination Is Common

8. d, Topic: Price Discrimination Is Common

9. a, Topic: Price Discrimination Is Common

10. d, Topic: Price Discrimination Is Common

11. b, Topic: Is Price Discrimination Bad?

12. c, Topic: Tying and Bundling

13. b, Topic: Tying and Bundling

14. c, Topic: Tying and Bundling

15. c, Topic: Tying and Bundling

16. c, Topic: Tying and Bundling

17. d, Topic: Tying and Bundling

18. c, Topic: Tying and Bundling

19. d, Topic: Tying and Bundling

20. a, Topic: Price Discrimination

Answers to Short-Answer Questions

21. Price discrimination is selling the same product at different prices to different customers. Price discrimination is most likely to increase total surplus when it increases output and when there are large fixed costs.

    Topic: Price Discrimination

22. Arbitrage is taking advantage of price differences for the same good in different markets by buying low in one market and selling high in another market. A price discriminator must prevent or limit arbitrage, otherwise the arbitrager will erode the profits from price discrimination and the price discriminator would just be selling its good for a low price.

    Topic: Price Discrimination

23. The principles of price discrimination are if the demand curves are different, it is more profitable to set different prices in different markets than to set a single price that covers all markets. To maximize profit, the firm should set a higher price in the markets with more inelastic demands. Arbitrage makes it difficult to set different prices in different markets, thereby reducing the profit from price discrimination.

    Topic: Price Discrimination

24. Perfect price discrimination is when the producer is able to determine maximum willingness to pay on the part of each potential customer. The firm charges each customer the maximum they are willing to pay for the product. In the graph mark the area above *MC* and below demand.

    Topic: Price Discrimination Is Common

25. Perfect price discriminators capture all the gains from trade and thus have an incentive to maximize gains from trade and eliminate any deadweight losses. So from an economic point of view, perfect price discrimination is not bad.

    Topic: Is Price Discrimination Bad?

26. Tying is a form of price discrimination in which one good, called the base good, is tied to a second good called the variable good. The price discrimination is due to the variable good purchase rate revealing elasticity of demand. Variable usage of the variable good leads to a different price for every customer with a different usage rate.

    Topic: Tying and Bundling

27. Though price discrimination might reduce deadweight losses and increase gains from trade, those are not goals of firms. Firms price discriminate to increase profits.

   Topic: Price Discrimination

28. Price discriminators will charge those customers with the most inelastic demands the highest prices.

   Topic: Price Discrimination

29. The table is filled in as follows:

	Maximum willingness to pay for FNC	Maximum willingness to pay for MTV	Revenue (Prices: FNC = $80; MTV = $65)	Revenue (Bundle Price: FNC + MTV = $90)
Bill	$80	$20	$80 for FNC	$90 for bundle
Mary	$25	$65	$65 for MTV	$90 for bundle
Company Revenues	N/A	N/A	$145	$180

   Topic: Tying and Bundling

30. Bundling requires that products are bought together in a bundle or package. The bundle price allows a firm to price discriminate, that is, it allows the firm to charge consumers a high price on those goods for which they have an inelastic demand and a low price for those goods for which they have an elastic demand.

   Topic: Tying and Bundling

13

Cartels, Games, and Network Goods

Why Learn about Cartels, Games, and Network Goods?

Interested Student: I understand cartels like OPEC, but do they play games?

Old Professor: Yes, they engage in strategic behavior or games like opponents in a football or basketball game engage in strategic behavior towards each other, except firms in an industry may sometimes want to cooperate sometime rather than compete.

Interested Student: That sounds interesting, but who is this important to?

Old Professor: Certainly business owners would be interested in strategic behavior and why forming an illegal cartel may or may not be worth the risks. Government officials would be interested in controlling cartels. Voters, of course, would want to be able to determine if elected officials were taking reasonable and effective actions in this area.

Interested Student: I can certainly see the interest on the part of all those groups.

Summary

A **cartel** is a group of suppliers who try to act as if they were a monopoly. If successful, cartel members can increase industry profits by agreeing to decrease industry output, which leads to a higher price for the product.

Cartels generally are not long lasting because of three reasons. The first reason is that members of a cartel each have an incentive to cheat on the cartel agreement. A second cause of cartel instability is new entrants and demand responses. The third reason for cartels breaking down is government prosecution where cartels are illegal.

The incentive that cartel members have to cheat on the cartel agreement to reduce output can be seen in Table 13.1 below, where each dollar figure is the oil revenues of each country (Russia is R and Saudi Arabia is SA) in millions of dollars.

Table 13.1

		Russia's Strategies	
		Cooperate	**Cheat**
Saudi Arabia's	**Cooperate**	$500 for each	$300 R, $600 SA
Strategies	**Cheat**	$600 SA, $300 R	$400 for each

Notice that the best the industry can do, collectively, is to cooperate and make industry revenue of $1 billion compared to $900 million, if either country cheats on the cartel agreement while the other keeps it, and $800 million, if both countries cheat on the cartel agreement. Even though cheating reduces industry revenues, each country has an incentive to cheat on the agreement.

A **dominant strategy** is a strategy that has a higher payoff than any other, no matter what the other party does. Notice in Table 13.1 that each country's dominant strategy is to cheat on the agreement. If the two countries cooperate, both earn $500 million in revenue. If Russia cheats on the agreement, Russia makes $600 million in revenue, which is more than it would make, if it cooperated and Saudi Arabia also cooperated. On the other hand, if Saudi Arabia cheats, Russia makes the most revenue ($400 million) by cheating too. By cheating, Russia makes $400 million compared to the $300 million it would have made by cooperating while Saudi Arabia cheated. Thus Russia's dominant strategy is to cheat no matter what Saudi Arabia does, because Russia makes more revenue no matter what Saudi Arabia does. The analysis is the same for Saudi Arabia whose dominant strategy is also to cheat no matter what Russia does.

Notice that this incentive to cheat causes the cartel members to jointly make the lowest revenue, $800 million, when both cheat, compared to $900 million they would make, if only one country cheats on the cartel. The cartel members could make $1 billion, if they both cooperated and lived up to the cartel agreement. A situation like this is known as the **prisoner's dilemma**. The prisoner's dilemma is a situation similar to that of Russia and Saudi Arabia where the pursuit of individual interest leads to a group outcome that is in the interest of no one. In this example, both parties cheat, thereby reducing group and individual country income that is in the interest of neither country.

Cartels might be successful to the extent that the reasons they are not long lasting are not present. The incentive to cheat is always there. If the cartel is in the production of a natural resource that is found in only a limited number of places, then new entrants and demand responses may be limited. Of course, even with a resource like oil, the OPEC, which stands for the Organization of the Petroleum Exporting Countries, is a cartel that led to more production as people searched for oil in new places and demand responses as people found substitutes. In a similar way with diamonds, the cartel has encouraged the production of manmade diamonds. Finally, to the extent that government regulation and prosecution is absent, cartels may be more stable.

Of course, with many of the resource cartels, not only is there an absence of government prosecution, governments are also responsible for creating and sponsoring the cartels. A single government cartel, such as the United States milk regulations, are more stable and put the interest of a particular group, suppliers, ahead of the interest of society, including consumers. With a single country government cartel, cheating on the cartel may be prosecuted reducing the incentive of members to cheat. This type of cartel is a serious problem in poor countries like Mexico, Russia, Indonesia, and many African countries. For government-sponsored natural resource cartels across several countries, for example OPEC, the incentive to cheat is still there. Government cartel members may dislike each other enough to go to war with each other. Such cartels may have more limited success than government sponsored cartels in one country.

A **network good** is a good whose value to one consumer increases the more that other consumers use the good. Examples include Internet message boards and fax machines. Most people enjoy posting on message boards when other people also post on the same message board and there is interaction among members.

Network goods are usually sold by monopolies or oligopolies. An **oligopoly** is a market dominated by a small number of firms. Standard wars are common when a market for network goods is being established. When networks are important, the "best" product may not always win. Competition in the market for network goods is "for the market" instead of "in the market."

The "best" product may not always win with a network good because the standard war may result in a Nash equilibrium, with a version of the good that is not the best (or later becomes not the best) as innovation takes place. A **Nash equilibrium** is a situation where no player has an incentive to change their strategy unilaterally. For example, Microsoft Windows may not be the "best" operating system, but most users have no incentive to change from it and make their computer incompatible with most other users in the world. However as the market for spreadsheet programs shows, competition for the market can cause changes in the standard network good, as domination in the spreadsheet market has moved from VisiCalc to Lotus 1-2-3 to Quattro Pro to Excel over the course of time.

Key Terms

cartel a group of suppliers that tries to act as if they were a monopoly

strategic decision making decision making in situations that are interactive

dominant strategy a strategy that has a higher payoff than any other strategy no matter what the other player does

prisoner's dilemma situations where the pursuit of individual interest leads to a group outcome that is in the interest of no one

network good a good whose value to one consumer increases the more that other consumers use the good

antitrust laws laws that give the government the power to regulate or prohibit business practices that may be anti-competitive

oligopoly a market dominated by a small number of firms

Nash equilibrium a situation in which no player has an incentive to change their strategy unilaterally

Traps, Hints, and Reminders

Cartel members have an incentive to cheat on their agreement.

The incentive to cheat on a cartel agreement can lead to a prisoner's dilemma where members acting in their own interest leads to an outcome in the interest of no single firm.

With a network good the competition is for the market more than among goods in the market.

A network good is a case where the "best" good does not necessarily win the competition for the market, but competition for the market still means that the dominant network good can change.

Government cartels put the interest of a group (that is, suppliers) above the interest of society in general and buyers in particular.

Practice Exercises: Learning by Doing

1. What is a cartel? What does a cartel do?

2. Why do cartels tend to lose their power and eventually collapse?

3. What is a dominant strategy?

4. The table below describes the possible oil revenues of two countries in millions. What is the best the two countries can do? What is the dominant strategy of each country?

Venezuela's Strategies

		Cooperate	Cheat
Saudi Arabia's	**Cooperate**	$700 for each	$300 SA, $900 V
Strategies	**Cheat**	$900 SA, $300 V	$400 for each

5. What is the result of a prisoner's dilemma?

6. What is a network good? What are the features of a market for a network good?

7. What is an oligopoly?

8. What is a Nash equilibrium?

*9. Your professor probably grades on a curve, implicitly if not explicitly. This means that you and your classmates could each agree to study half as much, and you would all earn the same grade you would have earned without the agreement. What do you think would happen if you tried to enact this agreement? Why? Which model in this chapter is most similar to this conspiracy?[1]

Multiple-Choice Questions

1. A cartel is a group of suppliers that try to act
   a. in the public interest.
   b. as if they were a network.
   c. as if they were a monopoly.
   d. All of the answers are correct.

2. Cartels tend to collapse due to
   a. government sponsorship.
   b. cheating by members.
   c. a lack of entry of new members.
   d. All of the answers are correct.

3. Cartels have a better chance of stability when the
   a. government sponsors the cartel rather than prosecutes the members.
   b. members cheat on the agreement.
   c. profit encourages entry.
   d. All of the answers are correct.

4. The prisoner's dilemma leads to an outcome that is
   a. best for one member of the group.
   b. in the interest of no one in the group.
   c. optimal for all members of the group.
   d. in the interest of all but the leading member of the group.

---

[1]Questions marked with a ★ are also end-of-chapter questions.

5. A dominant strategy is one that leads to

    a. a dominant payoff for the group collectively.

    b. the party with the dominant strategy dominating other cartel members.

    c. a government-sponsored cartel.

    d. a higher payoff for you regardless of what the other party does.

Use the following table to answer Questions 6 through 9.

		Russia's Strategies	
		Cooperate	**Cheat**
Mexico's	**Cooperate**	$300 for each	$100 M, $400 R
Strategies	**Cheat**	$400 M, $100 R	$200 for each

6. In the preceding table, the best the two countries can do jointly is to

    a. both cooperate.

    b. Russia cheats while Mexico cooperates.

    c. Russia cooperates while Mexico cheats.

    d. both cheat.

7. In the preceding table, Russia's dominant strategy is to

    a. do what Mexico does.

    b. do the opposite of what Mexico does.

    c. cooperate.

    d. cheat.

8. In the preceding table, if both countries follow their dominant strategy, then their combined revenues will be

    a. $200.

    b. $400.

    c. $600.

    d. None of the answers is correct.

9. In the preceding table, a way for the two countries to get to the best joint revenue result is to

    a. compete.

    b. form a cartel and cooperate.

    c. form a cartel and cheat.

    d. encourage entry.

10. With a government-sponsored cartel, the government is
    a. considering the interests of the suppliers and consumers equally.
    b. putting the interest of consumers ahead of the group of suppliers.
    c. putting the public interest first.
    d. putting the interest of the group of suppliers ahead of consumers.

11. A network good is one
    a. that requires other goods to work.
    b. whose value to the consumer increases as more consumers use it.
    c. whose value to the consumer comes from being an exclusive user.
    d. that is a complete network in itself.

12. Network goods
    a. are usually sold by competitive firms.
    b. commonly have standard wars in establishing networks.
    c. are always the best possible product.
    d. All of the answers are correct.

13. Network goods
    a. are usually sold by monopolies or oligopolies.
    b. have competition in the market not for the market.
    c. are when the best good wins.
    d. All of the answers are correct.

14. Network goods
    a. are usually sold by monopolies or oligopolies.
    b. have competition for the market not in the market.
    c. may not lead to the best version of the product winning the market.
    d. All of the answers are correct.

15. An oligopoly is a market
    a. with many competitors.
    b. with a single firm.
    c. with a few firms.
    d. controlled by the government.

16. A Nash equilibrium is a situation where
    a. the optimum result is achieved.
    b. the competitive optimum is achieved.
    c. no player has an incentive to change their strategy unilaterally.
    d. All of the answers are correct.

17. A network good may lead to other than the best product being adopted if consumers

    a. are irrational.

    b. reach a Nash equilibrium at a product other than the best product.

    c. cooperate.

    d. want to be among a small group of exclusive users of the good.

18. With a network good,

    a. the standard never changes.

    b. the standard can change as improved versions of the good are developed.

    c. the standard changes frequently.

    d. no standard is adopted.

19. Cartels

    a. are permanent.

    b. tend to be very stable.

    c. tend to lose their power and collapse.

    d. are never able to affect industry profits.

20. Cartels are often formed in natural resources like diamonds or oil because

    a. the incentive to cheat is less in these products.

    b. others who do not have the natural resource cannot enter the market.

    c. governments cannot prosecute cartel members in such industries.

    d. All of the answers are correct.

Short-Answer Questions

21. What is a cartel? What does a cartel do?

22. Why do cartels tend to lose their power and eventually collapse?

23. What is a dominant strategy and what can one lead to?

24. The table below describes the possible oil revenues of two countries in millions. What is the best the two countries can do? What is the dominant strategy of each country? If each country follows its dominant strategy, what is country and cartel revenue?

		Venezuela's Strategies	
		Cooperate	Cheat
Saudi Arabia's	**Cooperate**	$600 for each	$300 SA, $700 V
Strategies	**Cheat**	$700 SA, $300 V	$350 for each

25. What is the result of a prisoner's dilemma?

26. What is a network good? What are the features for the market for network goods?

27. What is an oligopoly?

28. What is a Nash equilibrium?

29. Under what conditions might a cartel be more successful or longer lasting?

30. Why might a government-sponsored cartel across several countries be less successful than a cartel in a single country?

Answer Key

Answers to Practice Exercises: Learning by Doing

1. A cartel is a group of suppliers that try to act as if they were a monopoly. A cartel reduces industry output and that leads to a higher industry profit.

Topic: Cartels

2. Cartels tend to lose their power and collapse due to cheating by cartel members, new entrants and demand responses, and government prosecution of cartel members.

Topic: Cartels

3. A dominant strategy is a strategy that has a higher payoff than any other strategy, no matter what the other player does.

Topic: No One Wins the Cheating Game

4. The best the two countries can do is to cooperate and generate a combined $1.4 billion in oil revenue. However, the dominant strategy of each country is to cheat on the cartel agreement because cheating maximizes each individual country's revenue no matter what the other country does.

Topic: No One Wins the Cheating Game

5. The prisoner's dilemma describes situations where the pursuit of individual interest leads to a group outcome that is in the interest of no one.

Topic: No One Wins the Cheating Game

6. A network good is a good whose value to one consumer increases the more that other consumers use the good. These goods are usually sold by monopolies or oligopolies, standard wars are common in establishing network goods, the best products may not always win, and competition is "for the market" instead of "in the market" for a network good.

Topic: Network Goods

7. An oligopoly is a market dominated by a small number of firms.

Topic: Network Goods Are Usually Sold by Monopolies or Oligopolies

8. A Nash equilibrium is a situation in which no player has an incentive to change their strategy unilaterally.

Topic: The "Best" Product May Not Always Win

9. Your class non-study agreement would probably break down as some individuals would cheat on the agreement and study to move up in the grade distribution. This would also cause others to study more, until the entire agreement fell apart. This happens because individual interest leads to a group outcome that is in the interest of no one. That is, this is a case of an unstable cartel or the prisoner's dilemma.

Topic: No One Wins the Cheating Game

Answers to Multiple-Choice Questions

1. c, Topic: Cartels

2. b, Topic: Cartels

3. a, Topic: Cartels

4. b, Topic: No One Wins the Cheating Game

5. d, Topic: No One Wins the Cheating Game

6. a, Topic: No One Wins the Cheating Game

7. d, Topic: No One Wins the Cheating Game

8. b, Topic: No One Wins the Cheating Game

9. b, Topic: No One Wins the Cheating Game

10. d, Topic: Government–Supported Cartels

11. b, Topic: Network Goods

12. b, Topic: Network Goods

13. a, Topic: Network Goods

14. d, Topic: Network Goods

15. c, Topic: The "Best" Product May Not Always Win

16. c, Topic: The "Best" Product May Not Always Win

17. b, Topic: The "Best" Product May Not Always Win

18. b, Topic: Competition "For the Market" instead of "In the Market"

19. c, Topic: Cartels

20. b, Topic: Sustainable Cartels in a Market Setting

Answers to Short-Answer Questions

21. A cartel is a group of suppliers that try to act as if they were a monopoly. A cartel reduces industry output and that leads to a higher industry profit.

    Topic: Cartels

22. Cartels tend to lose their power and collapse due to cheating by cartel members, new entrants and demand responses, and government prosecution of cartel members.

    Topic: Cartels

23. A dominant strategy is a strategy that has a higher payoff than any other strategy no matter what the other player does.

    Topic: No One Wins the Cheating Game

24. The best the two countries can do is to cooperate and generate a combined $1.2 billion in oil revenue. The dominant strategy of each country is to cheat on the cartel agreement because cheating maximizes each individual country's revenue, no matter what the other country does. If both countries follow their dominant strategy, each country would make $350 million or the industry would make a combined $700 million. That is $250 million less per country or $500 million less combined, than if they cooperated.

   Topic: No One Wins the Cheating Game

25. The prisoner's dilemma describes situations where the pursuit of individual interest leads to a group outcome that is in the interest of no one. A prisoner's dilemma can lead to group members acting against the interest of the group.

   Topic: No One Wins the Cheating Game

26. A network good is a good whose value to one consumer increases the more that other consumers use the good. These goods are usually sold by monopolies or oligopolies, standard wars are common in establishing network goods, the best products may not always win, and competition is "for the market" instead of "in the market" for a network good.

   Topic: Network Goods

27. An oligopoly is a market dominated by a small number of firms.

   Topic: Network Goods Are Usually Sold by Monopolies or Oligopolies

28. A Nash equilibrium is a situation in which no player has an incentive to change their strategy unilaterally.

   Topic: The "Best" Product May Not Always Win

29. A cartel has a better chance of lasting the more the reasons they break down are absent. That is, a cartel is more likely to be stable when there is less of an incentive for cheating, there are less entry and demand responses, and there is less government prosecution of members. With natural resource cartels, entry and demand responses are more limited. Government-sponsored cartels have no worry of prosecution. The incentive to cheat is always there, but with a government-sponsored single country cartel the government can prosecute members who cheat on the cartel agreement, thereby increasing the cost of cheating and reducing the incentive to cheat. Thus a government-sponsored resource cartel in a single country has the best chance to last.

   Topic: Summing Up: Successful Cartels

30. The incentive to cheat exists for countries just as much as it exists for firms. There is no one to enforce the cartel agreement on other governments similar to a government that can enforce the cartel agreement within its borders. Additionally, governments in a cartel may or may not like each other. Two member governments in OPEC had a bloody war with each other.

   Topic: Cheating on the OPEC Cartel

14

Labor Markets

Why Learn about Labor Markets?

Almost all of us have been employees or will be an employee some day. Some of us may have or hope to have employees. The wage rate that comes from the labor market is the single price that is the most important to most people.

Almost everyone is interested in the labor market. But who will be the most interested in labor markets?

> Employees and potential employees who want to earn as much as they can during their work life

> Employers and potential employers who will need to understand when they must pay their workers more and when they can get by with paying them less (as most employers would like to)

> Legislators, government officials, candidates, and voters who are interested in understanding how labor markets work and the effects government policies have on labor markets

> Students of economics, of course, both as employees or potential employees and employers or potential employers

Summary

Labor is the key good in the economy for most of us. The amount of time that we work and the price or wage we get for working determines how many goods we get to consume.

A worker is worth what they contribute to the firm. What a worker contributes can be measured by the **marginal product of labor (MPL)**. The MPL is the increase in a firm's revenues created by hiring an additional worker. If a lawn service mows 12 lawns a day, at $20 per lawn, hires another worker and then is able to mow 14 lawns per day, then the MPL of the last worker hired is $40.

Consider the data in Table 14.1 below.

Lawn Service Production Per Day

Number of Workers	Lawns Mowed @ $20 per lawn	Marginal Product of Labor (MPL) for the last worker hired
One	4	$80
Two	9	$100
Three	12	$60
Four	14	$40

When the firm hires one worker, the worker mows 4 lawns and at $20 per lawn has a MPL of $80. When the firm hires the second worker, the two workers are able to mow 9 lawns total or 5 additional lawns, so the MPL of the second worker is 5 lawns times $20 per lawn or $100. The third worker increases the number of lawns mowed by 3 and thus has an MPL of $60. The fourth worker is the example from the previous paragraph and has an MPL of 2 lawns times $20 and has an MPL of $40.

Firms want to hire those workers that cost them less than they contribute to the firm. If the firm in Table 14.1 must pay its workers $7 per hour during an 8 hour day, then each worker costs them $56 per day. Under these conditions the firm will want to hire workers 1-3, who each contribute more than $56 to the firm and not a fourth worker who would contribute only $40 to the firm. If, on the other hand, the firm must pay its workers $8 per hour for an 8-hour day, then each worker costs the firm $64 per day and the firm will want to hire workers 1 and 2 who contribute more to the firm than $64, and will not want to hire the third and fourth workers who each contribute less than $64 to the firm.

It is important to understand that the first hires are not necessarily "better" workers. Firms have the first worker hired do the most productive work. In our example, they cut the easiest lawns with the fewest steep slopes and fewest trees and other obstacles to work around. As later workers are hired, the firm puts them on less productive tasks. In our example, they cut yards that are more time intensive. So it may not matter in what order the workers are hired, the later hired workers will still have a lower MPL.

The MPL is the demand curve for labor and is downward sloping as usual. The market supply curve for labor is upward sloping as usual. This means higher wages lead to more work. Some individuals might work less if they are paid a higher wage, but the higher wage will attract other workers into the labor market.

The labor market is shown by Figure 14.1 below.

Figure 14.1

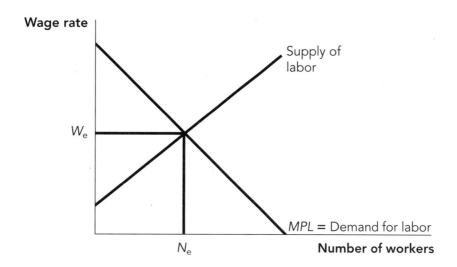

In Figure 14.1 the equilibrium wage is W_e, and the equilibrium number of workers hired is N_e, where the supply of labor equals the MPL or the demand for labor.

Workers in low-skilled jobs in a developed country like the United States tend to make more than workers doing the same job in a less-developed country like India. This is because the workers in the less-developed country work in a less-productive economy and thus have lower MPL than workers doing the same job in a more productive economy.

Human capital is the tools of the mind, the stuff in people's heads that makes them productive. It is not something we are born with, it is accumulation through investing time and other resources in education, training, and experience. Education is related to higher lifetime earnings. The return to education has grown over the last 60 years.

Some jobs pay more because they involve more risk or require workers to perform unpleasant tasks (or work in unpleasant circumstances). These differences in pay are called compensating differential. A **compensating differential** is a difference in wages that offsets differences in working conditions. Similar jobs must have similar compensation packages. If a fun job paid more than a job that was only a little fun, then everyone would want the fun job driving down its wage and few people would want the job with little fun driving up its wage. This is how the market creates compensating differentials.

Workers in wealthier countries can use that wealth to buy lower levels of risk. This leads to a 100 times higher death rate of coal miners in China compared to the United States.

Unions raise wages by reducing the supply of workers for a particular job. This is shown in Figure 14.2.

In Figure 14.2 the union reduces the supply of workers shifting it up and to the left. This causes the equilibrium wage to rise from W_1 to W_2 for those workers employed. But notice the amount of employment declines from N_1 to N_2. Unions can also possibly

Figure 14.2

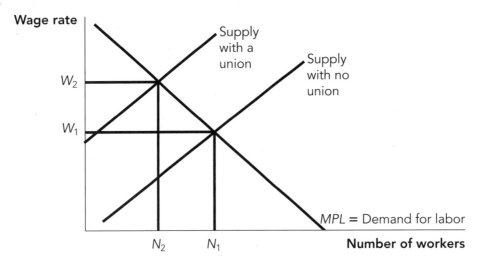

reduce wages over time if they slow growth in productivity. Finally not all unions call themselves unions. Professional associations, such as those for accountants or lawyers, restrict access to jobs and thus increase wages like any other union.

There is discrimination in the labor market. Some discrimination is good, for example, we would like our hospital to discriminate regarding who they let operate on us. Some of it is bad, if it is associated with characteristics that do not affect job performance.

There are two overall types of discrimination that can be bad. One is statistical discrimination. **Statistical discrimination** is using information about group averages to make conclusions about individuals. An example of this would be asking a very tall individual about basketball based on only knowing their height. Profit seeking business owners, who can make money finding the best workers, tend to reduce and can eliminate statistical discrimination in labor markets.

Preference-based discrimination is the second type of discrimination discussed in the textbook. There are three subdivisions of preference-based discrimination. They are employer discrimination, customer discrimination, and employee discrimination.

Employer discrimination like statistical discrimination is reduced and can be eliminated by market forces. The non-discriminating will be able to hire the discriminated-against workers more cheaply and compete the discriminating firm out of business or at least make the discriminating employer pay a price for the discrimination. Profit-seeking employers, by hiring more of the discriminated-against workers, tend to raise their wages and reduce the wages of the favored workers by reducing the demand for them.

Customer discrimination is tougher to solve. If women will not go to a gynecologist with a male nurse, then those gynecologists who hire male nurses may go out of business. If you expect Oriental-looking people in your Chinese restaurants, then Chinese restaurants who hire white or black servers and cooks may go out of business.

Discrimination by employees is when employees only want to work with a certain type of people. Like customer discrimination it is hard to overcome. If when you hire a mixed crew of workers one group all quit or the two groups have constant disagreements that reduce productivity, then businesses that do not meet their employees' preferences will be less productive and may go out of business.

Of course, as groups become less distinct, customer and employee discrimination may become less of a problem. Finally, it is important to note that government often enforces the discriminatory preferences on a society.

Key Terms

marginal product of labor (MPL) the increase in a firm's revenues created by hiring an additional laborer

human capital tools of the mind, the stuff in people's heads that makes them productive

compensating differential a difference in wages that offsets differences in working conditions

statistical discrimination using information about group averages to make conclusions about individual

Traps, Hints, and Reminders

The marginal product of labor (MPL) is the increase in revenue a firm gets from hiring another worker.

Unions raise member wages by restricting the supply of workers.

Preference-based labor market discrimination can be due to the preferences of business owners, customers, or employees.

Human capital is the tools of the mind. It is also produced not inborn.

Jobs may have different wages because they have different characteristics, but jobs must have similar compensation packages.

Practice Exercises: Learning by Doing

1. What is the marginal product of labor?

2. Why does the marginal product of labor decline as more workers are hired?

3. Fill in the third column of the table below.

Productivity of Painting

Number of Workers	Rooms painted @ $200 per room	Marginal Product of Labor (MPL) for the last worker hired
One	1	
Two	5	
Three	8	
Four	10	

4. What is human capital?

5. Why might one job pay more than another job?

6. How do unions get their members higher wages?

7. What is statistical discrimination in the labor market?

8. Explain the types of preference-based discrimination that are discussed in the textbook.

*9. Suppose that we tax CEO salaries very highly, as some are proposing in the United States. What is your prediction about CEO perks such as jets and in-house chefs?[1]

Multiple Choice Questions

1. The marginal product of labor is the change in the firm's revenue created by

   a. producing one more unit of output.

   b. selling one more unit of output.

   c. hiring an additional laborer.

   d. All of the answers are correct.

2. If a firm that charges $1,000 to paint a house can paint 3 houses a week with 4 workers and 5 houses a week with 5 workers, then the marginal product of the fifth worker is

   a. $400.

   b. $500.

   c. $1,000.

   d. $2,000.

3. The marginal product of workers declines as more workers are hired because

   a. the first worker is put to work on the most productive tasks.

   b. the first worker is a better worker than later hires.

   c. more workers are less efficient than fewer workers.

   d. more workers conspire to shirk their jobs.

4. Human capital is

   a. tools owned by people rather than corporations.

   b. tools of the mind.

   c. tools that human workers use on a job.

   d. tools owned by the government rather than corporations.

5. Human capital is

   a. innate abilities.

   b. acquired by investing resources in education, training and experience.

   c. acquired by exercise and physical training.

   d. the talents you are born with.

[1] Questions marked with a ★ are also end-of-chapter questions.

6. Workers in a rich country earn more than workers in a poor country because they
    a. benefit from scarcity of capital.
    b. benefit from the productivity of many other sectors in their economy.
    c. benefit from exploiting poor countries.
    d. benefit from protectionism.

7. While the individual labor supply might be backward bending, the market labor supply curve is positively sloped because higher wages
    a. make people wealthier.
    b. encourage people to take more leisure time.
    c. encourage business to hire more workers.
    d. encourage more people to enter the labor market.

8. More education is associated with
    a. higher lifetime wages.
    b. less productivity.
    c. reduced lifetime wages due to delayed working.
    d. reduced lifetime production.

9. Compensating differentials are
    a. a form of labor market discrimination.
    b. differences in working conditions.
    c. differences in wages that offset differences in working conditions.
    d. a form of human capital.

10. Jobs tend to pay more
    a. the safer the environment the work is performed in.
    b. the more unpleasant the tasks involved.
    c. the more fun they are.
    d. All of the answers are correct.

11. Statistical discrimination is
    a. using information about an individual to draw conclusions about a group.
    b. using information about an individual to draw conclusions about that individual.
    c. using information about group averages to draw conclusions about individuals.
    d. using information about group averages to draw conclusions about the group.

12. Preference-based labor market discrimination may be due to

  a. employees.

  b. employers.

  c. customers.

  d. All of the answers are correct.

13. The market may compete away employer discrimination by

  a. making discrimination profitable.

  b. making discriminating firms less profitable.

  c. making discrimination illegal.

  d. All of the answers are correct.

14. The job that would pay the most is one

  a. that is risky and unpleasant.

  b. that is safe and unpleasant.

  c. that is risky and pleasant.

  d. that is safe and pleasant.

15. A firm will hire workers so long as

  a. the marginal product of labor is falling.

  b. increased revenue from hiring an extra worker is less than the wage.

  c. increased revenue from hiring an extra worker is greater than the wage.

  d. the wage rate does not rise.

16. A firm will hire workers so long as the

  a. MPL is falling.

  b. MPL of the next worker is greater than the wage.

  c. MPL of the next worker is less than the wage.

  d. All of the answers is correct.

17. If you see a disproportionate number of female workers in a job then you know

  a. the customers of the firm are engaging in customer discrimination.

  b. the employer is engaging in hiring discrimination.

  c. the employees are engaging in employee discrimination.

  d. None of the answers is correct.

18. Discrimination may be caused by

  a. employees.

  b. government.

  c. customers.

  d. All of the answers is correct.

Use the following table to answer Questions 19 and 20.

Productivity of Repaving

Number of Workers	Driveways repaved @ $500 per driveway	Marginal Product of Labor (MPL) for the last worker hired
Two	5	
Three	7	
Four	11	
Five	13	

19. In the preceding table, the marginal product of labor (MPL) of the third worker is

    a. 2 driveways.

    b. $3,500.

    c. $1,000.

    d. 7 driveways.

20. In the preceding table, the marginal product of labor (MPL) of the fourth worker is

    a. 4 driveways.

    b. $5,500.

    c. $2,000.

    d. 11 driveways.

Short-Answer Questions

21. What is the marginal product of labor (MPL)?

22. Why does the marginal product of labor (MPL) decline as more workers are hired?

23. Fill in the third column of the table below.

Productivity of Roofing

Number of Workers	Roofs Shingled @ $4,000 per Roof	Marginal Product of Labor (MPL) for the last worker hired
One	2	
Two	5	
Three	7	
Four	8	

If each worker makes $7,000, how many workers will the firm hire?

24. What is human capital?

25. Why might two jobs with similar skill requirements pay different wages?

26. How do unions get their members higher wages?

27. What is statistical discrimination in the labor market?

28. Explain the types of preference-based discrimination that are discussed in the textbook.

29. Why might a carpenter in the United States make more than a carpenter in China?

30. How many workers will a firm hire?

Answer Key

Answers to Practice Exercises: Learning by Doing

1. The marginal product of labor is the increase in a firm's revenues that is created by hiring an additional laborer.

   Topic: The Demand for Labor and the Marginal Product of Labor

2. The first worker will focus on the most productive tasks so the marginal product of that worker is high. As more workers are hired, they are assigned to less productive tasks so the marginal product of labor falls.

   Topic: The Demand for Labor and the Marginal Product of Labor

3. The table is filled in as follows:

Productivity of Painting

Number of Workers	Rooms painted @ $200 per room	Marginal Product of Labor (MPL) for the last worker hired
One	1	$200
Two	5	$800
Three	8	$600
Four	10	$400

   Topic: The Demand for Labor and the Marginal Product of Labor

4. Human capital is the tools of the mind, the stuff in people's heads that make them productive.

   Topic: Human Capital

5. Wages differ between jobs because jobs have different characteristics. Higher wages are required to get people to take on jobs that are less fun, more unpleasant, or more risky. These differences in wages are called compensating differentials. Compensating differentials compensate those workers for accepting greater risk or doing more unpleasant or less fun jobs.

   Topic: Compensating Differentials

6. Unions raise member wages by restricting the supply of workers. As with any good, a reduction or restriction in supply causes price, in this case, the wage, to rise.

   Topic: Do Unions Raise Wages?

7. Statistical discrimination is using information about group averages to draw conclusions about individuals. For example, the person running at you with a knife may be trying to protect you from someone coming from behind you to do you harm. However, most people coming toward you with a knife are trying to do you harm and thus most people initially react defensively toward someone coming toward them with a knife.

   Topic: Statistical Discrimination

8. In the text three types of preference-based discrimination are discussed. These are employer, customer, and employee discrimination. An example of employer discrimination would be an employer only hiring people from their own church. A type of customer discrimination would be if diners would only eat in Chinese restaurants that employ Oriental-looking employees. An example of employee discrimination would be a firm's workers being only willing to work with other workers like themselves.

Topic: Preference-based Discrimination

9. If CEO salaries are taxed at a very high rate, one would expect CEO compensation to shift away from salaries toward perks like in-house chefs or corporate jets. The higher tax rate does not change the optimal compensation package, but it does make salary relatively more expensive than perks.

Topic: Compensating Differentials

Answers to Multiple-Choice Questions

1. c, Topic: The Demand for Labor and the Marginal Product of Labor
2. d, Topic: The Demand for Labor and the Marginal Product of Labor
3. a, Topic: The Demand for Labor and the Marginal Product of Labor
4. b, Topic: Human Capital
5. b, Topic: Human Capital
6. b, Topic: The Demand for Labor and the Marginal Product of Labor
7. d, Topic: The Demand for Labor and the Marginal Product of Labor
8. a, Topic: Human Capital
9. c, Topic: Compensating Differentials
10. b, Topic: Compensating Differentials
11. c, Topic: Statistical Discrimination
12. d, Topic: Preference-based Discrimination
13. b, Topic: Preference-based Discrimination
14. a, Topic: Compensating Differentials
15. c, Topic: The Demand for Labor and the Marginal Product of Labor
16. b, Topic: The Demand for Labor and the Marginal Product of Labor
17. d, Topic: Preference-based Discrimination
18. d, Topic: Preference-based Discrimination
19. c, Topic: The Demand for Labor and the Marginal Product of Labor
20. c, Topic: The Demand for Labor and the Marginal Product of Labor

Answers to Short-Answer Questions

21. The marginal product of labor (MPL) is the increase in a firm's revenues created by hiring an additional laborer.

Topic: The Demand for Labor and the Marginal Product of Labor

22. The first worker will focus on the most productive tasks so the marginal product of that worker is high. As more workers are hired, they are assigned to less productive tasks so the marginal product of labor falls.

Topic: The Demand for Labor and the Marginal Product of Labor

23. The table is filled in as follows:

Productivity of Roofing

Number of Workers	Roofs Shingled @ $4,000 per Roof	Marginal Product of Labor (MPL) for the last worker hired
One	2	$8,000
Two	5	$12,000
Three	7	$8,000
Four	8	$4,000

The firm will hire 3 workers but not the fourth, because the fourth worker's MPL is less than the wage.

Topic: The Demand for Labor and the Marginal Product of Labor

24. Human capital is the tools of the mind, the stuff in people's heads that makes them productive.

Topic: Human Capital

25. Wages differ between jobs because jobs have different characteristics. Higher wages are required to get people to take on jobs that are less fun, more unpleasant, or more risky. These differences in wages are called compensating differentials. Compensating differentials compensate those workers for accepting greater risk or doing more unpleasant jobs.

Topic: Compensating Differentials

26. Unions raise member wages by restricting the supply of workers. As with any good, a reduction or restriction in supply causes price, in this case the wage, to rise.

Topic: Do Unions Raise Wages?

27. Statistical discrimination is using information about group averages to draw conclusions about individuals. For example, the person running at you with a gun may be trying to protect you from someone coming from behind you to do you harm. However, most people coming toward you with a gun are trying to do you harm, and thus most people initially react defensively toward someone coming toward them with a gun.

    Topic: Statistical Discrimination

28. In the text, three types of preference-based discrimination are discussed. These are employer, customer, and employee discrimination. An example of employer discrimination would be an employer only hiring people from their own church. A type of customer discrimination would be if diners would only eat in Chinese restaurants that employ oriental-looking employees. An example of employee discrimination would be a firm's workers being only willing to work other workers like themselves.

    Topic: Preference-based Discrimination

29. Carpenters in the United States benefit from higher productivity throughout the United States economy compared to China. Thus the wages of United States for carpenters is higher than the wages for carpenters in China.

    Topic: The Demand for Labor and the Marginal Product of Labor

30. Firms hire workers as long as the marginal product of labor (MPL) of each worker is more than the wage the worker gets.

    Topic: The Demand for Labor and the Marginal Product of Labor

15

Getting Incentives Right: Lessons for Business, Sports, Politics, and Life

Why Learn about Incentives?

Interested Student: Incentives, I guess they are pretty important?
Old Professor: You are certainly correct there. Incentives as we have learned in prior chapters are fundamental to economics.
Interested Student: Sure, and they matter to pretty much everyone.
Old Professor: Right again, everyone from parents who want to get their children to behave to legislators who want to understand how people will react to actions of government.

Summary

Incentives matter. When an organization gets incentives right, it gets positive outcomes. When an organization gets incentives wrong, it can get very perverse outcomes.

A key concept of incentives is "you get what you pay for." This means that you should be careful and structure incentives toward that which is your direct goal. For example, businesses sometimes pay production workers a **piece rate**. A piece-rate system is any system that pays workers directly for their output. Such an incentive system directly targets output, which is what the firm wants from some production workers. There are however issues of quality and team production, which means a piece-rate system is not the best for all production workers.

A piece-rate system encourages existing workers to work harder and to miss less work. A piece-rate system also attracts more productive workers. However, firms must convince workers that more production will not lead to a lower piece rate.

A second key concept of incentives is that under certain circumstances weak incentives work better than strong incentives. Strong incentives put more risk on the worker. When factors, the worker does not control, affect output, then strong incentives may not translate into more or better effort. Weak incentives may also allow the owner to insure workers against the risk of those factors beyond their control.

An interesting type of weak incentive is a tournament. For example, a firm can link bonuses to relative rather than total individual sales. However tournaments still reduce the incentive to cooperate. Professors who grade competitively or on a curve essentially have set up a tournament for grades.

A third key concept of incentives is that money is not everything. Incentives are powerful but not all powerful incentives are for money. Organizations have a **corporate culture** that is the shared collection of values and norms that govern how people interact in the organization or firm. Workers who identify with their organization work harder. Employees who own stock in the firm they work for and members of teams, such as the military (or sport teams), all tend to work harder to support the organization with which they identify.

Key Terms

piece rate any payment system that pays workers directly for their output

tournament a compensation scheme in which payment is based on relative performance

corporate culture the shared collection of values and norms that govern how people interact in an organization or firm

Traps, Hints, and Reminders

You get what you pay for, thus it is important to set incentives to pay for what you actually want.

Weak incentives may be better than strong incentives when there are factors beyond the control of the worker affecting output.

Money is not everything. Non-monetary incentives, such as identification with the company or recognition, can be very effective at motivating workers particularly when combined with monetary incentives.

Some incentives like tournaments may discourage cooperation among workers or students in a class.

Practice Exercises: Learning by Doing

1. How do incentives work?

2. Under what circumstances are weak incentives better than strong incentives?

3. How does a tournament work as an incentive?

4. What is a piece rate? How does it act as an incentive?

5. What is corporate culture? What does it tell us about incentives?

6. In what way can incentives also act as insurance for workers?

7. Why might employers be partial to weak incentives that give workers insurance against random factors that affect production?

*8. Many professional athletes get a bonus if they win a championship. Is this kind of incentive better or worse than Tim Hardaway's assist bonus? Explain why.[1]

---

[1] Questions marked with a ★ are also end-of-chapter questions.

Multiple-Choice Questions

1. With incentives
   a. you get what you pay for.
   b. strong incentives always work best.
   c. money is the only incentive that really works.
   d. All of the answers are correct.

2. With incentives
   a. a company cannot really affect worker behavior.
   b. weak incentives can encourage worker cooperation.
   c. money is the only incentive that really works.
   d. All of the answers are correct.

3. With incentives
   a. a company cannot really affect worker behavior.
   b. strong incentives always work best.
   c. non-monetary incentives can be important.
   d. All of the answers are correct.

4. With incentives
   a. you get what you pay for.
   b. weak incentives can insure workers against things they cannot control.
   c. corporate culture can encourage worker effort.
   d. All of the answers are correct.

5. A piece rate is when each worker is paid
   a. by the number of hours the worker worked.
   b. by the amount of output the worker produces.
   c. by the amount the firm produces.
   d. a share of the profit the firm makes.

6. "You get what you pay for" is a warning that
   a. incentives do not matter.
   b. a firm must be careful in setting up incentives.
   c. incentives must be in terms of money.
   d. All of the answers are correct.

7. A tournament encourages effort by

    a. making effort more fun.

    b. encouraging cooperation among workers.

    c. having workers compete for a fixed pool of rewards.

    d. making effort harder to measure.

8. A tournament makes the factors that an agent does not control

    a. no longer influence rewards.

    b. have a greater influence on rewards.

    c. controllable by the agent.

    d. no longer influence output.

9. Tournaments can been used to increase effort in

    a. golf.

    b. classrooms.

    c. sales.

    d. All of the answers are correct.

10. Weak incentives can

    a. make workers face more risk from factors they cannot control.

    b. discourage workers from cooperating.

    c. limit the amount of risk workers face from the external environment.

    d. All of the answers are correct.

11. Weak incentives can

    a. reduce the risk workers face from factors they cannot control.

    b. discourage worker cooperation.

    c. increase the risk workers face from the external environment.

    d. All of the answers are correct.

12. Weak incentives can

    a. reduce the risk workers face from factors they cannot control.

    b. encourage worker cooperation.

    c. limit the risk workers face from the external environment.

    d. All of the answers are correct.

13. Weak incentives can

    a. increase the risk workers face from factors they cannot control.

    b. encourage worker cooperation.

    c. increase the risk workers face from the external environment.

    d. All of the answers are correct.

14. Tournaments
    a. encourage players to cooperate.
    b. make outside standards of achievement irrelevant.
    c. have prizes that depend on production.
    d. All of the answers are correct.

15. Tournaments
    a. encourage players to cooperate.
    b. make outside standards of achievement more important.
    c. have fixed prizes.
    d. All of the answers are correct.

16. Tournaments
    a. encourage players to compete against each other.
    b. make outside standards of achievement more important.
    c. have prizes that depend on how much is produced.
    d. All of the answers are correct.

17. Tournaments
    a. encourage players to compete against each other.
    b. make outside standards of achievement irrelevant.
    c. have fixed prizes.
    d. All of the answers are correct.

18. Corporate culture is the
    a. rules in the employee handbook.
    b. employment laws of a state.
    c. shared values that govern interaction in an organization.
    d. the natural law of human interaction.

19. The corporate culture at Wal-Mart led to employees
    a. hiding problems from management.
    b. forming a union.
    c. sharing information with managers who visited the stores regularly.
    d. not getting monetary incentives.

20. An example of a successful corporate culture is in
    a. most governments agencies.
    b. the United States military.
    c. Kmart.
    d. All of the answers are correct.

Short-Answer Questions

21. How do incentives work?

22. How is "you get what you pay for" a warning about incentives?

23. When might weak incentives work better than strong incentives?

24. What is a tournament?

25. How does a tournament work as an incentive?

26. What is a piece rate? What can undermine a piece rate as an incentive?

27. What is corporate culture?

28. What does corporate culture imply about incentives?

29. In what way can incentives also act as insurance for workers?

30. Why might employers be partial to weak incentives that give workers insurance against random factors that affect production?

Answer Key

Answers to Practice Exercises: Learning by Doing

1. Incentives tell people, workers, students, children, what you want from them. Incentives reward or punish people for certain actions. You get more of what you pay people to do and less of what you penalize people for doing.

   Topic: Lesson One: You Get What You Pay For

2. Weak incentives may be better than strong incentives in settings where the goal of incentives can be affected by factors that participants cannot control. For example, weak incentives for workers are effective when the workers' production is influenced by factors other than the efforts of the workers.

   Topic: Lesson Two: Tie Pay to Performance to Reduce Risk

3. A tournament rewards participants for results relative to each other rather than compared to an absolute standard. By making only relative results matter, tournaments encourage participants to try their best even if outside influences are making every participant less productive.

   Topic: Tournament Theory

4. A piece rate is any payment system that pays workers directly for their output. A piece rate acts as an incentive for workers to produce as much as possible because that will maximize their earnings.

   Topic: Piece Rates vs. Hourly Wages

5. Corporate culture is the shared values and norms that govern how people interact in an organization or firm. It tells us that people react to rewards other than monetary rewards. People generally want approval of those around them and thus will usually conform to the corporate culture of their organization.

   Topic: Lesson Three: Money Isn't Everything

6. Weak incentives can insulate participants against outside influence, such as fluctuations in the economy. If a business is better able to absorb economic fluctuation than its workers, it may want to use weak, rather than strong incentives, and thus insure its workers against economic downturns.

   Topic: Lesson Two: Tie Pay to Performance to Reduce Risk

7. Employers might like weak incentives that insure workers against random factors affecting production because such incentives encourage workers to cooperate with each other rather than only compete. This can be important to employers when cooperation can increase output. In addition, weak incentives that insure workers against macroeconomic fluctuations can help a firm keep its best workers during economic downturns.

   Topic: Lesson Two: Tie Pay to Performance to Reduce Risk

8. Yes, if what the owners want is championships rather than more assists by a particular player, bonuses for championships create better incentives than the example from the text, that is, the NBA guard, Tim Hardaway received a bonus for assists. The championship bonus gives players an incentive cooperate, that is, team play, rather than seek individual goals.

Topic: Lesson One: You Get What You Pay For

Answers to Multiple-Choice Questions

1. a, Topic: Lesson One: You Get What You Pay For

2. b, Topic: Lesson Two: Tie Pay to Performance to Reduce Risk

3. c, Topic: Lesson Three: Money Isn't Everything

4. d, Topic: Lesson Two: Tie Pay to Performance to Reduce Risk

5. b, Topic: Piece Rates vs. Hourly Wages

6. b, Topic: Lesson One: You Get What You Pay For

7. c, Topic: Tournament Theory

8. a, Topic: Tournament Theory

9. d, Topic: Tournament Theory

10. c, Topic: Lesson Two: Tie Pay to Performance to Reduce Risk

11. a, Topic: Lesson Two: Tie Pay to Performance to Reduce Risk

12. d, Topic: Lesson Two: Tie Pay to Performance to Reduce Risk

13. b, Topic: Lesson Two: Tie Pay to Performance to Reduce Risk

14. b, Topic: Tournament Theory

15. c, Topic: Tournament Theory

16. a, Topic: Tournament Theory

17. d, Topic: Tournament Theory

18. c, Topic: Lesson Three: Money Isn't Everything

19. c, Topic: Lesson Three: Money Isn't Everything

20. b, Topic: Lesson Three: Money Isn't Everything

Answers to Short-Answer Questions

21. Incentives tell people, workers, students, and children what you want from them. Incentives reward or punish people for certain actions. You get more of what you pay people to do and less of what you penalize people for doing.

    Topic: Lesson One: You Get What You Pay For

22. "You get what you pay for" is a warning to be careful in specifying incentives. If your incentive is incorrectly specified, you may get results that are different than what you had hoped for. In the example from the text, where the NBA guard was paid for assists, he went for assists (whether he got an assist or not) when he might have helped his team win more games by scoring or making a safer pass that would indirectly lead to a basket). If your incentive is wrong, you may harm your organization.

    Topic: Lesson One: You Get What You Pay For

23. Weak incentives may be better than strong incentives in settings where the goal of incentives can be affected by factors that participants cannot control. For example, weak incentives for workers are effective when the workers' production is influenced by factors other than the efforts of the workers.

    Topic: Lesson Two: Tie Pay to Performance to Reduce Risk

24. A tournament rewards participants for results relative to each other rather than compared to an absolute standard. Participants compete for fixed rewards against each other.

    Topic: Tournament Theory

25. By making only relative results matter, tournaments encourage participants to try their best, even if outside influences are making every participant less productive. For example, participants in the tournament will try as hard in bad weather as in good weather, because weather affects all participants. Thus if everyone's production is lower, but reward depends on relative production, effort will gain the worker as much in bad weather as in good weather.

    Topic: Tournament Theory

26. A piece rate is any payment system that pays workers directly for their output. A piece rate can be undermined as an incentive if the employer does not have the credibility that the piece rate will not be lowered later. If workers think that after they reveal how much they can produce, the employer will cut the piece rate, then the incentive of the piece rate will be undermined.

    Topic: Piece Rates vs. Hourly Wages

27. Corporate culture is the shared values and norms that govern how people interact in an organization or firm.

    Topic: Lesson Three: Money Isn't Everything

28. Corporate culture tells us that people react to other rewards rather than just money. People generally want approval of those around them and thus will usually conform to the corporate culture of their organization.

    Topic: Lesson Three: Money Isn't Everything

29. Weak incentives can insulate participants against outside influence, such as fluctuations in the economy. If a business is better able to absorb economic fluctuation it may want to use weak rather than strong incentives and thus insure its workers against economic downturns.

    Topic: Lesson Two: Tie Pay to Performance to Reduce Risk

30. Employers might like weak incentives that insure workers against random factors affecting production because such incentives encourage workers to cooperate with each other rather than only compete. This can be important to employers when cooperation can increase output. In addition, weak incentives that insure workers against macroeconomic fluctuations can help a firm keep its best workers during economic downturns.

    Topic: Lesson Two: Tie Pay to Performance to Reduce Risk

16

Stock Markets and Personal Finance

Why Learn about Stock Markets?

Business Student: Why should we learn about stock markets and personal finance from you? If you know so much, wouldn't you be too rich to teach economics?

Professor: Oddly, that is a very good question. You would think that I ought to be able to get rich quick just like those guys on late night TV. I will show you why that doesn't work and what you can do to get rich slow.

Who will be interested in stock markets? Any student who is at all interested in personal finance, building wealth, or avoiding scams will be interested in knowing more about the stock market.

Summary

This chapter illustrates the idea that there is no free lunch, even in personal finance. Knowing that there is no free lunch can help you avoid big mistakes in your personal finances. If an investment provides any benefit beyond its value as an investment, then that investment should provide a lower rate of return. Think of it this way: Imagine you were trying to decide whether to buy classic cars or stocks as investments. If they were both about as safe and both paid the same rate of return, you would always buy the classic cars. It would be fun to own classic cars. However, as lots of people buy classic cars, the price is pushed up and the rate of return is pushed down. You cannot have the free lunch of fun and high rate of return.

Similarly, there is a **risk–return trade-off**, which just means that safer financial assets have a lower return.

There are two basic types of investing: active and passive. Active investing is when you pay a manager to actively buy and sell stocks for you. Passive investing is when you purchase an index fund and then **buy and hold**. Index funds are collections of stocks that are in one of the main indices such as the Dow Jones Industrial Average, the Standard and Poor's 500 (S&P 500), or the NASDAQ (which stands for the National Association of Securities Dealers Automated Quotations). Passive funds and random stock picking beat active stock picking most of the time. Active fund managers have to know more than everyone else and be able to buy and sell stocks without everyone else catching on. Also, if fund managers start to do well, others will catch on and copy them. When all the other investors start following them, they have to pay more for stocks. Before you know it, the active managers cannot beat the market anymore. Even great stock managers might just be lucky. See graphic 16.2 to see how this would work. The **efficient markets hypothesis** is the idea that as soon as new information about a stock or bond becomes available, buyers and sellers very, very quickly use that information, and asset prices adjust very quickly. Very quickly (sometimes within minutes!) no one can use that information to make extra profits.

The other reason that passive funds are preferable to active funds is that active funds tend to have higher costs. Over time, those costs really add up. In the example in the text, the fund with higher fees cost an extra $16,582.

Other than watching fees, diversification is one of the few things that an individual can do to increase their wealth. Diversification is just the idea that spreading your wealth among many different investments is more successful than "putting all of your eggs in one basket."

Key Terms

efficient markets hypothesis the prices of traded assets reflect all publicly available information

buy and hold buying stocks and then holding them for the long run, regardless of what prices do in the short run

risk–return trade-off higher returns come at the price of higher risk

Traps, Hints, and Reminders

Sometimes students get confused about the trade-off between risk and return. They do not understand why the relationship exists. Imagine that there were two bonds you could buy. One is more risky than the other. Which would you pay more for? The less risky one, of course. But paying more for the less risky bond means that bond has a lower return.

The efficient markets hypothesis is similar to the idea that there is no such thing as a free lunch. If you could easily gather special information on stocks and make money, everyone would do that. That would get rid of your advantage.

Bubbles misallocate resources. For example, if there is a real estate bubble, then resources that would have gone to produce something else are drawn into real estate.

This does not mean that investing in housing is bad; it means that consumers valued something else more, and that investors were confused.

The authors do suggest ways to get rich slow. For example, by using the power of compounding, the longer your money is invested, the bigger it will be at the end. Small amounts of money saved over a long period of time can be much bigger than large amounts of money invested for a short period of time. Another way to get rich slow is by diversifying your portfolio to protect yourself against the risk from single stocks. It also helps build your wealth when you can avoid high fees when choosing stocks.

Practice Exercises: Learning by Doing

1. Briefly explain the difference between active and passive investing.

2. Imagine that your stock broker recommends a stock that will make a lot of money when some event everyone knows will happen happens. Your broker says this stock is sure to make lots of money. Explain why this analysis is incorrect.

3. What is the advantage of diversifying your portfolio?

4. Humberto is saving to send his children to college next year. Ling Ling is saving for her retirement in 30 years. Why should Humberto invest in more bonds than Ling Ling?

5. Imagine that a certain beer company provides free beer and free parties to all stock holders. Why would that stock be likely to have a lower rate of return?

6. Explain why it is hard to make money on the stock market or other asset bubbles.

7. Explain why the authors discuss getting rich slow.

Multiple-Choice Questions

1. According to Burton Malkeil, who could do as well as a stock guru at picking stocks?

   a. a bond guru

   b. the average citizen

   c. highly paid news reporters

   d. a blindfolded monkey with darts and the financial pages

2. If you pay someone to pick individual stocks for you instead of buying a broad index of stocks you are

   a. active investing.

   b. assuming efficient markets.

   c. exuberant.

   d. foregoing the risk-return trade-off.

3. What is the S&P 500?

   a. a NASCAR event

   b. a basket of 500 large firms that broadly mimic the United States economy

   c. a basket of 500 small tech firms

   d. a basket of 500 firms in Switzerland and the Philippines

4. In any given year about how many mutual funds beat the S&P 500?

   a. 40%

   b. 50%

   c. 1%

   d. 100%

5. If 3,000 stock market analysts flip a coin each year to see if a firm's price will go up or down, how many analysts will be expected to be correct every time after 6 years?

    a. just 1

    b. 0

    c. 500

    d. 47

6. The efficient markets hypothesis says that

    a. big firms are more efficient so they make all the money in stock markets.

    b. you cannot get rich buying and selling stocks based on public information.

    c. big firms are more efficient at picking stocks than individual investors.

    d. individuals are better at picking stocks than big firms.

7. Your stock broker tells you that today's news means that Google will make much more money next year than anyone had predicted. He recommends a buy. Why might this be poor advice?

    a. He is just trying to unload his own stock.

    b. If it was in today's news the price has already increased.

    c. Newspapers usually try to manipulate the stock market for their own gain.

    d. None of the answers are correct.

8. After the nuclear power plant in Chernobyl melted and contaminated the Ukraine with radiation, American potato prices increased. Why?

    a. People wanted to eat more potatoes.

    b. People were afraid to buy stocks.

    c. People were afraid to buy bonds.

    d. Traders quickly realized that when Ukrainian potatoes were contaminated, American potatoes would sell for more.

9. When financial economists talk about a stock's covariance they mean

    a. how much the stock price moves up and down.

    b. how much the stock moves up or down compared to its previous amount.

    c. how the stock moves up or down along with the rest of the market.

    d. how the price of the stock is.

10. When a stock price falls that means that

    a. the stock is undervalued and will rise.

    b. the stock will continue to fall.

    c. most buyers and sellers negatively reevaluated their opinion of the stock.

    d. the stock will suddenly have more variance.

11. The evidence for "technical analysis" is

    a. very strong; it works.

    b. mildly strong; it usually works.

    c. a mix of strong and weak.

    d. weak; it does not work.

12. According to diversification, if you work in the auto industry you should

    a. invest heavily in auto stocks.

    b. split your portfolio equally between auto stocks and non-auto stocks.

    c. have relatively few auto stocks.

    d. buy companies that supply auto companies.

13. Rank the following asset categories from lowest risk to highest risk (standard deviation).

    a. United States T-bills, small stocks, S&P 500, sorporate bonds

    b. Corporate bonds, small stocks, S&P 500, T-bills

    c. United States T-bills, corporate bonds, S&P 500, small stocks

    d. United States T-bills, small stocks, corporate bonds, S&P 500

14. According to finance economists, the riskiest stocks are

    a. stocks that move opposite of the overall economy.

    b. stocks that move with the overall economy.

    c. stocks that do well when the economy is doing well.

    d. stocks that do not do well when the economy is in a downturn.

15. The riskiest stocks are those with

    a. the least covariance with the market as a whole.

    b. the most covariance with the market as a whole.

    c. the most variance with the market as a whole.

    d. the least variance with the market as a whole.

16. An old family friend comes to you with a "can't fail" investment strategy. He has been making 5% more than the market for the past ten years and as a favor he will let you invest with him. You should

    a. remember the efficient market hypothesis and invest before everyone else does.

    b. be especially wary of your friend because there is no such thing as a free lunch.

    c. assume that your friend has found a bubble and ride it out before it bursts.

    d. use your friend as one of your assets.

17. Why is the stock market a better place to gamble than Las Vegas roulette tables?

    a. They actually have the same risk.

    b. Las Vegas is actually a safer place to gamble.

    c. The odds actually favor the stock investor while the odds are against the roulette gambler.

    d. The odds actually favor the roulette gambler while the odds are against the stock investor.

18. When economists talk about bubbles they mean

    a. you never know what will happen to the economy.

    b. sometimes investors bid up the price of an asset well above what the price should be.

    c. sometimes investors spend too much time focusing on core competencies.

    d. sometimes stock prices float back and forth like soap bubbles.

19. Right around the year 2000 there was a bubble in which market?

    a. real estate

    b. large stocks

    c. T-bills

    d. tech stocks

20. Bubbles and their bursts are painful to economies because

    a. they cause economies to invest in the wrong areas.

    b. people do not like to let asset prices get too high.

    c. bubbles are not actually painful. Paper profits go up then down. But only on paper.

    d. random stock pickers seem like geniuses when they just got lucky.

Short-Answer Questions

21. What is the difference between active and passive investing?

22. Why does your text recommend passive investing?

23. Some stock market analysts beat the market for many years in a row. If markets are efficient how is this possible?

24. Why is it hard for Warren Buffet to beat the market?

25. What are some simple ways to diversify?

26. What is meant by "technical analysis"?

27. Explain why you should be skeptical when your stock broker calls you with the "deal of a lifetime."

28. Explain why riskier stocks have higher returns.

29. If your economics professor says that housing prices will be at their very lowest next January, why might you be skeptical?

30. How do bubbles cause misallocation in markets?

Answer Key

Answers to Practice Exercises: Learning by Doing

1. Active investing is when you try to pick individual stocks and bonds. Passive investing is when you just pick a diversified portfolio and leave it alone.

   Topic: Passive vs. Active Investing

2. If the stock will make lots of money when global warming causes mass flooding and if the efficient market hypothesis is correct, then everyone would already know this information. Thus the stock price already includes this information.

   Topic: Why Is It Hard to Beat the Market?

3. Diversifying your portfolio protects investors from events that affect single stocks. If you own only XYZ company and XYZ goes bankrupt, you lose your entire portfolio.

   Topic: How to Really Pick Stocks, Seriously

4. Humberto does not have much time to get the benefit of earning higher returns and he needs to have safety. He cannot afford to have the stock market fall in the next year. Humberto needs bonds. Ling Ling has much more time to take advantage of the additional rate of return from stocks. Also, Ling Ling has time to weather the ups and downs of the stock market.

   Topic: Compound Returns Build Wealth

5. The beer company stock provides lots of extras in addition to the rate of return. People will be more likely to want to own that stock. As they bid up the price of the stock, the return will come down. If that were not the case, you could get better than a free lunch; you could have high stock returns and free beer.

   Topic: The No Free Lunch Principle or No Return Without Risk

6. It is hard to make money on bubbles because when you buy the asset to watch the price go up, you never know when the burst will come. When you bet on the burst coming, you could be wrong about the stock being a bubble or you could mistime the burst.

   Topic: Bubble, Bubble, Toil, and Trouble

7. The authors discuss getting rich slowly because efficient markets mean that ways of getting rich quickly are either non-existent (scams) or they are very risky. There is no free lunch.

   Topic: Introduction

Answers to Multiple-Choice Questions

1. d, Topic: Introduction

2. a, Topic: Passive vs. Active Investing

3. b, Topic: How to Really Pick Stocks, Seriously

4. a, Topics: Passive vs. Active Investing; How to Really Pick Stocks, Seriously

5. d, Topic: Passive vs. Active Investing

6. b, Topic: Why Is It Hard to Beat the Market?

7. b, Topic: Why Is It Hard to Beat the Market?

8. d, Topic: Why Is It Hard to Beat the Market?

9. c, Topic: How to Really Pick Stocks, Seriously

10. c, Topic: How to Really Pick Stocks, Seriously

11. d, Topic: How to Really Pick Stocks, Seriously

12. c, Topic: How to Really Pick Stocks, Seriously

13. c, Topic: The No Free Lunch Principle or No Return Without Risk

14. b, Topics: How to Really Pick Stocks, Seriously; The No Free Lunch Principle or No Return Without Risk

15. b, Topics: How to Really Pick Stocks, Seriously; The No Free Lunch Principle or No Return Without Risk

16. b, Topic: The No Free Lunch Principle or No Return Without Risk

17. c, Topic: The No Free Lunch Principle or No Return Without Risk

18. b, Topic: Bubble, Bubble, Toil, and Trouble

19. d, Topic: Bubble, Bubble, Toil, and Trouble

20. a, Topic: Bubble, Bubble, Toil, and Trouble

Answers to Short-Answer Questions

21. Active investing is trying to pick particular winners and losers whether they are stocks or some other asset. Passive is when you pick a diversified portfolio, not knowing which assets will be winners and losers. Passive investors hope that the majority of their portfolio will increase in value.

    Topic: Passive vs. Active Investing

22. The text recommends passive investing because fees are lower and it is very difficult to beat the market. Information is quickly adopted by the market. Further, diversifying your portfolio as a passive investor protects you from events that affect individual stocks. Remember that the S&P 500 beats most mutual funds most years.

    Topics: Why Is It Hard to Beat the Market? Avoid High Fees

23. While it is possible that some stock analysts are smarter than the market as a whole, another explanation is that if there are enough stock pickers some of them will be super lucky. The text provides a simple example of how this could work.

   Topics: Why Is It Hard to Beat the Market? How to Really Pick Stocks, Seriously

24. It is hard for Warren Buffet to beat the market because it is hard for anyone to have more knowledge than or to outwork the entire market. Buffet also has the difficulty that lots of people watch him. When Buffet buys a certain stock, lots of people want to buy that stock, and that pushes the stock price up.

   Topics: Why Is It Hard to Beat the Market? How to Really Pick Stocks, Seriously

25. A really simple way to diversify is to buy index funds. Pick something like the S&P 500. That is a broad collection of 500 different stocks.

   Topic: How to Really Pick Stocks, Seriously

26. "Technical analysis" is when stock pickers look at the past up and down pattern of stock prices to determine when they should buy and when they should sell. Unfortunately, it does not have very good results.

   Topics: How to Really Pick Stocks, Seriously The No Free Lunch Principle or No Return Without Risk

27. When your broker calls you with the "deal of a lifetime" you should be skeptical because if it was such a great deal the broker would buy all of the stock. Also, as soon as new information is available, the information is incorporated into the price. By the time your broker figures out a great deal and then calls you, it is not a great deal anymore.

   Topic: The No Free Lunch Principle or No Return Without Risk

28. Riskier stocks have higher returns because the less risky stocks have had their returns bid down. People would not buy a risky stock unless the risky stock had a higher return. People would rather buy the safer stock. When people buy the safer stock they bid safe stock returns downward.

   Topic: The No Free Lunch Principle or No Return Without Risk

29. How does your professor have this knowledge? Is he doing "technical analysis?" Is he making money off it? "Lowest in January" means that prices will start rising in February. If that is the case, is it not true that other people will figure this out too and be able to profit from this knowledge?

   Topic: The No Free Lunch Principle or No Return Without Risk

30. Bubbles encourage people to make mistakes regarding where they should invest. People see some asset prices rising and keep investing in that asset because they think that consumers want that asset. When the bubble pops, investors realize that they should have invested in something else.

   Topic: Bubble, Bubble, Toil, and Trouble

17

Public Goods and the Tragedy of the Commons

Why Learn about Public Goods and the Tragedy of the Commons?

Interested Student: Public goods, those are produced by the government, right?

Old Professor: Well, some public goods are produced by the government but as you will find out, some public goods are not produced by the government.

Interested Student: And tragedy sounds serious.

Old Professor: Well, it can be serious when incentives cause people to act in such ways that their way of life can be driven out of existence.

Interested Student: Yeah and, of course, voters and officials will care about this, right?

Old Professor: Exactly. Voters and officials who will want to know what to do about public goods and what can be done to avoid the tragedy of the commons.

Summary

A good can either be excludable or nonexcludable. An excludable good is one that the owner can prevent others from using at a low cost. A **nonexcludable good** is one that is difficult to prevent people from using at low cost.

A good can also be either rival or nonrival. A rival good is one that one person's use of it prevents others from using the good. For example, if I eat and enjoy a candy bar you cannot eat and enjoy that candy bar. A **nonrival good** is a good where one person's use of it does not reduce the ability of another person to use the good. For example, you watching a sunset will not reduce my ability to enjoy the same sunset.

A **free rider** enjoys the benefits of a public good without paying a share of the costs. A **forced rider** is someone who pays a share of the costs of a public good but who does not enjoy the benefits.

Private goods are rival and excludable. For example, if I eat a hamburger, then you cannot eat it, making a hamburger rival in consumption. Similarly, the owner of a hamburger can easily prevent others from using it, by eating it.

Public goods are nonrival and nonexcludable. For example, if I enjoy a sunset or the United States national defense, that does not prevent you from enjoying either of these goods. And it is very costly to try to prevent other people from consuming a sunset or national defense.

Advertising has made it possible for some public goods like broadcast television (TV) and radio to be produced by the market. Since everyone who watches or listens has the advertisements (commercials) broadcast to them, the advertisers pay for the public good and the broadcaster provides the programming to the viewer for free.

Nonrival private goods are nonrival but excludable. For example, you watching a movie channel like HBO (which stands for Home Box Office) on cable TV will not reduce my enjoyment of it. However, cable TV companies can cheaply exclude those that do not pay for their services from receiving their programming. All they must do is turn off their services to your house, if you do not pay.

Common resources are rival but nonexcludable. For example, if one fisherman catches a lobster, then other fishermen cannot catch that particular lobster. Thus lobsters are a rival good. But no one owns the lobsters. However, since no one owns the lobsters in the sea, and one fisherman cannot prevent another fisherman from fishing, lobsters are nonexcludable.

Because they are not excludable, common resources often lead to the tragedy of the commons. The **tragedy of the commons** is the tendency of any resource that is not owned to be overused and undermaintained. The tragedy is that in the case of common resources, such as fisheries, the fishermen have an incentive to overuse their resource (by fishing too much) and deplete the stock of fish, thus driving their way of life (livelihood) out of existence.

Governments have tried to overcome the tragedy of the commons by command and control. However command and control sometimes failed as firms just worked harder to use more of the resource, for example, by fishing more in a limited fishing season. A more successful government approach has been to assign property rights in the resource to a limited number of producers. Then these producers, like any owners, have an incentive to maintain the resource and use it at an optimal rate.

Key Terms

nonexcludable good a good that people who do not pay cannot be easily prevented from using the good

nonrival good a good that one person's use of the good does not reduce the ability of another person to use the same good

private goods goods that are excludable and rival

public goods goods that are nonexcludable and nonrival

free rider someone who enjoys the benefits of a public good without paying a share of the costs

forced rider someone who pays a share of the costs of a public good but who does not enjoy the benefits

nonrival private goods goods that are excludable but nonrival

common resources goods that are nonexcludable but rival

tragedy of the commons the tendency of any resource which is unowned and hence nonexcludable to be overused and under maintained

Traps, Hints, and Reminders

Private goods are rival and excludable.
Public goods are nonrival and nonexcludable.
Common resources are rival but nonexcludable.
Nonrival private goods are nonrival but excludable.
Public goods like a sunset need not be produced by the government.

Practice Exercises: Learning by Doing

1. What is the tragedy of the commons?

2. What is a nonexcludable good?

3. What is a nonrival good?

4. What is a private good? What is an example of a private good?

5. What are common resources? What is an example of a common resource?

6. What is a public good? What is an example of a public good?

7. What is a nonrival private good? How are they different from public goods?

8. What is a free rider?

*9. American bison used to freely roam the Great Plains. In the 1820s, there were some 30 million bison in the United States but a survey in 1889 counted just 1,091. Why were the bison driven to near extinction? How were the bison like tuna? At some restaurants and grocery stores, you can buy bison burgers, made from farm-raised bison. Is this good news or bad news if we want more bison around?[1]

---

[1] Questions marked with a ★ are also end-of-chapter questions.

Multiple-Choice Questions

1. If it is difficult to prevent a person from using a good at a low cost, then the good is

a. excludable.

b. nonexcludable.

c. rival.

d. nonrival.

2. If one person's use of a good does not reduce the ability of another person to use a good, then the good is

a. excludable.

b. nonexcludable.

c. rival.

d. nonrival.

3. A private good is one that is

a. rival and excludable.

b. rival and nonexcludable.

c. nonrival and excludable.

d. nonrival and nonexcludeable.

4. A public good is one that is

a. rival and excludable.

b. rival and nonexcludable.

c. nonrival and excludable.

d. nonrival and nonexcludeable

5. A nonrival private good is one that is

a. rival and excludable.

b. rival and nonexcludable.

c. nonrival and excludable.

d. nonrival and nonexcludable.

6. A common resource is one that is

a. rival and excludable.

b. rival and nonexcludable.

c. nonrival and excludable.

d. nonrival and nonexcludeable.

7. A free rider is someone who
   a. enjoys the benefits of a public good while paying a share of the costs.
   b. enjoys the benefits of a public good without paying a share of the costs.
   c. pays the costs of a public good without enjoying the benefits.
   d. All of the answers are correct.

8. A forced rider is someone who
   a. enjoys the benefits of a public good while paying a share of the costs.
   b. enjoys the benefits of a public good without paying a share of the costs.
   c. pays the costs of a public good without enjoying the benefits.
   d. All of the answers are correct.

9. A hamburger is an example of a
   a. private good.
   b. public good.
   c. nonrival private good.
   d. common resource.

10. A provider of satellite TV, such as Direct TV, is an example of a
    a. private good.
    b. public good.
    c. nonrival private good.
    d. common resource.

11. Asteroid deflection is an example of a
    a. private good.
    b. public good.
    c. nonrival private good.
    d. common resource.

12. A lobster in the ocean is an example of a
    a. private good.
    b. public good.
    c. nonrival private good.
    d. common resource.

13. Public goods are those that are
    a. produced by the government.
    b. nonrival and nonexcludable.
    c. owned by the public.
    d. All of the answers are correct.

14. Common resources

    a. tend to be undermaintained.

    b. are rival but nonexcludable.

    c. tend to be overused.

    d. All of the answers are correct.

15. The tragedy of the commons is that common resources tend to be

    a. nonrival.

    b. overused and undermaintained.

    c. produced by the market.

    d. excludable.

16. What makes the tragedy of the commons a tragedy is that people who overuse their common resource will tend to

    a. make too much profit.

    b. grow too big.

    c. drive their way of life out of existence.

    d. All of the answers is correct.

17. Governments have successfully solved the tragedy of the commons by

    a. assigning the right to use the common resource.

    b. taking over the market.

    c. allowing everyone to use the resource.

    d. None of the answers is correct.

18. Advertising has been used to increase the availability of

    a. nonrival private goods.

    b. private goods.

    c. common resources.

    d. All of the answers are correct.

19. The animals least likely to go extinct are

    a. wild animals.

    b. those that are owned.

    c. those animals that are a common resource.

    d. All of the answers are correct.

20. Which animal is most likely to go extinct?

    a. bears

    b. cows

    c. pigs

    d. chickens

Short-Answer Questions

21. What is a nonrival good?

22. What is a nonexcludable good?

23. What characterizes a private good? Give an example of one.

24. What characterizes a public good? Give an example of one.

25. What characterizes a nonrival private good? Give an example of one.

26. What are the characteristics of a common resource? Give an example of one.

27. What is the tragedy of the commons? Why is it tragic?

28. How can advertising affect public goods?

29. How can the government possibly solve the tragedy of the commons?

30. What is a free rider? What is a forced rider?

Answer Key

Answers to Practice Exercises: Learning by Doing

1. The tragedy of the commons is the tendency of any resource that is unowned to be overused and undermaintained.

   Topic: Common Resources and the Tragedy of the Commons

2. A nonexcludable good is one that is difficult to prevent other people from using at a low cost.

   Topic: Four Types of Goods

3. A nonrival good is one where one person's use does not reduce the ability of another person to use the good.

   Topic: Four Types of Goods

4. A private good is one that is excludable and rival. An example would be a candy bar. If you eat a candy bar, then I cannot enjoy it. The producers of the candy bar can exclude me from enjoying one by selling at a prohibitively high cost. Thus, I am "excluded" because I choose not pay to buy a candy bar at such a high price.

   Topic: Private Goods and Public Goods

5. Common resources are goods that are rival but nonexcludable. Alaskan king crabs are an example of a common resource. If one fisherman catches a crab, then others cannot catch that crab. However, no one owns the crabs in the sea and a fisherman cannot cheaply exclude other fisherman from the crab grounds.

   Topic: Common Resources and the Tragedy of the Commons

6. A public good is one that is nonrival and nonexcludable. An example of a public good is one like national defense, which is nonrival because more than one person can enjoy the benefits of it at the same time and it is nonexcludable because you cannot easily defend some people in an area or country without defending all of them.

   Topic: Private Goods and Public Goods

7. Nonrival private goods are those that are excludable but nonrival. The key is that these types of goods are excludable. This means that despite the fact that more than one person can enjoy the nonrival private good, producers will still produce the good because they are able to exclude those not willing to pay for the good. An example would be a basketball game. My enjoyment of a basketball game is not reduced by you also seeing it and the owners can exclude me from seeing it, unless I pay to see it.

   Topic: Nonrival Private Goods

8. A free rider is someone who is able to enjoy the benefits of a public good without paying a share of the costs.

   Topic: Private Goods and Public Goods

9. The bison population fell from 30 million to just above one thousand in about 70 years because they were a common resource like tuna. No one had an incentive to hunt the bison at the optimal rate because other hunters had the incentive to take any bison that were left behind to replenish the herd. Common resources are rival but not excludable. However, once a resource is owned or ranched the resource becomes excludable. Owners of ranch-raised bison have an incentive to maintain their herd, thus it is a good thing that stores and restaurants sell ranch-raised bison, if you want to see more bison around.

Topic: Common Resources and the Tragedy of the Commons

Answers to Multiple-Choice Questions

1. **b, Topic: Four Types of Goods**

2. **d, Topic: Four Types of Goods**

3. **a, Topic: Private Goods and Public Goods**

4. **d, Topic: Private Goods and Public Goods**

5. **c, Topic: Private Goods and Public Goods**

6. **b, Topic: Private Goods and Public Goods**

7. **b, Topic: Private Goods and Public Goods**

8. **c, Topic: Private Goods and Public Goods**

9. **a, Topic: Private Goods and Public Goods**

10. **c, Topic: Private Goods and Public Goods**

11. **b, Topic: Private Goods and Public Goods**

12. **d, Topic: Common Resources and the Tragedy of the Commons**

13. **b, Topic: Private Goods and Public Goods**

14. **d, Topic: Common Resources and the Tragedy of the Commons**

15. **b, Topic: Common Resources and the Tragedy of the Commons**

16. **c, Topic: Common Resources and the Tragedy of the Commons**

17. **a, Topic: Common Resources and the Tragedy of the Commons**

18. **a, Topic: Common Resources and the Tragedy of the Commons**

19. **b, Topic: Common Resources and the Tragedy of the Commons**

20. **a, Topic: Common Resources and the Tragedy of the Commons**

Answers to Short-Answer Questions

21. A nonrival good is one where one person's use does not reduce the ability of another person to use the good.

    Topic: Four Types of Goods

22. A nonexcludable good is one that is difficult to prevent other people from using at a low cost.

    Topic: Four Types of Goods

23. A private good is one that is excludable and rival. An example would be a slice of pizza. If you eat a slice of pizza, then I cannot enjoy it. The producers of the slice of pizza can exclude me from enjoying one at a low cost.

    Topic: Private Goods and Public Goods

24. A public good is one that is nonrival and nonexcludable. An example of a public good is one like police protection that more than one person can enjoy at the same time and is nonexcludable because you cannot easily protect some people in a neighborhood or city without protecting all of them.

    Topic: Private Goods and Public Goods

25. Nonrival goods are those that are excludable but nonrival. The key is that these types of goods are excludable. That means despite the fact that more than one person can enjoy the good, producers will still produce them because they are able to exclude those not willing to pay for the good. An example would be a basketball game. My enjoyment of a basketball game is not reduced by you also seeing it and the owners can exclude me from seeing the game, unless I pay to see it.

    Topic: Nonrival Private Goods

26. Common resources are goods that are rival but nonexcludable. Alaskan king crabs are an example of common resource. If one fisherman catches a crab, then others cannot catch that crab. However, no one owns the crabs in the sea and a fisherman cannot cheaply exclude other fisherman from the crab grounds.

    Topic: Common Resources and the Tragedy of the Commons

27. The tragedy of the commons is a tragedy because the users of a common resource have no incentive to maintain it. Thus, they can drive their way of life out of existence by completely using up a key resource.

    Topic: Common Resources and the Tragedy of the Commons

28. Advertising can take advantage of nonexcludable goods in the case of broadcast goods like TV and radio. Advertising can make it profitable to sell a nonrival public good that is nonrival but excludable.

    Topic: The Peculiar Case of Advertising

29. If a government has an entire common resource under its control, it can assign rights to producers. This way the usage of the resource can be limited and the resource maintained, because the rights holder are essentially the owners of the common resource. This is the example of New Zealand and their control of a common resource (fish).

    Topic: Common Resources and the Tragedy of the Commons

30. A free rider is someone who is able to enjoy the benefits of a public good without paying a share of the costs. A forced rider is someone who does not enjoy benefits from a public good but is forced to pay for a part of its costs.

    Topic: Private Goods and Public Goods

18

Economics, Ethics, and Public Policy

Why Learn about the Relationship of Economics to Ethics and Public Policy?

This is a chapter for those interested in the big picture and big ideas. This is also a chapter for the critic of economics. As you have seen in earlier chapters, economics shows that the market, when working, leads to the best outcome. If you want to intervene in the marketplace and you cannot find a market failure like a public good or a monopoly, then you are left appealing to moral authority like religion to argue the independent choices of people should be countermanded.

Thus those interested in the role of government will be interested in this material. So, who exactly would be interested in economics, ethics, and public policy?

> Legislators, government officials, and candidates who will be interested in making cases for government intervention

> Voters who will want to have a basis for deciding how much government intervention for which to vote

> Students of economics, of course, both as students and voters

Summary

This chapter deals with the question, should any and all voluntary trade or exchange be allowed. In this book, up until this point, we have studied positive economics. **Positive economics** is describing, explaining, or predicting without making recommendations. An example of a positive economic statement is that if the price ceiling on human organs were allowed to rise above the current level of zero, then the quantity supplied of human organs would rise.

Normative economics is recommendations or arguments about what economic policy should be. For example, what exchanges should be allowed. An example of a normative economic statement is that trade in human organs should not be allowed.

We learned in prior chapters that when the market works, free exchange leads to maximum consumer surplus plus producer surplus. To argue that such exchanges should not be allowed, a person needs a reason. This chapter discusses six such reasons that might be viewed as criticisms of economics. The authors generally dismiss these reasons, but then the authors, including the author of this study guide, are economists.

The first reason the authors discuss for not allowing some voluntary exchanges is exploitation. That is, the possibly one side of a trade is exploiting the other. The authors use a human organ donation example. Is the seller exploited if they do 1, 2, or 3?

1. Sell a kidney for zero dollars ($0), that is, donate it.
2. Sell a kidney for $5,000.
3. Sell a kidney for $5,000,000.

Situation 1, donation of human organs, is what is done now in the United States. Is that exploitive? Economists would say no, as long as the donation is voluntary. Clearly those who say monetary exchanges for kidneys should not be allowed, but view donated kidneys as a good thing, must not view donators as exploited. So if one is not exploited at a price of zero dollars, how can one be exploited at a price of $5,000, or at any price? Or if one is not exploited at a really high price like $5,000,000, how can one be exploited just because they voluntarily accept a lower price like $5,000?

The second reason for interfering in exchange between private individuals is what the authors call meddlesome preferences. Meddlesome preferences are when someone cares about an exchange that take place between two other people. An example used in the text is the prohibition in some states on serving horse meat in restaurants. Horse meat is on the menu in Europe and Japan. And, of course, beef that is regularly eaten in the United States is off the menu in India. Should the majority be able to keep some people from eating horse meat? What about other exchanges? Should the majority be able to prevent homosexuality, interracial marriage, some religious rites, or other such private transactions that some people do not like? One can begin to see the problem with meddlesome preferences. Meddlesome preferences may clash with other values like liberty and freedom.

The third reason for interfering in the market place that the authors discuss is fair and equal treatment. What is fair or equal may be very costly. In an example in the book, the authors discuss New York City spending a large sum of money to retrofit old city buses to make them wheelchair accessible. As the authors say in this section economics cannot answer questions about the sacred or the profane. If your religion tells you that pictures of naked people are bad, then it is irrelevant to you that exchanges involving this product are voluntary between other people. You may still think such exchanges should be banned. If equality in outcomes is your highest value, you may not care what economics says about the costs and benefits of assuring equal outcomes.

The fourth reason the authors examine for restricting market choices is cultural goods and paternalism. This is when a country like Canada discriminates in favor of domestically produced programming on government owned television. The criticism of this is that such subsidy schemes tend to be counterproductive and wasteful. Canadian program producers might make better programs, if they had to compete with those from the United States for airtime.

The fifth reason the authors explore for barring some exchanges is that one may not like the poverty, inequality, or income distribution that results from free exchanges. The authors turn to moral philosophy to help discuss the question, what is a just distribution of wealth.

The Rawls "maximin" principle says that government, without violating people's basic rights, maximize the benefit accruing to the most disadvantaged group in society. A person with a utilitarian philosophy would argue that we should try to implement outcomes that bring the greatest sum of utility or happiness to society. Nozick's entitlement theory is that outcomes do not matter. What matters is that the process leading to the outcome is just. That is, as long as the trades that lead to one person having more and another person having less are truly voluntary, they are moral. Consider the table below showing the incomes of two different three-person societies.

Society	Person 1	Person 2	Person 3	Average Income
A	$25,000	$20,000	$15,000	$20,000
B	$40,000	$25,000	$10,000	$25,000

A believer in the Rawls' "maximin" principle would prefer society A with the higher income for the poorest person. Someone who believed in Nozick's entitlement theory would not prefer either society based on outcomes, because to them only a fair process matters.

Since utilitarians are looking to maximize total society happiness, they would at times favor redistribution. So they would want some amount of money redistributed from the wealthy to the poor. But taking money from those that created the wealth reduces their incentive to create more wealth, which would make the entire society worse off. This acts as a check on the redistributive impulses of utilitarians, and thus we cannot know whether they would prefer society A or B above.

Next consider the same two societies with a third three-person society added in.

Society	Person 1	Person 2	Person 3	Average Income
A	$25,000	$20,000	$15,000	$20,000
B	$40,000	$25,000	$10,000	$25,000
C	$1,000,000	$150,000	$50,000	$400,000

A believer in Rawls' "maximin" principle would prefer society C despite its highly unequal distribution of income. Rawlsians would pick society C based on its highest income for the poorest person. Again someone who believed in Nozick's entitlement theory would not prefer either society based on outcomes, because to them only a fair process matters. Also, we still cannot know which society a utilitarian would pick because of their trade-off between happiness maximization and incentives for wealth creation.

The sixth and final reason the authors examine for interfering in private exchanges is who counts. Economists generally would count everyone involved in a decision. Politically though, people who do not live in or vote in a country do not count as much. This comes into play when a firm wants to hire someone from another country. The government may prohibit this exchange although both sides want to make it.

So while economists generally argue almost any voluntary exchange should be allowed, the majority or the government sometimes prohibit certain exchanges. This chapter tries to give and evaluate some of the reasons third parties sometimes use, to justify interfering with exchanges between two other individuals.

Key Terms

positive economics describing, explaining, or predicting without making recommendations

normative economics recommendations or arguments about what economic policy should be

Traps, Hints, and Reminders

Positive economics is about what is. An example of a positive economic statement is, if you raise the price, quantity demanded will fall.

Normative economics is about what should be. An example of a normative economic statement is a person should not be able to sell their kidney.

Voluntary exchange makes both people better off. Reasons explored in this chapter about why government might interfere with private exchange are possible exploitation, meddlesome preferences, fairness or equal treatment, protecting cultural goods and paternalism, poverty, inequality and the distribution of income, and should some people count more than others.

Practice Exercises: Learning by Doing

1. What is positive economics? What is an example of a positive economic statement?

2. What is normative economics? What is an example of a normative economic statement?

3. In the table below are incomes of three-person societies. Which distribution of income would a Rawlsian and a believer in Nozick's entitlement theory prefer? Explain why.

Society	Person 1	Person 2	Person 3	Average Income
A	$50,000	$30,000	$40,000	$40,000
B	$70,000	$60,000	$20,000	$50,000

4. What are meddlesome preferences? How might they conflict with other values like liberty and freedom?

5. Is someone who donates a kidney exploited? Is someone who sells a kidney exploited?

6. Whose happiness would an economist count in deciding foreign aid? How and why might that differ from who an elected official might count?

7. What is a utilitarian's view on the distribution of income?

*8. Of the three ethical theories we discuss (Rawlsian, utilitarian, and Nozickian), which two are most different from the third? In what way are the two different from the third?[1]

Multiple-Choice Questions

1. Positive economics is about

   a. what is.

   b. what should be.

   c. what is yet to be discovered in economics.

   d. macroeconomics.

2. Normative economics is about

   a. what is.

   b. what should be.

   c. old economic ideas that have been shown to be wrong.

   d. microeconomics.

3. Which of the following is a positive economic statement?

   a. The price of sugar is too high.

   b. People should use less sugar in their diets.

   c. If the price of sugar rises, then the quantity demanded of sugar will fall.

   d. All of the answers are correct.

4. Which of the following is a normative economic statement?

   a. Drug companies' profits rose last year.

   b. Drug companies should lower prices.

   c. If demand falls, drug company prices will fall.

   d. All of the answers are correct.

Use the following table to answer Questions 5 and 6.

Society	Person 1	Person 2	Person 3	Average Income
A	$25,000	$20,000	$15,000	$20,000
B	$40,000	$25,000	$10,000	$25,000

[1]Questions marked with an ★ are also end-of-chapter questions.

5. In the preceding table, Society A would be preferred by
   a. a Rawlsian.
   b. a utilitarian.
   c. a believer in Nozick's entitlement theory.
   d. None of the answers is correct.

6. In the preceding table, Society B would be preferred by
   a. a Rawlsian.
   b. a utilitarian.
   c. a believer in Nozick's entitlement theory.
   d. None of the answers is correct.

7. Meddlesome preferences often conflict with
   a. the majority.
   b. cultural goods.
   c. other values like freedom and liberty.
   d. All of the answers are correct.

8. Some people believe in interfering with private exchange
   a. to protect cultural goods.
   b. because of worries about exploitation.
   c. because of worries about lack of fairness.
   d. All of the answers are correct.

9. Some people do not believe in interfering in the marketplace, because as long as there is no market failure, the market
   a. does not maximize total surplus.
   b. counts everyone.
   c. does not produce an efficient amount of the good.
   d. All of the answers are correct.

10. A believer in Rawls believes the government should
    a. maximize the benefit accruing to the most disadvantaged group in society.
    b. maximize total happiness in society.
    c. ensure a just process to societal outcomes.
    d. All of the answers are correct.

11. A believer in utilitarian society believes the government should
    a. maximize the benefit accruing to the most disadvantaged group in society.
    b. maximize total happiness in society.
    c. ensure a just process to societal outcomes.
    d. All of the answers are correct.

12. A believer in Nozick's entitlement theory believes the government should

  a. maximize the benefit accruing to the most disadvantaged group in society.

  b. maximize total happiness in society.

  c. ensure a just process to societal outcomes.

  d. All of the answers are correct.

13. A believer in the Rawls maximin theory

  a. always prefers the most even distribution of income.

  b. may prefer a lower average income as long as the most disadvantage group is better off.

  c. always wants to minimize the wealth of the most favored group in society.

  d. may want the most disadvantaged group to have the least benefit.

Use the following table to answer Questions 14 through 16.

Society	Person 1	Person 2	Person 3	Average Income
A	$10,000	$10,000	$10,000	$10,000
B	$50,000	$40,000	$30,000	$40,000
C	$70,000	$60,000	$20,000	$50,000

14. Of the three societies in the table above a Rawlsian would prefer

  a. society A.

  b. society B.

  c. society C.

  d. Not enough information is given to choose.

15. Of the three societies in the table above a utilitarian would prefer

  a. society A.

  b. society B.

  c. society C.

  d. Not enough information is given to choose.

16. Of the three societies in the table above a believer in Nozick's entitlement theory would prefer

  a. society A.

  b. society B.

  c. society C.

  d. Not enough information is given to choose.

17. Utilitarians would redistribute money from the wealthy to poor people until

    a. everyone has the same income.

    b. total society happiness is maximized.

    c. everyone has the same happiness.

    d. All of the answers are correct.

18. Utilitarians might favor only a modest redistribution of income

    a. if wealth creators are very sensitive to incentives.

    b. if taking money from the rich greatly increases their incentive to earn.

    c. if wealth creators care little for the extra dollar of wealth they have.

    d. All of the answers are correct.

19. To an economist, which of the following people would count equally when evaluating a policy?

    a. an immigrant who wants to enter the United States for a job

    b. the owners of the United States firm who want to hire the immigrant

    c. the competing worker who would also like the job

    d. All of the answers are correct.

20. To a politician, which of the following people would count equally when evaluating a policy?

    a. an immigrant who wants to enter the United States for a job

    b. the owners of the United States firm who wants to hire the immigrant

    c. the relatives of the immigrant who hope to receive remittances

    d. All of the answers are correct.

Short-Answer Questions

21. What is positive economics? What is an example of a positive economic statement?

22. What is normative economics? What is an example of a normative economic statement?

23. In the table below are incomes of three-person societies. Which distribution of income would a Rawlsian and a believer in Nozick's entitlement theory prefer and why?

Society	Person 1	Person 2	Person 3	Average Income
A	$35,000	$15,000	$25,000	$25,000
B	$30,000	$40,000	$20,000	$30,000

24. What are meddlesome preferences? What other values might they conflict with and why?

25. Is someone who donates a kidney exploited? Is there a price at which someone could sell a kidney and not be exploited?

26. Whose utility would an economist count in deciding immigration law? How and why might that differ from who an elected official might count?

27. What is a utilitarian's view on the distribution of income? What effect might incentives have on this view?

28. What is Nozick's entitlement theory?

29. What does a Rawlsian think the government should do?

30. What are cultural goods? What happens to the producers of them if the government helps them out?

Answer Key

Answers to Practice Exercises: Learning by Doing

1. Positive economics is describing, explaining, or predicting without making recommendations. An example of a positive economic statement is when the price of a good goes up quantity demanded for that good goes down. Many other such statements would also be correct.

Topic: Introduction

2. Normative economics is recommendations or arguments about what economic policy should be. An example of normative a normative economic statement is gasoline prices should be higher to reduce pollution. Many other such statements would also be correct.

Topic: Introduction

3. A Rawlsian would pick society A where the least well off person makes $30,000 over society B where the worst well off person only makes $20,000. Believers in Nozick's entitlement theory care about a just process not outcomes and thus we cannot say which society they would prefer.

Topic: Poverty, Inequality, and the Distribution of Income

4. Meddlesome preferences are when some third party cares what two other people do. Meddlesome preferences might seem a good idea, when it is something we are for or against, but they may conflict with other values like freedom and liberty. For example, if you are against eating horse meat, then telling others they cannot eat horse meat might seem like a great idea to you. But what if the majority wants to ban a religion or homosexuality or some other thing you view as your individual right to decide?

Topic: Meddlesome Preferences

5. Most people would feel that someone who donated a kidney to a person who needed a kidney was doing a good thing. So it is puzzling how donating the same kidney but getting some amount of money in the exchange makes people worry about the exchange being exploitive. If there is any amount of money that one would sell a kidney for and not consider the exchange exploitive, then it is hard to call any amount of money the person with the kidney accepts as exploitive. Further it is hard to explain why giving up a kidney without any compensation would not also be exploitive.

Topic: Exploitation

6. An economist would say everyone involved in a policy counts. For example, with foreign aid, the recipients count and the taxpayers who provide the money also count. An elected official might see it very differently. The recipients of foreign aid cannot vote, thus they cannot help the politician. On the other hand many taxpayers are also voters so they might count much more to an elected official who wants to be reelected.

Topic: Who Counts? Immigration

7. The utilitarian view of the distribution of income is that if the poor value the next dollar spent more than the rich value a loss of a dollar of spending, then money should be transferred from the rich to the poor until there are no more gains to be had.

   Topic: Poverty, Inequality, and the Distribution of Income

8. Nozickian ethical theory is the most different from Rawlsian and utilitarian theory. Rawlsian and utilitarian ethical theory focus on fair outcomes, while Nozickian theory focuses on fair processes that lead to outcomes.

   Topic: Poverty, Inequality, and the Distribution of Income

Answers to Multiple-Choice Questions

1. a, Topic: **Introduction**

2. b, Topic: **Introduction**

3. c, Topic: **Introduction**

4. b, Topic: **Introduction**

5. a, Topic: **Poverty, Inequality, and the Distribution of Income**

6. d, Topic: **Poverty, Inequality, and the Distribution of Income**

7. c, Topic: **Meddlesome Preferences**

8. d, Topic: **The Case for Exporting Pollution and Importing Kidneys**

9. b, Topic: **The Case for Exporting Pollution and Importing Kidneys**

10. a, Topic: **Poverty, Inequality, and the Distribution of Income**

11. b, Topic: **Poverty, Inequality, and the Distribution of Income**

12. c, Topic: **Poverty, Inequality, and the Distribution of Income**

13. b, Topic: **Poverty, Inequality, and the Distribution of Income**

14. b, Topic: **Poverty, Inequality, and the Distribution of Income**

15. d, Topic: **Poverty, Inequality, and the Distribution of Income**

16. d, Topic: **Poverty, Inequality, and the Distribution of Income**

17. b, Topic: **Poverty, Inequality, and the Distribution of Income**

18. a, Topic: **Poverty, Inequality, and the Distribution of Income**

19. d, Topic: **Who Counts? Immigration**

20. b, Topic: **Who Counts? Immigration**

Answers to Short-Answer Questions

21. Positive economics is describing, explaining, or predicting without making recommendations. An example of a positive economic statement is when the price of a substitute good for butter goes up, the demand for butter rises. Many other such statements would also be correct.

Topic: Introduction

22. Normative economics is recommendations or arguments about what economic policy should be. An example of a normative economic statement is prescription drugs should be cheaper because everyone should have health care. Many other such statements would also be correct.

Topic: Introduction

23. A Rawlsian would pick society B where the least well off person makes $20,000 over society A where the worst well off person only makes $15,000. Believers in Nozick's entitlement theory care about a just process not outcomes and thus we cannot say which society they would prefer.

Topic: Poverty, Inequality, and the Distribution of Income

24. Meddlesome preferences are when some third party cares what two other people do. Meddlesome preferences might seem a good idea, when it is something we are for or against, but they may conflict with other values like freedom and liberty. For example, if you are against eating horse meat, then telling others they cannot eat horse meat might seem like a great idea to you. But what if the majority wants to ban a religion or homosexuality or some other thing you view as your individual right to decide?

Topic: Meddlesome Preferences

25. Most people would feel that someone who donated a kidney to a person who needed a kidney was doing a good thing. So it is puzzling how donating the same kidney but getting some amount of money in the exchange makes people worry about the exchange being exploitive. If there is any amount of money that one would sell a kidney for and not consider the exchange exploitive, then it is hard to call any amount of money the person with the kidney accepts as exploitive. Further it is hard to explain why giving up a kidney without any compensation would not also be exploitive.

Topic: Exploitation

26. An economist would say everyone involved in a policy counts. For example with immigration policy, the immigrants, the employer who wants to hire the immigrant, those left in the home country of the immigrant who hope to get remittances, and host country workers who would compete against the immigrant all count to the economist. An elected official might see if very differently. The immigrant and those at home receiving remittances cannot vote and thus cannot help the politician. On the other hand, the owners of the host country firm who wants to hire the immigrant and host country workers who would compete against the immigrant for a job are likely also voters, so they might count much more to an elected official who wants to be reelected.

Topic: Who Counts? Immigration

27. The utilitarian view of the distribution of income is that if the poor value the next dollar spent more than the rich could value a loss of a dollar of spending, money should be transferred from the rich to the poor until there are no more gains to be had. If however the rich are sensitive to the lower incentive to create wealth from having it transferred from them, the utilitarian would favor more modest transfers from the rich to the poor.

Topic: Poverty, Inequality, and the Distribution of Income

28. Nozick's entitlement theory is that outcomes need not be equal as long as the process is fair. Thus, they do not prefer one society to the other base on outcomes, but rather prefer one society to another based on process that leads to outcomes. They prefer a just process.

Topic: Poverty, Inequality, and the Distribution of Income

29. A Rawlsian thinks the government should maximize the benefits to the least-advantaged group in society.

Topic: Poverty, Inequality, and the Distribution of Income

30. Cultural goods are goods associated with a particular culture, such as opera, which is associated with Western culture or silk robes associated with Japanese culture. If a government protects such goods, then the producer may become even more inefficient and the public may come to want these goods less and less.

Topic: Cultural Goods and Paternalism

19

Political Economy

Why Learn about the Political Economy?

This chapter is for those interested in economic policy. This chapter explores the intersection between economics and political science while focusing on why economic analysis is often ignored in the political arena. In this chapter, we examine voter behavior, the behavior of special interest groups, and how democracy and a free press enhance government responsiveness to the public.

Thus those interested in government will be interested in this material. So who will be the most interested in the political economy?

> Legislators, government officials, candidates, and voters who will be interested in making cases for government intervention

> Voters who will want to have a basis for deciding how much government intervention for which to vote

> Students of economics, of course, both as students and voters

Summary

This chapter begins by asking why mainstream economics is often ignored in the political realm. The authors offer three possibilities: the criticism of economics in Chapter 18 are correct, so politicians are right to ignore economic analysis; the possibility that mainstream economists are just wrong about economics; or that the voting public and politicians have incentives that encourage them to ignore economics.

The first bad incentive comes from the fact that each voter knows that their vote is unlikely to decide a particular election. So voters individually decide not to become as informed as they might about various issues. Or voters individually decide to remain rationally ignorant. **Rational ignorance** is when the benefits from acquiring more information are less than the costs.

Rational ignorance matters because if voters are uninformed, then it is hard for them to make informed choices about what policies to support. Also, voters who are rationally ignorant will often make decisions for irrational reasons. Finally, rational ignorance matters because not everyone is rationally ignorant and those who are not may have an advantage in getting the policies that benefit them at the expense of taxpayers as a whole.

A *special interest group* is a small group of people with a common interest. A special interest group can have an incentive to be informed. Any benefit a small group receives is spread over fewer people (a small percentage) than the voting public as a whole. Also, the benefits a special interest group can achieve for its members may, on a per member basis, be more, even much more, than the share of taxes per member that will be needed to support the government providing the benefit.

The book discusses that the United States sugar industry benefits from a government imposed quota on sugar imports. Sugar interests also donate to members of both political parties on the Senate Agriculture Committee who vote on the quota. In this case, sugar producers are rationally informed as they each gain large benefits from the sugar quota and voters are rationally ignorant as the sugar quota cost them a cent or a few cents on any particular product that contains sugar.

The sugar example is a case of *concentrated benefits* and *diffused costs*. Concentrated benefits are benefits that accrue to a few individuals. Diffused costs are costs like taxes that are spread out widely, for example, falling on all taxpayers. Concentrated benefits and diffused costs provide an opportunity for a special interest group to get a benefit at the expense of taxpayers. It also provides an incentive to waste resources.

For example, if a policy costs society $500 and would provide a special interest group that pays 2% of the total tax bill of society a $400 benefit, then the group will certainly favor and push for this policy. The special interest group would get its $400 benefit while paying $10 (or .02 × $500). So, the net gain of the special interest group is $390, that is, $400 − $10. However, society is wasting resources on this policy. It cost society $500 to provide a $400 benefit, so $100 (or $500 − $400) is wasted. If enough policies are adopted that waste resources, then the people of society will see their standard of living erode.

A possible macroeconomic case of rational ignorance is that the winner of United States presidential election can be accurately predicted by the state of the macroeconomy and the length of time the incumbent party has held the White House. This is called the *political business cycle*. Maybe people in the United States that vote for president are myopic and do not consider to what extent the president is responsible for current economic conditions or maybe the economy is the single issue to United States presidential voters. This voting pattern, of course, has created an incentive for incumbent presidents. They naturally do what they can to make United States economic conditions as favorable as they can when heading into a presidential election, even if economic conditions are only made artificially to appear better. The book gives an example of social security payments being increased before a presidential election while the corresponding tax increase was delayed until the following year. And the data shows that United States personal income has grown faster in election years than in non-election years and the difference is enough that it is likely not due to chance. This movement in United States personal income around elections is called the political business cycle.

Up to this point in the chapter, democracy with rationally ignorant voters, special interest groups, and wasted resources does not look so good. However, when you look around the world, democracies are the richest countries, so they must be doing something right.

The alternative is often an autocratic government that seeks through control of the press to keep the people uninformed. While voters in democracies may sometimes be rationally ignorant, they are often better informed than people in autocratic societies where the government controls the press. The evidence is that famines happened not due to lack of food in a country, but in countries where the government is not responsive to the public because of a lack of a free press and a lack of representative government.

Key Terms

rational ignorance when the benefits of being informed are less than the costs of becoming informed

median voter theorem when voters vote for the policy that is closest to their ideal point on a line, then the ideal point of the median voter will beat any other policy in a majority rule election

Traps, Hints, and Reminders

Rational ignorance is when a person does not find it worthwhile to acquire information.

Concentrated benefits and diffused costs provide an incentive for special interest groups to be informed and may provide an incentive for the government to waste resources.

Practice Exercises: Learning by Doing

1. When is it rational to be ignorant?

2. What incentive do special interest groups have to be rationally informed?

3. If a special intrest group that pays 2% of taxes can get itself an $800 benefit that costs the government $1,000, is this worthwhile for the special interest group and society?

4. What incentive does diffused costs and concentrated benefits create?

5. What problems does rational ignorance potentially cause?

*6. The "median voter theorem" is sometimes called the "pivotal voter theorem." This is actually a pretty good way to think of the theorem. Explain why.[1]

Multiple-Choice Questions

1. It is rational to remain ignorant when the costs of information
   a. are positive.
   b. are negative.
   c. are greater than the benefits from the information.
   d. are less than the benefits from the information.

2. Among the problems created by rational ignorance is
   a. more costly information.
   b. voters may decide based on irrational criteria.
   c. old economic ideas that have been shown to be wrong.
   d. microeconomics.

[1]Questions marked with a ★ are also end-of-chapter questions.

3. Special interest groups can get gains for their members if

    a. benefits and costs are concentrated.

    b. benefits and cost are diffused.

    c. benefits are concentrated and costs are diffused.

    d. benefits are diffuse and costs are concentrated.

Use Scenario 1 to answer Questions 4 through 7.

Scenario 1

    A. The interest group pays 5% of all taxes.
    B. The interest group can get a $500 benefit from the government.
    C. The policy benefit given the interest group costs the government $700.

4. In Scenario 1, the part of the cost of the benefit paid by members of the special interest group is

    a. $35.

    b. $465.

    c. $500.

    d. $700.

5. In Scenario 1, the net benefit to the members of the special interest group is

    a. $35.

    b. $465.

    c. $500.

    d. $700.

6. In Scenario 1, the net benefit to society is

    a. −$200 (minus $200).

    b. $35.

    c. $665.

    d. $700.

7. If the government in Scenario 1 adopts this policy it will be

    a. maximizing societal happiness.

    b. wasting resources.

    c. rationally ignorant.

    d. maximizing GDP.

8. Famines are least likely when

    a. the press is free under a dictator.

    b. the press is government-controlled under democracy.

    c. the press is free under democracy.

    d. the press is government-controlled under a dictator.

9. In the United States, personal income grows the fastest
    a. in non–election years.
    b. in election years.
    c. in random years.
    d. in odd–numbered years.

10. Special interest groups seek
    a. concentrated costs.
    b. diffused benefits.
    c. concentrated benefits.
    d. All of the answers are correct.

Short-Answer Questions

11. When is it rational for a voter to remain ignorant?

12. What incentive do special interest groups have to be rationally informed?

13. If a special group that pays 3% of taxes can get itself a $700 benefit, that cost the government $1,000, is this worthwhile for the special interest group and society?

14. What incentive does diffused costs and concentrated benefits create?

15. What problems does rational ignorance potentially cause?

Answer Key

Answers to Practice Exercises: Learning by Doing

1. Rational ignorance is when the benefits from acquiring more information are less than the costs.

   Topic: Voters and the Incentive to Be Ignorant

2. Because they are small and any benefit they can get from the government is spread over a relatively small number of people. Since the costs are borne by a much larger group, usually taxpayers, special interest groups have an incentive to be rationally informed about their particular area of interest.

   Topic: Special Interests and the Incentive to Be Informed

3. This scenario is certainly worth it for the interest group. They get an $800 benefit while only paying $20 of the cost for a net benefit of $780. It is not in the interest of society because the government spends $1,000 to get a group an $800 benefit which means $200 worth of resources are wasted.

   Topic: Special Interests and the Incentive to Be Informed

4. Concentrated benefits and diffused costs give a special interest group the incentive to seek a benefit from the government most of which will be paid for by taxpayers. Taxpayers will not complain because each taxpayer's share of the costs is relatively small.

   Topic: One Formula for Political Success: Diffuse Costs, Concentrate Benefits

5. Rational ignorance matters because if voters are uninformed, then it is hard for them to make informed choices about what policies to support. Also, voters who are rationally ignorant will often make decisions for irrational reasons. Finally, rational ignorance matters because not everyone is rationally ignorant, and those who are not may have an advantage in getting the policies they want.

   Topic: Why Rational Ignorance Matters

6. The median voter can be thought of as the pivotal voter because it is the preference of the median or pivotal voter that becomes the policy option. The median voter is pivotal because if the median voter's ideal policy changes, then the policy favored by the election winner will change too.

   Topic: Two Cheers for Democracy

Answers to Multiple-Choice Questions

1. c, Topic: Voters and the Incentive to Be Ignorant

2. b, Topic: Why Rational Ignorance Matters

3. c, Topic: One Formula for Political Success: Diffuse Costs, Concentrate Benefits

4. a, Topic: Special Interests and the Incentive to Be Informed

5. b, Topic: Special Interests and the Incentive to Be Informed

6. a, Topic: Special Interests and the Incentive to Be Informed

7. b, Topic: Special Interests and the Incentive to Be Informed

8. c, Topic: Democracy and Famine

9. b, Topic: Voter Myopia and Political Business Cycles

10. c, Topic: Special Interests and the Incentive to Be Informed

Answers to Short-Answer Questions

11. Rational ignorance is when the benefits from acquiring more information are less than the costs. Voters who know their vote is very unlikely to decide an election have an incentive not to spend much to acquire information about candidates and remain rationally ignorant.

    Topic: Voters and the Incentive to Be Ignorant

12. Because they are small and any benefit they can get from the government is spread over a relatively small number of people. Since the costs are born by a much larger group, usually taxpayers, special interest groups have an incentive to be rationally informed about their particular area of interest.

    Topic: Special Interests and the Incentive to Be Informed

13. This scenario is certainly worth it for the interest group. They get a $700 benefit while only paying $30 of the cost for a net benefit of $670. It is not in the interest of society because the government spends $1,000 to get a group a $700 benefit which means $300 worth of resources are wasted.

    Topic: Special Interests and the Incentive to Be Informed

14. Concentrated benefits and diffused costs give a special interest group the incentive to seek a benefit from the government most of which will be paid for by taxpayers. Taxpayers will not complain because each taxpayer's share of the costs is relatively small.

    Topic: One Formula for Political Success: Diffuse Costs, Concentrate Benefits

15. Rational ignorance matters because if voters are uninformed, then it is hard for them to make informed choices about what policies to support. Also, voters who are rationally ignorant will often make decisions for irrational reasons. Finally, rational ignorance matters because not everyone is rationally ignorant, and those who are not may have an advantage in getting the policies they want at the expense of taxpayers as a whole.

    Topic: Why Rational Ignorance Matters